The Unending Hunger

The Unending Hunger

Tracing Women and
Food Insecurity across Borders

Megan A. Carney

UNIVERSITY OF CALIFORNIA PRESS

University of California Press, one of the most
distinguished university presses in the United
States, enriches lives around the world by
advancing scholarship in the humanities, social
sciences, and natural sciences. Its activities are
supported by the UC Press Foundation and by
philanthropic contributions from individuals and
institutions. For more information, visit
www.ucpress.edu.

University of California Press
Oakland, California

Library of Congress Cataloging-in-Publication Data

Carney, Megan A., 1984–
    The unending hunger : tracing women and food
insecurity across borders / Megan A. Carney.
        pages   cm
    Includes bibliographical references and index.
    ISBN 978-0-520-28400-5 (hardcover : alk. paper)—
ISBN 978-0-520-95967-5 (pbk. : alk. paper)—
    1. Women immigrants—United States.
    2. Mexicans—United States.   3. Central
Americans—United States.   4. Food security—United
States.   5. Food security—Government policy—United
States.   I. Title.
    JV6602.C37 2015
    362.83′9812083—dc23

                                          2014035669

Manufactured in the United States of America

24   23   22   21   20   19   18   17   16   15
10   9   8   7   6   5   4   3   2   1

In keeping with a commitment to support environmen-
tally responsible and sustainable printing practices, UC
Press has printed this book on Natures Natural, a fiber
that contains 30% post-consumer waste and meets the
minimum requirements of ANSI/NISO Z39.48-1992 (R 1997)
(*Permanence of Paper*).

For my ancestors, especially for my grandparents—Joan Vedder, Murman Vedder, Isabel Carney, and Edward F. Carney—as well as for the generations yet to come. May you be born into a better world.

CONTENTS

1

ILLUSTRATIONS

ACKNOWLEDGMENTS

First and foremost, my deepest gratitude goes to the women at the heart of this book who graciously invited me into their lives and injected this work with the stories that follow. This work is as much a product of their labor as it is of my own.

The seeds for this project were planted long ago, both literally and metaphorically, while I was an undergraduate at the University of California–Los Angeles. It was during these years that I became involved with a student-led, grassroots alternative food movement. This movement formed part of a larger push for sustainability policies within institutions of higher education. I worked with dozens of fellow student organizers through the California Student Sustainability Coalition to advocate for a sustainable food policy in the University of California system, and to cultivate the first small organic farm on UCLA's campus. I am incredibly thankful to all of those with whom I shared this experience, especially Tim Galarneau, Melissa Haft, and Dorothy Le, and for the friendships that have endured since then. The anthropology department at UCLA was extremely supportive in helping me to link my student activism with my academic pursuits. The anthropology honors program—including Doug Hollan, the chair at the time, and my thesis advisers Alessandro Duranti and Monica Smith—offered the perfect balance of structure and freedom, particularly in exploring and experimenting with one's intellectual curiosity. I thank the Wasserman family for providing me with my first research grant to conduct anthropological fieldwork, and my peers in the honors program for their continual insights and feedback. I'd also like to thank my college roommate Yanira Lemus for inspiring me to study immigrant foodways in sharing with me her family's recipes from El Salvador. I am humbled by our friendship and the hospitality that her family has shown me over the years as I also marvel at the story of how her parents were able to escape from civil war in El Salvador and to create a new life for their family in the United States.

There are those who provided critical guidance and feedback as I further refined my research interests during graduate school at the University of California–Santa Barbara. My dissertation committee could not have been more supportive and encouraging throughout the various phases of this project. In her five years of service as my dissertation chair, Susan Stonich bestowed me with an immense appreciation and respect for all aspects of research. I am especially thankful to her for valuing my ambitions toward an engaged anthropology and for supporting my decision to foreground social outcomes in my work. I am also indebted to the other members of this committee, including Melissa Caldwell, Teresa Figueroa, Leila Rupp, and Casey Walsh. Melissa Caldwell has continued to be an unrelenting champion for this project; she has always provided timely and thoughtful feedback, and has been a beacon of inspiration for encouraging me to move the project forward into the development of a book. I am also thankful to her for steering me toward theory that would have otherwise been off my radar. Casey Walsh helped me to scale this project from the level of theory down to the ground and back up again. As the department adviser to graduate students at UCSB, he was also a steady source of moral support. I always walked away from meetings at his office feeling more grounded in my project and optimistic about the future. Leila Rupp illuminated the interdisciplinary significance of my research, and provided necessary feminist critique as I began writing. Last but not least, Teresa Figueroa enhanced this project with her rich knowledge of immigrant communities in Santa Barbara County. I also credit her, along with Travis Du Bry, with diversifying my familiarity with the vast literatures of political economy, transborder migration, and Chicano studies. Aside from these individuals I am also indebted to Patricia Allen, Molly Anderson, Allison Carruth, Susan Greenhalgh, Julie Guthman, Lisa Jacobson, Erika Rappaport, and Lois Stanford for the mentoring they provided me while I was completing my graduate studies. In addition, my graduate student peers enriched my experience in the classroom as well as in the field. In particular, my gratitude goes to Heather Berg, Martin Brix, Alison Hendley, Eric Humel, Maritza Maksimow, Rani Mclean, Heather Thakar, Lindsay Vogt, and Laura-Anne Minkoff-Zern.

During graduate school, I also had the fortune of participating in several interdisciplinary research groups. The University of California Multicampus Research Program on Food and the Body provided ample opportunity for circulating works in progress and connecting with esteemed scholars in related fields. The Interdisciplinary Humanities Center (IHC) at UCSB served as my "home away from home" on campus. I am especially grateful to Ann Bermingham and Emily Zinn from the IHC for connecting me to sources of funding and opportunities for presenting my work to diverse audiences.

There are several members of the community in Santa Barbara to whom I am grateful for welcoming me into their lives and offering various forms of support during the course of my fieldwork. Raquel Lopez was a steadfast liaison, as well as a patient and gifted focus group facilitator. Amy Lopez from the Foodbank of Santa Barbara County (FSBC) was generous with her time and in allowing me to learn more about her work while she also connected me with many important individuals for the purposes of this research; she never ceases to impress me with her boundless energy and passion for improving people's lives, and I feel honored to call her my friend. Other members of the FSBC staff were equally accommodating and supportive. In addition, I am thankful to those individuals who were involved with the development of the Santa Barbara County Food Policy Council in its infant stages, the Santa Barbara County Public Health Department, and my many fellow organizers over the years who continue to prove themselves as talented and dynamic movers and shakers, including Bridget Dobrowski, Jasper Eiler, Gina Fischer, Gerri French, Heather Hartley, Alison Hensley, and Eric Lohela.

I received additional mentoring while in postdoctoral appointments at the University of Washington and at Arizona State University. It was during this time that I was able to further develop and refine the arguments from my dissertation for the production of this book. The UW Department of Anthropology and the Latin American and Caribbean studies program provided many opportunities for exchange with a talented array of scholars. I am especially grateful to professors Ann Anagnost, Rachel Chapman, and Janelle Taylor from the Department of

Anthropology, as well as professor José Antonio Lucero for welcoming me into his Sawyer Seminar, "B/ordering Violence." Ann Anagnost provided a very warm welcome by helping to organize a series of workshops in the spring around the theme of food in which I was able to circulate an early draft of one of the chapters of this book. I also thank professor Bettina Shell-Duncan for supporting this series through the UW Medical Anthropology and Global Health program.

The Comparative Border Studies Institute and the School of Transborder Studies at ASU generously provided the time and space in which to put the finishing touches on my manuscript and submit it for publication. In particular, I thank professors Edward Escobar, Desiree Garcia, Matt Garcia, and Cecilia Menjívar for coordinating the postdoctoral fellowship in comparative border studies, and several members of the ASU faculty and staff for supporting me throughout the course of the yearlong fellowship, including Elizabeth Cantu, Maria Luz Cruz-Torres, Yasmina Katsulis, Airín Martinez, Luis Plascencia, and Carlos Vélez-Ibáñez. In addition, the Institute for Humanities Research Immigration Research Cluster, as well as the School of Human Evolution and Social Change, connected me with opportunities to present my work and to receive feedback. Last but not least, I was constantly inspired and supported by my CBS postdoctoral colleagues Holly Karibo and Laia Soto-Bermant.

A small handful of individuals exceeded all expectations of generosity in reading earlier versions of the manuscript and providing essential feedback that undoubtedly enabled its thorough enhancement. Ann Anagnost and Emily Yates-Doerr both graciously agreed to be the first reviewers of the work in its (almost complete) entirety. Reviewers Leo Chavez and Teresa Mares assessed the work with their vast expertise in the topic and offered extremely helpful suggestions for developing the final version.

This project would not have been possible without the generous support of several funding sources. I received a dissertation grant to cover the fieldwork expenses from the University of California Institute for Mexico and the United States. This grant allowed me to train and hire a small number of undergraduate research assistants from UCSB. Some of these students were more involved than others, but Mary Alvarado, Jessie Fidler, Fatima Segura, and Emily Terrill had a significant role at various stages of the project. I received additional funding for preliminary phases of research and for writing from the UCLA Center for Labor and Employment, the Chicano Studies Institute at UCSB, the UCSB Graduate Division, the UCSB Department of Anthropology, and the UCSB IHC Predoctoral Fellows Program.

The staff at University of California Press has been incredibly supportive at all stages of bringing this book to publication. I am thankful especially to Kate Marshall for championing this work and believing in its potential impact. Stacy Eisenstark has also been very helpful in offering her valuable technical assistance. I very much appreciate their patience in working with a first-time book author; it has been a true pleasure to work with both of them.

Because so many people have undoubtedly touched my life and have shaped my thinking in a number of ways, I apologize to those whose names I may have left out here by accident.

It is sometimes assumed that authors (as well as scholars, for that matter) lead isolated and lonely lives. I feel incredibly blessed to say that this is not at all true in my case. In the years culminating in the work that follows, there has been a large circle of family and friends I have been able to call on for various forms of support. For their unconditional love and encouragement I especially thank my parents Edward Carney and Danna Vedder; my stepmother Linda Carney; my siblings Matthew Carney, Alexandra Dunn, and Aerin Ginsberg; my grandparents, to whom this book is dedicated; my in-laws Karl Johnson, Barbara Johnson, and Steve Johnson; Carol Lorraine and Ted Massart; and some of my dearest friends Jessica Alder, Gina Mesiti-Miller, Jessica Robles, and Lynzy Smeenk. Jessica Lanuza has also been a faithful tutor and incredible friend over the years. *Muchísimas gracias por todo lo que me has enseñado.*

Finally, I am most indebted to Lucas Johnson, my loving husband and enduring companion in life, who believes in me more than anyone else and never allows me to give up.

Introduction

Struggling to feed her children and fearing the possibility of hunger, Malena perceived no other option but to migrate in search of work from her home state of Guerrero, Mexico, to the United States. She lived with relatives in Santa Barbara, California, while she tried to find employment. Both the language barrier and the risks associated with her unauthorized status instilled fear in Malena and posed further challenges to surviving her surroundings. Despite finally securing a job as a hotel housekeeper in which she regularly clocked more than seventy hours per week, there was still never enough time or money to alleviate the painful, everyday constraints on feeding and eating that had followed her from Mexico. In the language of public health practitioners and emergency food programs, chronic food insecurity continued to haunt Malena in the United States. As one aspect of the material scarcity experienced by Malena, chronic food insecurity not only reflected how limited resources could be harming the health of Malena and her family but also signaled a weakening of the social relations once regularly enacted and sustained through food.

Sadly, Malena blamed herself for failing to overcome this material scarcity. Contrary to her original expectations, life in the United States did not offer much reprieve from the suffering she had experienced in Mexico. Estranged from her children and without much hope for the future, she had been rendered to feel powerless, anxious, socially isolated, and excluded.

Malena was not at all alone in her experience.

Indeed, stories such as Malena's are all too common. They speak to how disruptions to eating and feeding register at both the personal and social levels and articulate the experiences of women migrating across borders. Yet, curiously, these women's stories have hitherto been overlooked in the rich literature on migration from Mexico and Central America to the United States. This book brings these women's stories to the fore.

WHAT'S GROWING IN YOUR OWN
BACKYARD: SANTA BARBARA COUNTY
AS A MICROCOSM OF THE GLOBAL

This book features the experiences of migrant women who are living in Southern California, and specifically in the coastal region of Santa Barbara County, a place that has come to epitomize the concept of "hunger in the land of plenty." Boasted of in travel brochures and real estate magazines as the "American Riviera," Santa Barbara County is popularly depicted as a place brimming with material affluence and natural beauty that is enjoyed by all who go there. Yet this depiction could not be any farther from reality.

As is increasingly the case in the United States, extreme disparities of wealth prevail in the county, where an increasing number of poverty-stricken households exist alongside some of the nation's wealthiest households. As of the 2010 census, almost one in five residents (18 percent) of Santa Barbara County were living below the federal poverty level (US Census Bureau 2010). Although the economic recession most likely had an effect on figures in the 2010 census, poverty had risen significantly since prior assessments (up from 11.9 percent of households in 2007). Rather than representing an exception, the upward trending of poverty in Santa Barbara County is consistent with that of much of the United States, a situation that has sparked much vitriol and debate in recent years around "class warfare," "the 99 percent," and the "haves and have-nots." It is perhaps not so surprising or coincidental that the research on which this book is based coincided with the emergence of the Occupy movement in the United States that has since swept across many parts of the globe.

Of course, there are many historical and geographical characteristics that distinguish Santa Barbara County from other popular tourist destinations and desired places to live in the United States (and the world); I will expand on those unique characteristics in the coming pages. Yet fundamentally, it is not so different from any of these other places. I imagine that many readers will have their own version(s) of Santa Barbara in drawing from the list of places they have lived and traveled. It may even include their own backyards.

FOOD SECURITY AS A
BIOPOLITICAL PROJECT

Scholars of globalization have identified a central contradiction of neoliberal capitalism—namely, that capital and commodities move uninhibitedly across geopolitical borders while the movement of labor is restrained. To this relatively recent discussion in the social sciences I lend the following revision: food, in its commodity form and as a site of capital accumulation, moves uninhibitedly across geopolitical borders while growing numbers of people face fewer and fewer options for guaranteeing their means of survival. Food consistently ranks at the top of this list. In an arrangement that some are now calling the "neoliberal food regime" (Pechlaner and Otero 2010), the corporate takeover of the global food system is predicated on a system of values that places profits before people (Nally 2011). The global reach of this arrangement continues to displace millions from rural agrarian livelihoods who must then migrate as a means to find economic alternatives and to alleviate food insecurity.

I approach food insecurity as an object of ethnographic inquiry for the reasons that its meaning is anything but simple and its location is all too imprecise. As I explain herein, this concept has come to index an array of technical definitions as well as a host of politics wherein these definitions are constructed. In addition, the term *food insecurity* has also garnered wider usage in recent years as part of the popular vernacular in the United States, being adopted by media and the realm of emergency food assistance. Rather than passively engaging with this concept, I suggest we need to unpack its multiple meanings and usages, particularly when it becomes a label to infer the competencies of individual human beings.

The sister concepts of *food insecurity* and *food security* were formally launched at the first World Food Conference in 1974 (Pottier 1999), and have since undergone several iterations. The latest definition put forth by the Food and Agriculture Organization of the United Nations (FAO) describes food security as "a situation that exists when all people, at all times, have physical, social and economic access to sufficient, safe and nutritious food that meets their dietary needs and food preferences for an active and healthy life" (FAO 2002). The FAO identifies four dimensions of food security: food availability, economic and physical access to food, food utilization, and stability over time. Food insecurity, by contrast, is outlined as "[a] situation that exists when people lack secure access to sufficient amounts of safe and nutritious food for normal growth and development and an active and healthy life" (FAO 2002).

Although in many cases "expert opinion" continues to dominate policy discussions about global food security (Page-Reeves 2014; Pottier 1999), the goal with subsequent definitions and annual measurements issued by the FAO has been to better approximate the lived experiences of vulnerable populations. The 2013 *State of Food Insecurity in the World* report, for instance, claims to go "beyond measuring chronic food deprivation. It presents a broader suite of indicators that aims to capture the multidimensional nature of food insecurity, its determinants, and outcomes" (FAO 2013, 4).

As with many large-scale development projects, global interventions to food insecurity have usually been administered in a top-down method through which the agents of development appear to act "paternalistically" toward a group or population of so-called beneficiaries. The Green Revolution of the 1960s and '70s serves as an apt example. In response to widespread hunger and malnutrition during the 1960s, the Rockefeller and Ford Foundations funded agricultural research and the transfer of technological packages for agriculture, particularly for rice and wheat production in developing countries and specifically in the regions of Asia (primarily India) and Latin America (primarily Mexico). In delivering agricultural inputs to resource-poor farmers in the third world, proponents of the Green Revolution predicted increased agricultural productivity. These technological packages transferred to Asia and Latin America included high-yielding crop varieties, chemical inputs and fertilizers, and irrigation (International Food Policy Research Institute 2002). While larger, wealthier farms prospered from higher yields, and a growing population could hypothetically access an enhanced supply of grains available through the market, critics of the Green Revolution claim that its benefits were "distributed unevenly" (Simmonds and Smartt 1999, 353). Not only were many small farmers displaced because of labor-saving techniques brought about through new technological packages and the ensuing expansion of big agriculture; economic purchasing power also became further concentrated among elites, causing hunger to spike in many parts of the world (Simmonds and Smartt 1999). Because Mexico served as a primary site of the Green Revolution experiment, its elevated status as one of the world's top agricultural exporting countries is undoubtedly linked to the lingering effects of this experiment. Other traces of the experiment are also visible in the continued widespread displacement from traditional agrarian livelihoods, increased industrialization of agriculture, and increased labor migration to other parts of Mexico and to the United States.

"Trickle-down" schemes designed to improve food security, as observed with the Green Revolution or with more recent international development and global health projects such as fortification or biofortification of the food supply (Kimura 2013), tend to obscure how disparities in food and health are actually structural in origin. Many projects falling under the aegis of food security, insofar as they reproduce rather than dismantle structures of inequality, represent elusive forms of violence. Paul Farmer has defined structural violence as "a series of large-scale forces—ranging from gender inequality to racism and power—which structure unequal access to goods and social services" (1996, 369). The US food system is one vehicle of structural violence, as evidenced by survey findings showing that food insecurity occurs disproportionately among women and people of color (Allen 2008; Coleman-Jensen et al. 2011; Gottlieb and Joshi 2010; Poppendieck 1997). Structural violence is visible yet again in the processes required for those who experience food insecurity to ask for support. There are few, if any, redeeming or dignified qualities ascribed to those individuals relying on a system that society views as providing needs-based "emergency" relief or government "handouts." These processes would likely appear much different if society viewed food as a basic human right.

FOOD: A RIGHT OR A COMMODITY?

The global-industrial food system—characterized by privatization, deregulation, and trade liberalization—has rendered food a "commodity" (Li Ching 2008). The 2007–9 global food crisis demonstrated the vulnerability of resource-poor people around the world to price speculation on commodity crops (Holt-Giménez and Patel 2009). *Harper's* magazine's July 2010 feature story aptly titled "The Food Bubble: How Wall Street Starved Millions and Got Away with It" (Kaufman 2010), explained how the unprecedented expansion in the number of hungry people globally could be traced to unregulated trading practices among Wall Street stockholders and financiers.

Although the right to food was declared "binding international law" through the International Covenant on Economic, Social and Cultural Rights, few nation-states uphold this right in practice (FAO 2003; Messer and Cohen 2007; Pimbert 2007, 2008; Rae 2008; Spieldoch 2007). Multilateral financial aid and lending institutions such as the World Bank and the International Monetary Fund (IMF), and international trade agreements promoted through the

General Agreement on Tariffs and Trade and the World Trade Organization (WTO), have significantly shaped agricultural production and policies (De Schutter 2009), thus leading many critical social scientists to observe how food has been governed "within and beyond nation-states" (Phillips 2006, 42). Institutions setting the parameters of the global food economy also oversee measuring and designing interventions for food security, but these activities are rarely coordinated (Holt-Giménez and Patel 2009). In arguing against a continuation of paternalistic policies, Molly Anderson contends, "The right to food cannot be met long-term through external donations. It requires local control over practices and policies to reinforce the ability to grow or buy stable amounts of nutritious food for one's household and community" (2008, 602).

The WTO, the IMF, and the FAO have been criticized by scholars and activists alike for disarticulating economic development goals from those for health and food security (Carney 2011a; Pottier 1999). In other words, they critique the tendency of policy makers to segregate trade rules from human rights' goals in addressing global food insecurity (FAO 2003; Messer and Cohen 2007; Pimbert 2007; Pimbert 2008; Rae 2008; Spieldoch 2007). Finding inherent contradictions in the bifurcated discussion of economic development and food insecurity, these scholars and activists argue for more integrated food and agriculture policies (Pottier 1999). The transnational social movement for food sovereignty has led this critique in recent years, calling attention to the lack of democracy in food systems, widespread global food insecurity and hunger, destruction of local ecologies, and limited levels of participation afforded to women in determining food policies. The food sovereignty movement interprets these conditions as part and parcel of increased corporate control of the global food system (Carney 2011b; McMichael 2009; Patel 2009; Pimbert 2007; Rosset and Martinez-Torres 2010).

In response to domestic food insecurity, the US government has endorsed needs-based approaches, meaning that it provides nutritional "handouts" based on a household's income and constructs recipients as "beneficiaries" rather than viewing them as rights-holding citizens (Anderson 2008). This approach thus predicts, and contributes to, much of the stigma around welfare assistance. Instead of holding the state accountable for people's right to food, blame for food insecurity is directed at individuals who are perceived as having failed to maximize their economic potential in caring for the nutritional needs of themselves and their families. Janet Page-Reeves eschews the needs-based approach for being "antithetical to a rights-based conceptualization of food insecurity" (2014, 4) and poses important questions: "Are we merely concerned with feeding the hungry? Or are we interested in ending hunger? And can we realistically imagine that we can end hunger without dealing with poverty and inequality?" (10).

A fuller understanding of food insecurity takes into consideration broader political and economic contexts, wherein the gradual dismantling of the social safety net and subsequent privatization of social services have made it increasingly difficult for people to provide for themselves (Carney 2011a; Carney 2014a). The network of private food aid (i.e., charitable food assistance) in the United States, which continues to serve an ever growing number of people, is but one example of these changes.

A HUNGER THAT IS UNENDING

Based on original research from ethnographic fieldwork that I conducted between 2008 and 2011 in Southern California, this book critically examines the role of food insecurity in shaping migration from Mexico and Central America. Specifically, I present the lived experience of Mexican and Central American women with food insecurity in the United States. As part of presenting this lived experience I discuss efforts by state agencies and nongovernmental organizations to promote food security and the repercussions of these trends for women's subjectivities (i.e., beliefs, desires, feelings, and other ways of experiencing one's being in the world). I discuss the agency of women in both complying with and resisting everyday attempts by the state to produce neoliberal, "caring," and food secure subjects, and I allude to the ways that food insecurity and the conditions of unauthorized migration conspire to compound the structural vulnerability of these women. Furthermore, I interpret Mexican and Central American women's role in this project as another instance of the state transferring its reproductive burdens to a foreign "other" amid deepening "deficits of care." Notably, I underscore how the biopolitics of food insecurity and the biopolitical project of food security translate to further social suffering and the continued erosion of state entitlements. By invoking a language of biopolitics and the biopolitical, I mean to reference how life itself is made into an object of political maneuvering. Thus, I find a biopolitics of food insecurity visible in the uneven distribution of vital resources—specifically food—and food security as a biopolitical project being waged in the segmenting of populations that later subjects them to differential treatment by state institutions. Women find scarce opportunities to escape these biopolitical modes as they also grapple with a hunger that is unending.

In making the claim that food security approaches are a platform for contemporary biopolitics and that much of today's global migration by women is entangled with biopolitics, this book presents a threefold argument. First, this book sheds light on the realities of women who have migrated from Mexico and Central America to the United States in order to improve their life chances, only to then (re)encounter similar constraints once living in the United States. These women's lived experiences attest to how *food insecurity—as a series of structural constraints on everyday eating and feeding—is a vehicle for contemporary biopolitics.* I defer to Arthur Kleinman's framing of lived experience: "the dialectic between cultural category and personal signification on the one side, and brute materiality ... on the other" (1989, 55). One may compare lived experience to that which results from the combined forces of structure and agency.

Second, as governments create so-called favorable market conditions and gradually roll back welfare programs, I argue that they increasingly transfer responsibility to individuals to rectify the problem of food insecurity through getting them to adopt a prescribed set of values, beliefs, and practices. I refer to this arrangement herein as the *biopolitical project of food security.*

Third, in charging individuals to redress the problem of food insecurity, states also rely on a gendered division of labor in which reproductive labors are generally assigned to women. Unlike labor that is deemed "productive," reproductive labor tends to merit less prestige in market economies. In this book I argue that the contemporary biopolitical project of food security rests on the shoulders of those who perform caring labor—namely women—but whose contribution to this aspect of everyday social reproduction is generally devalued by society.

A rich anthropological literature examines the experiences of Mexican and indigenous migrants as farmworkers in the United States (Holmes 2013; Palerm 2002; Stephen 2007). Although I do not wish to deemphasize the importance of focusing on the embodied forms of structural vulnerability migrants endure as *producers* in the industrial food system (see especially Holmes 2013), the present volume offers a counterpoint to this literature by delving into a thick description of the experiences of people at the other end of this spectrum—specifically in the realms of feeding and eating. In shifting the analytic frame to those who oversee these activities—particularly women—I demonstrate how much of the social suffering documented by anthropologists is gendered. This book is therefore an active response to calls by scholars for broader representation of migrant women in the ethnographic literature on migration from Mexico and Central America while it also advances the argument that this endeavor requires more explicit attention to global food policy and local food systems. In the chapters that follow I underscore how feeding and eating, as both personally necessary activities and core aspects of social life, are mediated by processes from above (i.e., neoliberal economic development, trade agreements), below (everyday negotiations around crises of care), and the spaces in between (i.e., bureaucratic decision making, local and state policies).

FOOD INSECURITY IN THE UNITED STATES

The United States Department of Agriculture (USDA) reports that food insecurity currently affects roughly forty-nine million people, or close to one-fifth of the US civilian population (Coleman-Jensen, Gregory, and Singh 2014). The USDA conceptualizes and measures food insecurity at the household level and defines it as "uncertain, insufficient, or unacceptable availability, access, or utilization of food" (Wunderlich and Norwood 2006, 4). Public health advocates estimate that this national epidemic costs about $90 billion per year in increased medical care expenses, lost educational attainment and worker productivity, and investment burden into the emergency food system (Brown et al. 2007). Food insecurity rose steadily in absolute and relative numbers from 1993 to 2009 (Coleman-Jensen et al. 2011), a fact highlighted by some to argue that society has not made any genuine attempts to eradicate food insecurity in the United States (Chilton and Rose 2009).

The US government released its formal definition of food security and corresponding procedures for monitoring food insecurity in the early 1990s (Wunderlich and Norwood 2006). Heretofore the government gave the following characteristics of food security: "Access by all people, at all times, to enough food for an active, healthy life and includes at a minimum: (a) the ready availability of nutritionally adequate and safe foods and (b) the assured ability to acquire acceptable food in socially acceptable ways (e.g., without resorting to emergency food supplies, scavenging, stealing, and other coping strategies)" (Anderson 1990, 1598).

Changes to the USDA's system of classification for food security and food insecurity reveal how these discourses are heavily politicized (Himmelgreen and Romero-Daza 2010). For instance, the USDA revised its terminology in 2006, eradicating the term *hunger* from all official research and reporting. As Stephen Haering and Shamsuzzoha Syed explain it, "The purpose of the elimination of the word hunger from the classification schemes was to reflect both the evolution of the understanding of hunger as a phenomenon distinct from, though closely related to food insecurity, as well as to recognize the limitations of extant measurement instruments for accurately gaging hunger" (2009, 13). Households in the United States are now classified as either "food secure," "low food secure," or "very low food secure" (Wunderlich and Norwood 2006). Critics of revisions to the USDA's formal language purport that the department has effectively attempted to "depo-liticize" the experience of food insecurity and hunger, ironically providing further evidence of how this experience is indeed entrenched in a flurry of politics (Allen 2007). Regrettably, those in US policy circles with minimal insight into on-the-ground issues also risk the possibility of misrepresenting "the very nature of food insecurity and what it means to those households most affected" (Stanford 2014, 105).

Efforts to alleviate food insecurity in the United States broadly filter into the rubric of either public (federal/governmental) or private (nonprofit/emergency) programs. The USDA spends $45.39 billion, or 48.4 percent—the largest share of its total annual budget—on food stamps and nutrition programs (Imhoff 2007), although recent legislation by Congress warns of drastic reductions to food stamp spending. The US government established the Food Stamp Program during the Great Depression to address both the surplus being produced by American farmers and the chronic conditions of hunger experienced by poor families (Biggerstaff, Morris, and Nichols-Casebolt 2002; Imhoff 2007). The USDA revised its terminology in 2008 with respect to the Food Stamp Program, renaming it the Supplemental Nutrition Assistance Program (SNAP), and individual states have further rebranded the program (e.g., California's CalFresh Program). Since 2008 enrollment in SNAP has soared, growing by nearly 40 percent, or ten million recipients, from 2007 to 2009 alone (DeParle and Gebeloff 2009), for a total in January 2014 of 46.5 million.[1] The Food Research and Action Center (2011) estimated that the program was feeding about one in seven adults and one in four children.

Other forms of federal food assistance include the national school lunch and breakfast programs; the Women, Infants, and

Children Supplementary Nutrition (WIC) Program; and the Emergency Food Assistance Program. Despite increased enrollment in SNAP and WIC, the USDA—by order of the US Congress—has made numerous cuts to both programs. In May 2013, the House Agriculture Committee proposed cutting $20 billion from SNAP following a trend in budget cuts that resulted in a 13 percent reduction in funding for SNAP benefits at the end of 2012 (Nixon 2013; Vauthier 2011). The WIC program also awaits severe budget cuts that were expected to amount to over $340 million in 2013. In commenting on these proposed cuts to the WIC program, the *New York Times* reported that pregnant and breast-feeding women as well as infants would be given priority enrollment, while women not breast-feeding along with children over one year old could be put on an indefinite waiting list ("As the Cuts Hit Home" 2013). Participation in the program has already declined as WIC agencies have adopted cost-saving measures such as downsizing staff, consolidating clinics, reducing office hours, or closing offices altogether. These conditions prevent many low-income women from applying for benefits, especially among those who are only able to visit WIC offices during the evening or weekend hours to avoid missing work (Neuberger and Greenstein 2013).

Another area of USDA funding goes toward community food security projects. The concept of *community food security* "emerged from the North American context in the late 1980s and early 1990s to expand international food security theory beyond the medical model developed by international health organizations and to include more subjective dimensions of hunger" (Johnston and Baker 2005, 341). As a result of lobbying efforts in the mid-1990s, the 1996 Farm Bill included the Community Food Security Act with a pool of annual funds ($5 million) to support community food security projects through the Community Food Projects

Competitive Grants Program. Between 1996 and 2003, more than $22 million in grants was distributed to 166 awardees (Tauber and Fisher 2004). Although the granting program has been important to community food security efforts, it makes up a negligible proportion of the total USDA budget ($146 billion in 2014; US Department of Agriculture 2014).

Despite contributions by the USDA to welfare assistance and community food security initiatives, Mariana Chilton and Donald Rose (2009) argue that the United States has made no real advances in reducing national food insecurity, asserting that needs-based, federal food assistance programs at best mitigate the experience of food insecurity but do nothing to dismantle the forms of institutionalized oppression and structural inequality that allow for an unevenness in the distribution of vital resources. At the height of economic recession for instance, rates of food insecurity were substantially higher than the national average for households with incomes below the official poverty line (42.2 percent), households with children headed by single women (37.2 percent, almost three times the national average), households with children headed by single men (27.6 percent), black households (25.7 percent), and Hispanic households (26.9 percent; Nord, Andrews, and Carlson 2009, 8). And "very low food security" was higher than the national average (5.7 percent) for households with children headed by single women (13.3 percent), women living alone (7.7 percent), men living alone (6.8 percent), black and Hispanic households (10.1 and 8.8 percent, respectively), households with incomes below the poverty line (19.3 percent), and households located in principal cities of metropolitan areas (6.6 percent; Nord, Andrews, and Carlson 2009, 11). Kami Pothukuchi argues that structural changes such as "living wages, better jobs, education, and health and child care"

(2004, 360) should be at the forefront of policy reform for improving food security in the United States.

FOOD SECURITY MEETS DIETARY HEALTH:
A LENS INTO BIOPOLITICS

Insofar as the process of defining food security is highly politicized, the various steps assumed in orienting and disciplining a population toward the goal of food security delineate a biopolitical project. A repeated theme of discussion in this book is how state institutions act upon populations differentially to discipline them in the biopolitical project of food security. By focusing on the individual body as the locus of intervention, and entrenched as they are in the neoliberal food regime (McMichael 2009), food security approaches have more to reveal about contemporary biopolitics than they do about any genuine attempt to alleviate food insecurity.

I employ the term *biopolitics* in reference to the politicization of life, specifically natural life, a topic of inquiry inspired by Michel Foucault that has garnered much attention from those with interests in critical studies of health, science and technology, reproduction, and the state. In his claim that "modern man is an animal whose politics calls his existence as a living being into question" (1978, 188), Foucault accounted for how this politicization of life represented the primary mode of contemporary *governmentality* comprising technologies of domination through top-down regulation and technologies of the self through individuals' internalization of disciplinary processes (Foucault 1991). To name a practice or project "biopolitical" suggests that it has taken life "as the object of its politics" (Murphy 2012, 10). Building on Foucault's formulation of a biopolitical logic as it underpins contemporary governmentality, feminist historian Michelle Murphy gestures to the notion of differential governance: "as populations were understood to be made up of internal differences . . . variation—marked as race, class, pathology, caste, or even sex—could be differentially governed, enhancing some forms of life, neglecting or actively destroying other aspects of life, to bring forth the desired future of that population" (2012, 13). She thus notes how the effects of biopolitical practices are always "profoundly uneven" and calls for an approach that acknowledges the "confluence of multiple biopolitical modes at work in any given place" (12).

A core theoretical aim of this book is to demonstrate how the contemporary *biopolitics of food insecurity* overlap with and articulate the *biopolitical project of food security*. On the one hand, I underscore how multilateral trade agreements, the industrialization of agriculture, and a deregulation of markets are part and parcel of a political economic redistribution of life chances. On the other hand, I illustrate how the unevenness of life chances is approached as a problem of governmentality, with individuals being charged with the bulk of responsibility for the problem. I argue that the embodied experiences of Mexican and Central American women living in the United States provide a unique and vivid example of the overlap of these different biopolitical modes, as these women are often the first to absorb the impacts of economic restructuring in their home countries and to become the designated targets of biopolitical scrutiny upon entering host countries. Moreover, the effects of projects intended to bolster food security are profoundly uneven: as a biopolitical project, food security holds individuals responsible for their own dietary health while at the same time producing failure among those who have always already been rendered into a position of abject marginality. Giorgio Agamben's (1998) concept of "bare life" is particularly applicable here, as it indexes life that has been stripped of political rights. The operating idea is that of the "bootstrap" approach, which assumes that anyone anywhere should be able obtain necessary, life-sustaining resources, including food. Yet this idea entirely neglects how populations, being governed differentially, are either afforded or denied the formal means to stake claims on such resources.

RESEARCH METHODOLOGY

Santa Barbara County is part of the Tri-County Region that connects California's Central Coast to Southern California. As it is only about one hundred miles north of Los Angeles and accessible via a major highway, the city of Santa Barbara and its outskirts regularly attract a flood of urbanites who are seeking a respite from crowded city life. Santa Barbara County has also appealed to many celebrities and others from the entertainment industry as a place either to retire or to maintain a quieter residence that is outside the Hollywood limelight.

Tourism, agriculture, and construction rank among the county's principle economic activities (County of Santa Barbara 2008); these industries annually employ several thousand migrants who work as hotel cleaning staff, janitors, cooks, gardeners, farmworkers, and construction workers. The southern portion of the county, commonly referred to as the South Coast, attracts tourists because of its scenic beaches, water-based activities, fine dining, and wine tasting rooms. The northern portion of the county, which includes the areas of Santa Maria, Lompoc, Santa Ynez, and Cuyama, provides the bulk of agricultural and viticultural production as well as wine tourism. Revenues from tourism exceed $1.5 billion annually for the county, of which $612 million comes from the city of Santa Barbara (Lauren Schlau Consulting 2008). Notably, the majority of employees in the hospitality, agriculture, and construction sectors receive paltry earnings that make it difficult to reside near sites of employment, and local organizations like PUEBLO have been at the forefront of advocacy efforts to get employers to adopt a living wage policy.

According to the latest census findings, Latinos comprised 43.8 percent of Santa Barbara County's population (comparable to the rest of California, at 38.2 percent) but also 59.2 percent of the enrollment in K–12 public schools, indicating that there will likely be substantial growth in this segment of the population in coming years (Bureau of Population Statistics 2010; California Health Interview Survey 2009; US Census Bureau 2014). This is also consistent with recent reports projecting that in 2014 Latinos will surpass whites as the largest racial/ethnic group in California (Lopez 2014). Relegation of Latinos into unskilled, low-wage jobs in this region, a trend with historical precedence, has translated to disproportionate levels of poverty among them: Latinos account for 69 percent of the county's population living at 200 percent the Federal Poverty Level or below (California Health Interview Survey 2009).

Aside from it being a common destination for migrant labor, and within close proximity to my graduate institution, I ultimately chose Santa Barbara County for my fieldwork because of the complexities and contradictions of its food system. The county has one of the most profitable agricultural sectors in the state of California, grossing over $1 billion in annual revenues from a variety of crops, but primarily strawberries, wine grapes, and broccoli (Agriculture Future Trust 2007). Given Santa Barbara County's agricultural productivity, one might deduce that its cornucopia of locally grown fruits and vegetables would foreclose any potential for food insecurity, but this is not at all the case. For the year

2008 the California Health Interview Survey (2009) found that 37.1 percent of low-income households were food insecure. Notably, the survey defined *low-income* as households with incomes at 200 percent and below the Federal Poverty Level. In contrast, reports from those on the front lines of emergency food assistance suggest that these survey findings are extremely conservative. In its 2011 annual report, the Foodbank of Santa Barbara County claimed that one in four county residents—representing over 100,000 individuals—had sought private food assistance sometime during the previous year. That so many local households struggle to obtain adequate supplies of food can be partially explained by global demand and California's role in being a major agricultural exporter for the world; a recent study estimated that more than 97 percent of Santa Barbara County crops were marked for export and that less than 2 percent of these crops were reserved for consumption within the county (Cleveland et al. 2011).

Many residents thus rely on emergency or government programs for supplying nutrition assistance, the latter category including options such as SNAP, WIC, and the federal school meals program. While SNAP has been notoriously underutilized in California, and Santa Barbara County has one of the lowest enrollment rates in the state (Shimada 2009), underenrollment is less of an issue for the WIC program; 56 percent of mothers who had a child in 2009 in Santa Barbara County enrolled in WIC (Santa Barbara County 2011). Unlike other areas of the United States where the free and reduced-price school meal program is severely underutilized and underfunded (Poppendieck 2010), Santa Barbara County has almost full participation from those who are eligible for the program: 53 percent of the county's schoolchildren were enrolled in 2009 (California Department of Education 2010). There has also been a concerted effort to improve the quality of the meals provided to schoolchildren through this program. The Orfalea Foundation's School Food Initiative has coordinated efforts to train school food service workers in how to cook from scratch and to source food from local farmers, thereby piggybacking on the success of like-minded initiatives in other parts of the country such as that in the Berkeley Unified School District.

When I first moved to Santa Barbara to attend graduate school, I arrived with enthusiasm for community activism that had been cultivated both through my years of student organizing and my upbringing in a progressively minded Northern California surf town. The social causes with which I aligned myself, both within the university and in the larger community, frequently related to food and subsequently positioned me as an "insider" to many facets of my future research. My involvements ranged from advocacy in farm-to-school programs, volunteering for the food bank, organizing for and serving on the local food policy council, and planning for a local food festival. During the course of these activities I interacted with many of the individuals whom I later interviewed for the purposes of this research, including staff members of nonprofit organizations, public health practitioners, and grassroots activists.

Alternatively, I was also an "outsider" in conducting this research, as my key informants were women who had migrated from Mexico and Central America to the United States. I recruited twenty-five Mexican and Central American women from three cities along the South Coast of Santa Barbara County: Santa Barbara, Goleta, and Carpinteria. I conducted outreach with prospective research participants through established community organizations in Santa Barbara County—specifically private food assistance distributions and Head Start programs. The only

Figure 1. A residential street in the community of fieldwork in
Santa Barbara. Photo by the author.

three eligibility criteria I specified for recruiting participants
were that women be of age eighteen or older, have migrated from
Mexico or Central America, and have had previous experience
utilizing some form of food assistance while in the United
States.[2]

My key informants ranged in age from twenty-four to sixty
(with a mean age of thirty-eight); they were migrants from
Mexico, Honduras, and Guatemala, although the majority of
them came from Guerrero, Michoacán, and Oaxaca, Mexican
states that commonly send a lot of migrants to the United States.
Five of the women had obtained legal status in the United States,
including a Guatemalan woman who had been granted asylum,
but most (twenty out of twenty-five) were *sin papeles* (without
papers—that is, undocumented). Length of residency in the
United States among my key informants spanned from as short

Figure 2. A storefront in Goleta. Photo by the author.

as three months to as long as thirty years. With the exception of one woman who was in the process of adopting a child through familial networks in Mexico, all of the women had children, with an average of two children per household. Of the twenty-five women, eleven held full- or part-time employment, nine described themselves as being underemployed, four were being supported by a spouse, and one was on disability. Two of the women reported obtaining postsecondary training at a university or vocational school, while the others had attended anywhere from one to six years of primary school. Only two of them had received some formal secondary education in the United States. Sixteen of the women were married or living with a spouse, four had never been married, and five were divorced. These details and more are summarized in a full list of the participants in appendix 2. I have intentionally withheld the actual names of key informants and other forms of identifying information.

Semistructured and life history interviews, dietary surveys, participant observation, and focus group discussions served as the primary instruments of data collection from key informants.

Figure 3. A storefront in Goleta. Photo by the author.

I arranged interview times with the women in advance over the phone, and they chose the locations for our meetings. Most often they elected to meet in their homes, but occasionally we met at parks, schools, and community centers. With the women's permission or by their invitation, I accompanied them in daily activities that ranged from grocery shopping to informal work, and from picking up kids at school to preparing meals. Toward the end of my fieldwork I organized three focus groups that met a total of three times each. These were facilitated by a moderator who was also a native resident of Santa Barbara and herself from a Mexican immigrant family; as the leader of a local nonprofit organization she had many years of experience with facilitating stakeholder and focus groups. All of the interviews and focus group interactions were conducted in Spanish. I recorded these interactions with the women's verbal consent and transcribed the recordings with the help of undergraduate research assistants who were also native Spanish speakers. The portions of the transcriptions that appear throughout this book I have translated from Spanish into English.

For interviews with key informants I began with a structured format to gather baseline data, and I reserved more sensitive topics for the second and third rounds of interviews. In these subsequent interviews I employed a life history interview approach, which seeks to understand past and present influences on people's perceptions and behaviors (Goldman et al. 2003; Langness and Frank 1981). The life history method has been championed for use in food- and health-related research especially for its potential to reveal "beliefs, transformations, [and] transmissions" (Hubert 2004, 46), thereby giving context and background to studies of contemporary dietary behavior (Counihan 2004; Goldman, et al. 2003; Hubert 2004). Annie Hubert suggests this method allows informants to tell "the food story of their lives" (2004, 46) and to contextualize transformations that have occurred in the process of acquiring and preparing foods.

Aside from my interactions with key informants, I also had numerous interactions with others in the women's families, social networks, and communities. I conducted semistructured interviews with front-line workers in the public health and nonprofit sectors; this group included an outreach worker for CalFresh; two staff members of a local food bank; the executive director of a local nonprofit specifically serving the Latino and Chicano communities of Santa Barbara; three officials from the Santa Barbara County Public Health Department; five *promotoras* (bilingual/bicultural community health workers); and the cofounder of the Santa Barbara SOL (Sustainable, Organic, Local) Food Festival. In these interviews I was particularly interested in comparing how public and nonprofit agencies, as well as grassroots activists, perceived and framed the experience of food insecurity differently from the

Figure 4. A Mexican *tienda* in Carpinteria. Photo by the author.

people who were being targeted by interventions to improve food security. I also conducted informal interviews with additional individuals working in all of the above contexts.

Like most anthropologists entering the field, never could I have imagined carrying out this research without integrating the method of participant observation. Kathleen and Billie DeWalt describe participant observation as the foundation of ethnographic research design, a tool for both data collection and analysis (2002). While the method is not without its challenges, requiring that researchers learn to straddle the divide between participant and observer and maintain integrity in this endeavor, it is invaluable in acting as a sort of sounding board for other sources of data. As articulated by F. Xavier Medina, participant observation "allows us to correct biases that may be present in interlocutors' discourses," noting that "these biases are always part of an informant's subjectivity, which, of course interacts with the also inevitable subjectivity of the researcher" (2004, 61). My goals as a participant observer were thus to enhance the quality of research data, the interpretation of that data, and the continual reassessment of research questions. For instance, participant observation data enhanced and brought to life data that I had collected through dietary surveys, as I was able to observe the women's kitchens, cooking facilities, cooking instruments, storage conditions, and foods and to participate in cooking activities and the sharing of meals (Hubert 2004). In addition to employing this method in the women's homes, I conducted participant observation in a variety of public health, food assistance, and community event settings, including private food distributions, health fairs, coalition meetings of public health advocates, meetings of *promotores*, community festivals, nutrition outreach events, and SNAP outreach events.

The focus groups comprised six to ten women each and were arranged by area of residence (Morgan and Krueger 1998; Stewart et al. 2007). The assistance provided by a hired moderator ensured that I was able to record data completely and accurately, while also engaging as an active participant in all focus group discussions (Morgan and Krueger 1998; Stewart, Shamdasani, and Rook 2007). I chose to incorporate focus groups into my research design for their purported potential to disrupt the power relationships embedded in the traditional research process and for the reason that they have been demonstrated as highly effective in the context of community-based planning with low-income groups and other marginalized populations (Greves et al. 2007; Jowett and O'Toole 2006; Kieffer et al. 2004; Minkler and Wallerstein 2003; Sarkisian et al. 2005; Sloane et al. 2003; Williams and Blackwell 2004). Prior to the commencement of the focus groups, the moderator and I collaborated in developing an interview guide that would be conducive to a semistructured moderating approach

Figure 5. A Virgen de Guadalupe altar at a trailer park in Carpinteria. Photo by the author.

Figure 6. A Virgen de Guadalupe altar at a trailer park in Carpinteria. Photo by the author.

(Morgan and Krueger 1998; Stewart et al. 2007). Each group met a total of three times over the span of two months for approximately one and one-half to two hours per session at venues that were located within walking distance of the women's homes (Bernard 2006; Morgan and Krueger 1998; Stewart et al. 2007).

Positionality and Feminist Approaches to Fieldwork: Inverting the Gaze

Several of the challenges anthropologists identify in conducting fieldwork, particularly fieldwork that is committed to a decolonization of the discipline, surfaced in the course of my research. For instance, privileged aspects of my own identity, such as being an Anglo-American woman of middle-class background and having US citizenship by birth, distinguished me in certain respects from the structurally disadvantaged position of my key informants. Some of my colleagues and superiors in academia called these aspects of my identity into question when considering my competencies for this fieldwork, noting the methodological and epistemological disadvantages of being an "outsider" to my research population. I see these concerns as completely sensible and relevant, and I expect that some of my readers may also have these considerations in mind. In addition to my commitment to social justice I have the utmost respect for taking a critical stance on positionality in the social sciences, and it is for these reasons that I sought to disrupt the conventional power dynamics historically characterizing a Western tradition of research. Despite the differences that exist between anthropologists (or other social scientists) and a research population, it is also my conviction that we as researchers are much more enmeshed in the social worlds of the people we study than we tend to recognize. Notably, the women in my research informed me that it was actually my identity as an outsider that made them feel more comfortable when sharing stories of deeply personal experiences. Of course, I still went through a period of establishing rapport with key informants prior to arriving at this level of interaction, but they trusted that because I had limited contact with others in their communities I would not engage in gossip about them.

There is an established tradition of feminist ethnography that emphasizes a democratization of knowledge production and shared authority in the research process (Behar and Gordon 1995). While the women in my research did not engage in the process of ethnographic writing per se (many were limited by only a few years of formal schooling), I have sought to balance the contributions of key informants with my own during both the research process and the production of this book. During the research process I emphasized a flexible methodology, one that was participatory and open to the ingenuity of research participants. For instance, in conducting interviews with my informants I sought to frame the work as a collaboration (Yow 2005, 2) by asking them what questions they thought were important as in regards to certain lived experiences. I also asked the women what aspects of their own lives they would want brought to the attention of a wider audience, following Aihwa Ong's insight: "By presenting informants' stories, we help marginal groups intervene in global narratives by putting into circulation alternative circuits of discursive power," (1995, 354). Finally, as a component of the focus groups, I asked the women if they would be willing to produce miniature autoethnographies via the use of disposable cameras. Specifically, the moderator and I asked participants to photograph those aspects of their everyday lives that brought them feelings of pride, peace, or happiness, and some of these self-portraits appear in this book.

These images serve partially as a means of self-expression and empowerment for those who are often stigmatized and silenced by our society; including them here is to stand in solidarity not only with these women in confronting these everyday oppressive forces but also with an emerging generation of anthropologists whose ambition it is to redistribute ethnographic authority across a collective. This approach stands in contrast to the business-as-usual research scenario in which the collective takes a backseat while a single individual charters the entire process of "speaking *for.*" The women's self-portraits and my own photographs are reproduced herein with the express permission of the women portrayed.

Finally, there has been some ambivalence among scholars around what constitutes *immigration,* versus *migration,* and relatedly what distinguishes an *immigrant* from a *migrant.* While the former term has a connotation of intractability and intentionality around obtaining formal citizenship, the latter is slightly more ambiguous. Some scholars express explicit preference for a particular phraseology over others, demonstrated for instance by Patricia Zavella's logic in deciding to employ the term *migrant* in discussing her research with Mexicanos in Northern California. She explains that this term allowed her "to evoke the ambiguities and indeterminacies that are involved in the process of migration … [and] to disrupt the U.S.-centric, assimilationist framework and remind us that migration is not necessarily linear but processual and contingent upon changing circumstances" (2011, xiii–xiv). While I am also tempted to exclusively refer to my key informants as migrants, there is simultaneously a part of me that feels uncomfortable with doing so. This discomfort stems mainly from the plain and basic reality that the circumstances of my study participants were by no means uniform. As I will demonstrate with my research findings, the lives of my key informants were in perpetual states of suspension, in part driven by estrangement from family and loved ones that may have or have not resulted in reunification. Not all of these women were committed to becoming US citizens or to remaining in the United States for the rest of their lives, but many of them spoke of or hinted at these aspirations nonetheless. Therefore my discussion shifts among *immigration, migration, immigrant,* and *migrant* as fluid categories. The women in my research also sometimes used the terms *Latino* or *Latina* for self-identification or for describing the community to which they belonged, so I occasionally incorporate these in the text as well to denote individuals who claim Mexican or Central American heritage. However, I do so while also recognizing that not all people of Mexican or Central American descent identify with this frame of reference. Thus, I see an ideal analysis in this context as one that mirrors the language of the research participants, even though this language may contradict itself at times.

OUTLINE OF THE CHAPTERS

In chapter 1, "'We Had Nothing to Eat': The Biopolitics of Food Insecurity," I trace the gendered effects of structural violence as waged through neoliberal economic policies that have direct implications for food insecurity in rural communities. Women's migration, I argue, has much to do with food in this context. Engaging with research that attempts to account for and explain women's migration from Mexico and Central America to the United States, while also incorporating theory on the relationship of gender to *foodwork* (a concept whose meaning I unpack in chapter 1), I argue for a research agenda that devotes more explicit attention to the prominence of chronic food deprivation in my informants' decisions to migrate. Combining life history data with ethnographies of Mexican and Central American women in Santa Barbara County, I demonstrate how food operates both literally and metaphorically across borders as an indicator of broader struggles in women's lives. Because migration thus serves as a strategy employed by many women for alleviating food insecurity, I suggest that concern for food animates various aspects of contemporary migration by women from Mexico and Central America to the United States and therefore merits broader recognition in the ways that we conceptualize "deservingness" and authorize entry to those seeking relief in one form or another in migrant-receiving countries.

Chapter 2, "Caring through Food: 'La Lucha Diaria,'" explores the gendered dimensions of social reproduction and its constraints in the United States, particularly as these articulate with one's immigration status. For many Mexican and Central American women, the act of feeding, or *alimentarse*—specifically the provision of what they consider *comida saludable* (healthy food)—ranks above all other obligations to different caring labors and also epitomizes the concept of motherhood. Yet a host of prohibitive social, political, and economic variables conspire to render the practice of feeding in the United States "una lucha diaria" (a daily struggle).

Chapter 3, "Nourishing Neoliberalism? Narratives of *Sufrimiento*," highlights the different forms of anguish and disappointment that shape Mexican and Central American women's encounters with food insecurity in the United States as well as the effects of these (re)encounters for women's subjectivities and overall well-being. In narrating experiences with social isolation, violence, material scarcity, and longing for "home," my informants bring attention to the multiple layers of suffering that accompany post-migration struggles for survival. Food is a prominent discursive theme in these narratives and provides a tangible medium through which these women reinterpret the past and situate the present. They allude to what they understand as the embodied effects of this suffering, such as struggles with weight, diabetes, and depression. Thus I borrow from syndemic theory—a conceptual framework that interprets the aggregation of diseases and how they interact within given social and environmental contexts—to argue that food insecurity and the conditions of unauthorized migration conspire with extant health vulnerabilities to compound and normalize women's social suffering.

Chapter 4, "Disciplining Caring Subjects: Food Security as a Biopolitical Project," focuses on the experiences of Mexican and Central American women with different forms of food assistance in the United States and the strategies of private food aid programs in operationalizing a preventative health approach toward clients, specifically by organizing around the objective of preventing diet-related disease. Organizations tailor programs to meet several desired criteria: transferring knowledge and skills to clients, reforming individual behavior, and empowering clients to take control of their dietary needs and propensity for health problems. I argue that these sites of food aid become proxies for the state in facilitating the transfer of responsibility for care from the realm of the collective to the individual through aligning with public health interventions. This invoking of clients to assume a larger share of responsibility for diet and health implies that women are disproportionately burdened with this task. Although I acknowledge the will of those working with or for these organizations to improve the lives of people in underserved communities even while operating within significant financial and institutional constraints, I also suggest that interventions become sites of epistemic violence in failing to disrupt narratives about the poor as being culpable for their own health problems. In avoiding conflicts with state institutions or private industry to push for structural change, much of the work of these organizations is not only complicit with but also becomes a vehicle for the biopolitical project of food security.

In chapter 5, "Managing Care: Strategies of Resistance and Healing," I highlight modes of resistance, cooperation, and "making do" deployed by Mexican and Central American women in responding to everyday crises of care in the United States. These women sometimes subvert the biopolitical project of food security and associated attempts by state institutions to discipline "caring" subjects in the ways that they choose to engage (or not) with different aid programs while also reproducing symbolically violent discourses about users of welfare. Even though the women are able to partially subvert disciplinary processes on the part of state institutions, they are also impelled by a fear of surveillance. I conclude this chapter with a discussion of the women's calls for social change while also gesturing to possibilities for resistance.

The conclusion summarizes the core contributions of my research. In it I revisit the structures of inequality that articulate a biopolitics of food insecurity and implicate disproportionate burdens for women—and especially for women migrating across borders. Notably, I gesture to the "winners" and "losers" in this biopolitical scheme, suggesting that biopolitical projects linked to food insecurity portend long-term devastation for the health of the nation, not to mention the ripple effects of such projects in perpetuating an uneven distribution of life chances throughout the world. I conclude by calling for new modes of conceptualizing social change. The epilogue continues with this theme in delineating some of the applied contributions of my fieldwork in Santa Barbara County.

On a personal note, I began fieldwork as a food justice activist (or so I thought), but I became quickly disillusioned with this aspect of my identity as I further immersed myself into the everyday lives of migrant women. As a platform for activism, I found the concept of food justice to be overloaded with preconceived notions of what it should look like on the ground and that the important question of "whose food justice?" was often lost in the frenzy to organize diverse groups of people and to build a cohesive campaign message. Because food is the basic sustenance of human life, demanding that each woman, child, and man have enough food simply does not go far enough. I still consider myself an activist, but I refuse to limit myself to the realm of food, as I believe that a focus on food justice distracts us from the innumerable other forms of marginalization and inequality that shape the human experience.

On numerous occasions throughout my fieldwork, I witnessed women of different ages, nationalities, and personal backgrounds banding together in the face of everyday struggles. One of these occasions was the last meeting of one of the focus groups. As women were imagining possible improvements to community programs, one of the participants, Celeste, confessed as she broke into quiet tears that her husband had been without work for the past month. Her family was going hungry, but she had not been able to attend any of the private food assistance distributions in recent weeks because they coincided with the English lessons that her five-year-old son needed for entry to kindergarten in the fall. At the end of the meeting, as all of us embraced in emotional farewells, one woman retrieved cash from her wallet and placed it firmly into Celeste's hand. Others in the room began to gather left-over items from our small meal to send home with Celeste and the moderator of our focus group promised that in the next week she would connect Celeste with a staff member who could drive her to and from her son's English lessons as well as area food distributions.

These small acts of kindness, while not offering much in the way of transforming the parameters of the experience of living as an unauthorized migrant in the United States, in some way help to mitigate the pain and suffering that accompany everyday forms of structural vulnerability, including feelings of isolation and displacement. How anthropology may help in facilitating such acts beyond the context of fieldwork—for example, by inducing a sympathetic reader or public through the production of ethnography—should be a central focus of our work. The ethnographic work thus functions as a "birthplace of sorts, out of which a mode of inquiry and a method of narration as well as the possibility of a public [comes] into existence," and it is "a reader, a community of sorts, neither the character nor the writer which will manifest and carry forward anthropology's potential to become a mobilizing force in the world" (Biehl 2013, 577). The women whose lives unfold in the following pages imparted this wisdom to me, for which I am forever indebted. I can only hope that throughout this work and successive writings I am able, even if only in some small way, to do them justice.

CHAPTER ONE

"We Had Nothing to Eat"

The Biopolitics of Food Insecurity

IN SEARCH OF FOOD

It is mid-December 2010 and I am arriving at the home of Betanía, a woman in her early sixties whom I met at a nutrition outreach event organized by the food bank. The address she provided me over the phone takes me to the Eastside neighborhood of Santa Barbara, a predominantly Latino residential area flanked on one side by the range of mountains that separate Santa Barbara from Montecito and on the other side by the commercial zone of Milpas Street. As I approach the carport leading up to a side entrance of the small, nondescript house whose address I hope matches the one I was given by Betanía, I notice the door is slightly ajar. Betanía beckons me in with a wave and shouts "Pásale!" from inside. As I push through the doorway, she dusts off a white plastic chair for me in the center of the kitchen. In the corner of the room stands an artificial Christmas tree decorated with colorful lights and various ornaments. Joining us is Betanía's daughter Paula, who hovers over the table making cheese enchiladas, as well as Betanía's grandson, who is sent to play in another room shortly after we begin conversing. Paula occasionally chimes in during the interview to help answer my questions.

I learn from both women that four families live together in this two-bedroom home and that they help each other—"cooperamos todos"—by sharing household resources and expenses. Betanía's husband earns money as a dishwasher at a Chinese restaurant, where he has been employed for the past nine years. Sometimes he collects aluminum cans and glass bottles to turn in at a local recycling station for extra cash. Betanía explains that she tends to domestic chores such as grocery shopping and helps with preparing meals for everyone in the household.

Responding to questions on my dietary survey, Betanía and Paula explain that they have had to limit themselves to eating only one meal per day because that is all they can afford right now. Also referring to others in the household, they report regular instances of hunger, reduced food intake, and diets that they consider to be unbalanced, even among the children. They complain that often they have "solo frijoles . . . y arroz" (only beans and rice) to feed the children. Betanía further discloses that food is especially scarce around the time that rent is due to the landlord, the fourth or fifth day of each month.

Since arriving in the United States, both Betanía and her husband have developed diabetes. Without access to health insurance they must pay out of pocket for any medical expenses related to their condition. Betanía's US-born granddaughter has also been hospitalized from a serious illness for the past couple of years, but some of this care is subsidized. Although Betanía visits her granddaughter in the hospital almost daily, she notes that others in the household also take turns in making these visits. Between expenses related to Betanía's diabetes and her granddaughter's hospitalization, the family does not see an end to the medical debt they have accumulated over the years.

Betanía and Paula describe life in Santa Barbara as "muy difícil" (very difficult) because there is "poco trabajo" (little work). They shop at the stores within closest proximity to their home, seeking "las especiales" (specials) because they do not have access to a car and cannot afford items at full price. Any supply of fruits and vegetables they have comes from the food bank. Unfortunately, however, Betanía is often unable to attend distributions organized by the food bank because of scheduling conflicts with her medical appointments. She rarely buys meat because she says that it is "tan caro" (too expensive). Toward the end of my visit on this day in December, Betanía leans over to me and whispers out of earshot from her daughter that although she often lacks meat or vegetables, she can always whip up an egg with beans, or beans with salsa, or *huevos a la Mexicana*, all the while gesturing with her hands.

Despite the family's struggles with limited resources, Betanía reports that her diet has improved since coming to the United States. In Mexico she could not buy rice, beans, or vegetables, for instance, because she and her husband had no source of income. Her town lacked much in the way of employment opportunities, and although her family farmed for subsistence, severe droughts prevented them from producing enough food for the household. "No lo quiero recordar porque estábamos bien pobre" (I'd rather not remember because we were so poor), she says in attempting to recall the inevitable hunger that would follow unfavorable harvests. Season after season of poor yields and poor earnings prompted Betanía's family to leave the Mexican state of Guerrero for the United States. Her husband was the first to arrive, almost a decade before Betanía; he strived to regularly send home a portion of his earnings, but he was only able to do so occasionally. By the time I met Betanía, she had been living in the United States for nine years.

Betanía learned to cook from her mother, like many other women in my research, and to grow corn and other crops from her father. In Mexico, her family lived in a *casita* (small house) and they were very poor. She went to school for only one year and never pursued employment outside of the home. She married at age fifteen and had her first child two years later. She is the mother of eight children, five of whom are living in the United States; two daughters and one son are still living in Guerrero. All of her daughters, both in the United States and Guerrero, have followed in their mother's footsteps of becoming traditional housewives, and they do not have formal employment outside of the home. Her son in Mexico is a farmworker, while her sons in the United States are employed as landscapers or as restaurant kitchen staff.

I continue to regularly visit Betanía at her residence in Santa Barbara, specifically—and of all places—in her kitchen, which doubles as the site of sleeping quarters with her husband. On a rainy day some months following my initial visit, I arrive again at Betanía's home at our scheduled time. Her daughter Paula greets me at the door and informs me that Betanía has gone to the store but should be returning shortly. It seems that Betanía had missed the food bank distribution the prior day because of the rain and has gone to the store in hopes that she might find items on sale today. A few of Betanía's grandchildren wave from the corner of the room and motion for me to take a seat. Paula explains that the children stayed home from school today because they woke up feeling sick. One has a sore throat, and three have the flu. The four of them sit wedged together in their pajamas on a short stack of twin mattresses set against the wall, watching cartoons on a small television set. As I wait for Betanía to return from her shopping excursion I watch as Paula proceeds to prepare food for the children. She lifts the lids of a couple steaming pots on the stove to reveal their contents: pinto beans in one and a *caldito de pollo con verduras* (soup of chicken and vegetables) in the other. Perched on the wall shelves behind me are packages of store-bought tortillas, bags of dried beans and lentils, crates of eggs, and a bottle of Nutralife tablets. I am reminded of the Nutralife brochures that have been left behind by Spanish-speaking sales representatives in the homes of my other research participants; I have learned that mothers sometimes substitute these tablets for fruits and vegetables when finances are not available to purchase the latter.

Around the kitchen there are also decorations such as silver streamers hanging from the ceiling and a sign on the wall that reads Es Niño, Es Niño, Es Niño (It's a Boy, It's a Boy, It's a Boy), left over from a recent celebration to welcome Betanía's newest grandson into the family. Paula orders all of the children to wash their hands before eating. The older boy does not like anything in his soup, and carefully removes each sliver of onion from the broth and sets it aside. In coaxing the children to try the soup, Paula tells them that "caldito es bueno para la gripe" (a little soup is good for the flu) and "te curarás" (you will heal). Meanwhile, Paula's two-year-old daughter sits in her stroller in front of the television, intermittently crying to her mother for attention. Paula gives her Cheerios, asking if she would like some milk; the little girl nods. Paula proceeds to heat milk on the stove and then adds it to the cereal. Stacking plastic chairs one on top of another to function as a high chair, Paula props her daughter up at the table, yet the two-year-old still refuses to eat her Cheerios. For the boy who won't eat his soup Paula begins to prepare a sandwich of fried eggs, cheese, ham, slices of hot dog links, and mayonnaise.

About an hour past our scheduled meeting time Betanía finally returns home from the store, but with empty hands. She closes her umbrella and sits next to me with a look of resignation, indicating that her excursion was not a success.

These scenes from Betanía's home attest to the everyday constraints faced by many low-income, immigrant women in meeting the nutritional needs of households. With limited material means, they must resort to exercising their creativity and finding alternatives in this endeavor. While women such as Betanía attribute their decision to migrate to conditions of food insecurity, they regretfully report only minimal improvements to their household food resources after arriving in the United States. These constraints on nutritional needs compound the embodied aspects of *structural vulnerability*: "a positionality that imposes physical/emotional suffering on specific population groups and individuals in patterned ways ... it is a product of class-based economic exploitation and cultural, gender/sexual, and racialized discrimination" (Quesada, Hart, and Bourgois 2011, 340). The cumulated effects of structural vulnerability, James Quesada and colleagues (2011) argue, translate to "very real consequences: shorter lives subject to a disproportionate load of intimate suffering" (351). This chapter examines how women attempt to subvert the structural violence of food insecurity through migration, even if they are reacquainted with food insecurity once living in the United States.

OUT OF LATIN AMERICA: TRACING THE
GENDERED EFFECTS OF NEOLIBERALISM

Multilateral trade agreements, structural adjustment programs, and other modes of uneven economic development have contributed to widespread displacement of people from agrarian occupations and livelihoods in the world's less wealthy countries, as well as to mass migration of those displaced (Green 2011). A lack of economic opportunity in the home countries of migrants and a demand for workers abroad in the service sector has also translated to increased feminization of migration in the past two decades. In fact, a 2013 report by the United Nations estimated that women accounted for 48 percent of the total international migrant population, and that female-to-male ratios were even higher when looking at migration to the United States and Europe (United Nations Department of Economic and Social Affairs Population Division 2013). Migration from Latin America has specifically been linked to global capitalism, neoliberal economic development, and geopolitical instability in the region (Durand and Massey 2010; Kearney 1995; Robinson 2008). Jorge Durand and Douglas Massey (2010) identify three predominant channels of this outward migration: intraregional migration (i.e., migration within Latin America), south-to-north migration, and transoceanic migration. This book focuses on south-to-north migration, specifically from Mexico and Central America to the United States.

Since the late 1970s women have migrated from Mexico to the United States in equal numbers as men as a result of increased "economic integration of Mexico and the United States" and "feminization of labor" (Segura and Zavella 2007, 2). Much of this migration is unauthorized, meaning that individuals who are migrating do not have formal permission to do so. However, some scholars have actually argued that such migration is indeed authorized but that it is only fashioned as such "informally" through the labor demands waged by US-based employers (Plascencia 2012). Eleven million unauthorized immigrants are estimated to be living in the United States (Passel and Cohn 2011), one-third of whom are women (Segura and Zavella 2007). Compared to other states, California has the largest number of foreign-born residents from Latin America and the largest number of unauthorized immigrants employed in its economy (US Census Bureau 2010; Van Hook, Bean, and Passel 2005). Recent studies have suggested, however, that economic conditions related to recession accounted for a decline in the number of people migrating to the United States and even prompted some return migration to Mexico (Passel, Cohn, and Gonzalez-Barrera 2012). Durand and Massey (2010) note that although rates of Latin American intraregional and transoceanic migration are likely to intensify if the US economy slips into further decline, the actual number of immigrants from Latin America living in the United States continues to exceed populations in other regions. Thus, despite a temporary tapering off in the number of people arriving from Mexico, the United States continues to be an important site for analyzing migration from Latin America.

The ways in which women form a large part of this migration have received considerably little scholarly attention. Denise Segura and Patricia Zavella have, for instance, alluded to an underrepresentation of women "in the vast literature on migration from Mexico" (2007, 3); they note that migrant women's strategies for "[coping] with social inequalities based on racial, gender, class and/or sexual differences ... of feeling 'in between' cultures, languages, or places" (4) are often masked by "negative representations" circulated through the media and cultural norms (11), therefore adding insult to injury. These negative representations of Mexican (and Central American) women living in the United States insinuate that they lack "agency, resources, and knowledge—a portrayal that fuels a continual disavowal of their central role in sustaining the wellbeing of their families, cultural traditions, and a workforce upon which many of us depend" (Mares 2014, 46). For instance, US-Mexico borderlands anthropologist Deborah Boehm highlights the double standard in which a man migrating without legal authorization is valorized as a "good man," while an undocumented migrant woman proceeds with shame (2012, 97). Feminist scholar Grace Chang has also critiqued the popular misconception that Latina women represent a "new menace" to US society, being portrayed as "idle, welfare-dependent mothers and inordinate breeders of dependents" (2000, 4). She claims that a focus on allegedly high birth rates and immigrants' consumption of public resources "is clearly not gender neutral" (5). She writes, "Just as black women have babies in order to suck up welfare, we are told, immigrant women come to the United States to have babies and consume all of the natural resources in sight" (34). Chang finds that some women come to accept these portrayals, even engaging in rhetoric that is self-effacing, for the reason that they find few outlets for formal social belonging in US society.

Ethnographic research on women's migration from Mexico and Central America to the United States has identified several factors that influence women's decisions to migrate: desire for reunification with family members; desire for improved economic opportunities; intimate partner violence; and political violence and instability (Boehm 2012; Chang 2000; Segura and Zavella 2007). Women's levels of education, their prior marital status, and the strength of their social networks in the United States are also important predictors of migration. Segura and Zavella contend that the numbers of women migrating within the US-Mexico borderlands specifically are increasing: "More and more women migrate within Mexico and from Mexico to the United States, a development that exacts particular regional effects in both countries, including women's incorporation into the labor market and the feminization of specific occupations on both sides of the border" (2007, 5). They suggest that migrant women's entry into the labor market facilitates their negotiation "for an enhanced social space in households, local communities, and the state" (3). It is important to point out that in noting how women's migration is now almost on par with or surpassing that of men Segura and Zavella call for research that will enable us "to understand better the nature of this shift in the gender composition of transnational migrants and what it means for women's work and family experiences as well as women's identities and cultural expressions in the United States and in Mexico" (2007, 7). A fundamental aspect of endeavoring to understand shifts in the gender composition of transnational migrants is inquiring into how the very notion of gender is constituted through the process of migration. Given Judith Butler's assertion that "[g]ender is in no way a stable identity or locus of agency from which various acts proceed; rather, it is an identity tenuously constituted in time—an identity instituted through a *stylized repetition of acts*" (1998, 519), research on women's migration might delve into how women contest, negotiate, and enact social expectations tethered to gender identity.

As populations have been displaced from agrarian livelihoods in Mexico and Central America through neoliberal policies of structural adjustment and trade liberalization, women from these communities have faced a unique set of challenges. Much of this has to do with the ways in which women are disproportionately burdened with the labor of *social reproduction*: "the creation of people as cultural and social, as well as physical beings" (Glenn 1992, 4). While the "double-duty" workday extracts value from women both as wage earners and caregivers, these activities do not yield equal compensation. Susana Narotzky (1997) claims this is because the act of caring is believed to inherently provide its own rewards. Despite evidence presented by feminist scholars warranting compensation for the reproductive labor that undergirds "productive" labor and enables capital accumulation (Barker 2005; Narotzky 1997), reproductive labor has been consistently devalued.

Food Insecurity as Structural Violence

The North American Free Trade Agreement, signed in 1994 by the United States, Mexico, and Canada, serves as a prime example of legislation that has displaced many rural Mexican households from farming as an occupation because they are unable to compete with subsidized, imported commodities (Fernandez-Kelley and Massey 2007). The Central American Free Trade Agreement has had similar repercussions on Central American rural households. Shahra Razavi (2002) elaborates on the effects of these policies, particularly for women; she writes, "Rather than *shifting the terms of trade* toward agriculture, neoliberal policies have been, in effect, *shifting the burdens* of adjustment toward small farmers, and especially the women in rural households who often bear the double burden of farm (and off-farm) work and the care of human beings" (2002, 2; emphasis in the original). Stated bluntly, the effects of neoliberal economic policies have not been gender neutral. Rather, women have experienced uneven consequences of these policy shifts and have had to make "invisible adjustments" along the way. Razavi further elaborates, "As governments have abandoned essential elements of public social provision, social responsibility has shifted to families and communities, throwing a disproportionate burden on women's shoulders" (8–9), including the burden of the provision of food. Moreover, the demise of the welfare state brought about by structural adjustment, as well as the inability to compete with cheap agricultural inputs rendered through trade liberalization, has compromised the capacity of rural households to avoid food insecurity. Although Penny Van Esterik argues that "states have a duty to avoid depriving, to protect from depriving, and to aid the deprived" (1999b, 226), food insecurity, as a palpable consequence of these policy shifts, represents the biopolitics of the state and "states themselves often do the depriving intentionally or unintentionally" (226).

As Van Esterik (1999) contends, "Women's identity and sense of self is often based on their ability to feed their families and others; food insecurity denies them this right" (225). Food procurement, preparation, and allocation are inherently social activities through which women may sustain and negotiate relations with others while also asserting some level of influence over these relations (Abarca 2006; Allen and Sachs 2007). Carole Counihan (1999) stresses the historical precedence of these activities, and of feeding in particular, as they have been asserted by women throughout the world. Drawing on Counihan's influential work on food and gender, Masha Sukovic and colleagues underscore that "women have always had a special relationship with food, as they have universal responsibility for food preparation and consumption, are often defined as nurturers, and carry out this role mainly through feeding" (2011, 229). Feeding and its accompanying labors—what Brenda Beagan (2008) calls foodwork—therefore comprise a central aspect of social reproduction. As such, impediments to these activities have very real social consequences. As Van Esterik notes, "For women who are normally responsible for feeding their families, the experience of being unable to feed their children is tantamount to torture" (1999, 230).

Notably, the literature on women's migration from Mexico and Central America to the United States has yet to identify or consider with much resolve the role of structural violence in the global industrial food system and the gendered division of foodwork in shaping human transnational flows. Teresa Mares's (2012; 2013) research on Latino immigrants' engagements with different food programs in the Seattle area in some ways stands as an exception. In examining Latino immigrants' reliance on emergency food programs and how they view these programs as complementing ties of mutual aid, she finds that "the provisioning of emergency food remains an inadequate solution to transnational material inequalities that disparately impact the lives" of these immigrants (2013, 2). She also extends her thinking to the structural violence of a food system that has transnational implications, gesturing to the possible ways that food insecurity patterns migration, noting, "The stripping of rights and agency is indicative of the inequalities that persist not only in the emergency food system but also in the transnational economic disparities that impel people to migrate in the first place ... this reliance on emergency food and the absence of self-sufficiency must be placed into a transnational context whereby the crossing of borders becomes a strategy to survive neoliberal policies that have impoverished millions" (2013, 19). Despite Mares's astute critique, her speculation about how food insecurity interacts with people's decisions to migrate remains a secondary area of interest in her overall analysis. Her data also do not necessarily allow her to explore the extent to which these patterns of displacement are gendered.

Indeed, few scholars have explicitly questioned the reciprocal relationship of food insecurity to migration (Crush 2013), an issue that merits further attention. One explanation for why this gap exists, at least in terms of the ethnographic literature, could be that informants and researchers often implicate one another in the production of nostalgic narratives of food and homeland. For instance, the isolated or rare occasion of feasting during a festive celebration might override the everyday scarcity or monotony of food in informants' retelling of the past. Experiences of food insecurity and hunger prove to be undoubtedly painful and even traumatic, and as such they are often folded into a more generalized discourse of poverty or suffering in informants' narratives. Veena Das's insight that "[r]esearch on gender and violence is not only about how worlds are unmade by violence but also how they are remade" (2008, 293) suggests here that part of the process of healing or distancing oneself from traumatic experience involves informants reconstructing the past as they would like for it to be remembered.

In the following section I turn again to the experiences of my key informants to suggest that women's decisions to migrate may indeed exhibit a desire to uphold social obligations in the realm of food amid massive structural shifts that translate to livelihood displacement in rural communities. I highlight the prominence of food insecurity in these women's decisions to migrate. Specifically, the act of *alimentarse*—a verb from Spanish translating as "to feed"—occupies a central place in these women's conceptualizations of motherhood, with subsequent implications for women's decisions around migration. Despite the ubiquity with which women throughout the world are assigned to overseeing this aspect of social reproduction, I also wish to push back against depictions of all women as "natural" nurturers; it is this sort of bio-

logical essentialism that sustains and supports a continued deval-
uation of reproductive, caring labors.

With these women's stories I also suggest that resistance to recognizing migration as a survival strategy of many has the dual
effect of dehumanizing those who suffer and obscuring experiences of poverty. By highlighting the experience of food insecurity as a consequence of poverty and primary impetus for wom-
en's migration, I question in the chapter's concluding section why
the moral economy through which categories of inclusion and
exclusion are constructed and enacted currently does not allow
for recognizing the violence of being denied adequate food.

THE PROMINENCE OF FOOD
IN GENDERED MIGRATION

As I listened to women's histories of migration in conducting my
research, I was slightly surprised to hear one phrase uttered over
and over again: "Allá no tenemos nada que comer" (Back there we
had nothing to eat). In invoking this past, many women were alluding to everyday struggles to uphold obligations to family shaped
by overall material scarcity but epitomized in the constraints on
feeding and eating. I am by no means the first to make this observation. Deborah Boehm accounts for the "intimate relations," for
instance, that shape women's migration from Latin America to the
United States, and Melanie Nicholson (2006) observes how Mexican women "are literally providing food for their children" by
migrating to the United States: "[They] are also constructing
visions of their children's futures that would have been impossible
without migration. [These women see] the present separation
from their children as a *sacrifice* that [will] lead to improved standards of living for the family as a whole, and particularly for their

children, in both the present and the future" (2012, 21). The following vignettes reveal a framing of migration through the language of feeding and eating as they also underscore the forms of grief, conflict, and exploitation that intersect with women's decisions to migrate and their aspirations to overcome the structural conditions that constrain them as mothers.

"There Isn't Enough Money"

Linda, a mother of three, found solace in having spared her children from the hunger she knew as a child. Growing up in Michoacán, Linda's family could not afford to buy any food. Instead, they relied on a diet of *básicos* (basic foods): "If one desires fruit or vegetables, *one must buy them* and our parents didn't have enough money to buy. We ate almost no meat because it was very expensive. So we ate beans, chilies, tortillas; this is what one ate most because we didn't have money for fruits and vegetables." Her father tended to the land and her mother to fruit trees; these activities provided an important source of food for her family despite the unpredictability of harvests. Her parents suffered from different health problems, including diabetes (her mother) and complications from alcoholism (her father). In reflecting on how diabetes eventually led to her mother's death, Linda speculated on the extent to which this disease was brought on and exacerbated by a diet lacking in quality sources of nutrition. Despite her resentment toward her father for having been an abusive alcoholic while she was growing up, she exhibited some sympathy toward him in relaying how the economic desperation of her family could have had a similar effect on anyone.

As a child Linda was expected by her mother to clean the house, launder clothes by hand, and iron things for money from others in town. She did not attend school for long because her parents needed the children in her family to work. She recalled the shame of not being able to even afford shoes. At the age of twelve Linda began working in *el campo* (the fields) "cortando la fresa" (harvesting strawberries), then broccoli, and later tomatoes. Even with the combined income among her siblings the family was never able to accumulate enough money to buy nutritious food ("no alcanza dinero para comida nutritiva"), nor were the children permitted to eat the food that they picked as farmworkers.

In her early twenties and anticipating her first child, Linda decided to migrate to the small Southern California city of Carpinteria, where her husband had been working in the local flower nurseries. Linda's husband paid $1,200 to a *coyote* for her crossing into the United States, an experience that proved highly traumatic. She had been racked with anxiety prior to crossing, and the person waiting to escort her on the other side—her uncle—attempted to molest her.

I meet Linda when she is in her early thirties, almost ten years after her arrival in the United States. She and her husband do not have papers, but all of their children, now ages twelve, seven, and five, are US citizens by birth. On a typical day Linda drives her husband to work in the morning in their used minivan, makes breakfast, brings her children to school, cleans the house, goes to the grocery store, does laundry, makes dinner, and bathes her children. Linda also does the majority of cooking for her husband's parents who live nearby; Linda and her husband bring them food every other day on the way to or from his work. Linda earns some money on the side doing laundry for her neighbors, and she has a job cleaning a woman's house about thirty miles away once a week.

Although she considers her present living circumstances vastly better than those she experienced as a child, and access to food in the United States as "mejor que nuestro pueblo" (better than in our town [in Mexico]), Linda laments that frequently she does not have the resources to provide what she considers to be a balanced diet to her children. She has also been making pleas to her husband to curtail his drinking habit so that they can have a little more money for food. To save money on groceries, she risks driving without a license forty minutes south to the city of Oxnard because she can find foods there at a cheaper price. However, much of the food in her household comes from charitable local food pantries because "no hay suficiente dinero para comprar" (there isn't enough money to buy [food]). She collects produce through charitable distributions at a church on the first and third Wednesday of each month and also once per month at a community center. Although her family never goes without eating, she worries that the food they eat is insufficient for maintaining good health.

Linda was not the only one of her siblings to leave Michoacán in search of a better life; her sister Luisa had migrated, also to Carpinteria, for similar reasons. Luisa's recollections of her childhood, especially in terms of food, mirror those of her sister: *básicos* such as beans, a piece of cheese, chilies in vinegar, *hecho de mano* (handmade) tortillas, and on rare occasions, meat: "Here [in the United States]," she explains, "you don't lack for an apple, an orange, fruit, anything. In Mexico, it is very different. In Mexico they raised us on beans. When she could, our mom bought us a piece of cheese and chilies in vinegar to add to our meal.... When they had money they sometimes bought us soup or meat. But very little meat because it was so expensive and our parents didn't have the money to buy it for us. We ate whatever there was for us to eat."

Like her sister, Luisa had helped around the household and attended only a few years of school but was sent to work in the fields at the age of twelve. She was twenty-two years old when she

Figure 7. The nursery grounds—the site of Linda's husband's employment—in Carpinteria. Photo by the author.

migrated to the United States with her husband, as they were soon going to start a family. By the time they married, her husband had been migrating seasonally between the United States and Mexico for ten years.

When I meet Luisa she has been living in the United States for fifteen years and shares a home with her husband, son (age fifteen), and daughter (age twelve). I usually visit Luisa on weekdays at her apartment, which is located mere blocks from Carpinteria State Beach; her husband is always at work, so I never have the opportunity to meet him. Often when I visit Luisa she is caring for others' children as a means to earning some income. She enjoys taking these children with her on beach walks as part of her daily exercise. During our mornings together, chatting over coffee and the *telenovelas* resounding from Luisa's television, she complains of heated arguments with her husband from the night before; she implies that increased financial stress at home has prompted many of these arguments. Moreover, she worries that her husband is siphoning away the already meager amount of money that she has earmarked for food through his worsening drinking habit. Fortunately, she is able to partially make up for these losses through help from food stamps and provisions from local food pantries that she frequents with her sister. She thinks about leaving her husband and taking her children with her, but she fears lacking the means to feed them. During a focus group discussion, Luisa informs us all that she is on a waiting list for family counseling services.

"I Fight for Their Well-Being"

Tensions with her husband and an inability to provide for her children, especially in the way of food, had informed Malena's decision to migrate from the Mexican state of Guerrero to the United States. While living estranged from her husband for several years as he migrated to and from the United States, Malena had relied on him to send remittances home in support of the family: "He left me with my child when he was only two months old; he came here [to the United States]. He had been coming here since 1984. So he already knew the country well." These remittances from her husband had been helping Malena to procure foods for her children until one day when this support suddenly stopped.

When I meet Malena, she is forty-four years old, working more than seventy hours per week as a hotel housekeeper and living with her youngest daughter (age four), who has US citizenship by birth. Three of her children (ages thirteen, fourteen, and eighteen) are still living in Guerrero with their grandmother and she has since gone through a divorce from her husband.

Although Malena expresses tremendous grief in being away from her children, she rationalizes her decision to migrate to the United States for the primary reason that she was no longer able to fulfill her responsibilities as a mother while remaining in Mexico. Her husband had forfeited his obligations to the family by discontinuing financial support and communication, and she had a debt that was accumulating from needing to borrow money to buy food: "The debt that I had there [in Mexico] ... this is what was worrying me. So I thought and said, 'When I am going to pay this money?' So, I thought and thought only of this, and I had faith and hope that I'd arrive here [in the United States]. Ultimately I was thinking of work because I came to work, to find a job."

With limited resources to feed her children, and desiring to reconcile her marriage, Malena decided to seek work and reunite with her husband in the United States. Malena's husband begrudgingly assisted with the $1,500 they paid to a *coyote* to help her cross the border. When she arrived in the United States, however, she struggled to find work. Her husband was of no help, and he berated her for being a financial drain on him and others in their shared household. He also tried intimidating her with accusations that she would never find work and that she was incapable of supporting herself.

Food was especially difficult for Malena to manage during those times when she did not have a job. There are often long pauses whenever I ask about hunger or reductions to one's food intake; she'll then open up about times in the past that she would lock herself away in her room for days at a time, forgoing meals entirely.

Almost a year after her arrival in the United States, Malena's brother was finally able to arrange a job for her picking and packing peaches, grapes, and cherries in a Northern California town near San Francisco. Malena credited her five months working in Northern California, and living away from her husband, with having doused her fears and cultivating in her a newfound strength

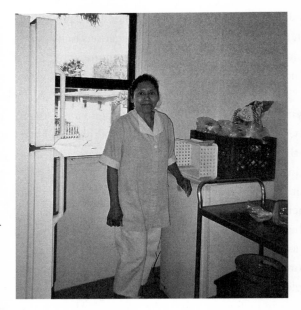

Figure 8. Malena's self-portrait at work. Photo courtesy of Malena.

that allowed her to stand up to her husband: "perdí mi miedo... me dio una esperanza" (I lost my fear... and [this experience] gave me hope). Since this experience, work has provided an important source of pride for Malena, perhaps partially because food has been so difficult to manage without a job. Her self-portrait while dressed in uniform at work is a testament of this pride.

Malena attributes the end of her marriage to irreconcilable differences. Her husband felt no sense of obligation to the family and did not care to comport himself in the manner of a faithful companion or devoted father. "He does not live for his children, they do not merit his attention, and he didn't even want to speak to them. He didn't like the responsibility of having children," she explains. Her children wanted to hear from their father but he rarely called or visited. Malena describes him as someone who preferred to drink and party with friends. Whenever she would confront him about his behavior, their exchanges always escalated into "conversaciones fuertes" (heated conversations). Eventually she gave him the option of divorce, which he accepted. She has since been caring for the family entirely on her own.

Malena has not seen three of her children for five years, as they remain in Guerrero with their grandmother. Her undocumented status makes it nearly impossible for her to visit them without risking reentry to the United States. During one focus group discussion Malena becomes visibly distressed as she reflects on being away from her children in Mexico; she wants them to know that "Esforzarme para dejarlos bien" (I fight for their well-being). She adds, "I hope to do something better for them because they are young and they still need me." They frequently ask when they will be able to visit, but she fears she won't be able to provide for them in the United States, as she has already needed to significantly reduce the amount of money she sends home each month. Without anyone else to help take care of her youngest daughter here, the two of them sometimes eat at fast food establishments such as McDonald's because they are the cheapest option: "el precio mas que nada" (price more than anything).

AN UNENDING HUNGER: FOOD INSECURITY IN ACCOUNTS OF RETURN MIGRATION

While constraints on eating and feeding might precede women's decisions to migrate from their home countries, as in the experiences of Linda, Luisa, and Malena, it is also the case that these constraints could factor into decisions around return migration. Following economic recession, many of my research participants relayed stories of return migration on the part of relatives, friends, or neighbors, or even speculated on their own plans for return.

Mothers who are living estranged from children increasingly perceive fewer advantages to remaining in the United States. Yolanda, for instance, a mother with children on both sides of the US-Mexico border, has been contemplating a return to Acapulco. She cites how continuing effects of the economic crisis have jeopardized her ability to feed her children. Originally, Yolanda migrated to the United States to assist her husband, who was not earning enough money to support her and their two daughters (ages fourteen and eight) in Acapulco. She arrived in the United States in 2004. "I was sad because my husband was gone," she explains. "[Our daughters] wanted to see him too. He was here and sending us money. It was hard because I was used to his company and at times I felt lonely. He decided to bring me here but I had to leave my daughters behind." Yolanda and her husband reimbursed "poco a poco" (little by little) the $1,700 owed to a *coyote* for helping her to cross the border. When she first arrived they were sharing a room with another family in an apartment, but later transitioned to having their own room in an apartment shared with two other families. She collected cans and bottles on the street as a way to earn some cash and then worked in a cracker factory for six years until its closure the previous October. Presently, her husband is working as a painter and she as a housecleaner, but she reveals some frustration with the job because her *patrona* is always scolding her and threatening to reduce her hours.

In the six years they have been working in the United States, Yolanda and her husband have had two more children. She agonizes about her family's living situation: "I have two [children] here and it's difficult because I want to see my other daughters [in Mexico]. I tell them 'soon,' but I don't really know. We're going to see what happens with the economy and decide whether it is better for me to stay or to return." She is pleased that her children in the United States will benefit someday in the workplace from having learned "dos idiomas" (two languages). Previously, when she had more stable employment, Yolanda had been able to send money to her two children in Mexico every two weeks for food and school-related costs, including books, notebooks, backpacks, and clothes. While Yolanda longs to reunite with her children in Mexico, she also doesn't want to deprive her US-born children of the privileges of citizenship. Nonetheless, a decline in wages and fewer opportunities for employment in the United States increasingly interferes with her ability to put food on the table.

On one of my visits to her home situated within a large apartment complex in Santa Barbara, Yolanda tells me that she is preparing a soup with chicken that she found discounted at the store. She explains her preference for making soups over *comida seca* (dry food), and for preparing meat in soups rather than *seca* (out of water), because the broth absorbs the flavor and the nutrition. Yolanda cuts and washes broccoli, potatoes, and baby carrots. She makes a salsa in the blender using water, tomatoes, and garlic; this salsa will provide a flavor base for the soup. She lights her gas stove with a match. Meanwhile her husband watches television in the other room and her children play outside enjoying the extra hours of summer light. Occasionally they peer into the window to watch their mother in the kitchen.

Food insecurity has been rampant in Yolanda's household—especially four months ago, when neither she nor her husband could find work. They never go hungry because they at least always have basic items such as bread and milk, she explains, which they obtain through vouchers from the WIC program. There have been times, however, when she has had to reduce the amount of food she gives to her children, and rarely do they have the ingredients necessary to attain her vision of a balanced diet. For these reasons, Yolanda has become extra vigilant about stretching what few resources they have to feed her family.

"DESERVING" TO CROSS BORDERS

Sukovic and colleagues call for bringing "a more prominent gendered or feminist perspective into the emerging field of food studies, especially the connection between food preparation and empowerment" (2011, 234). In the preceding pages I have argued that we should expand our analysis of gendered migration to be more attentive to how food scarcity undergirds women's decisions to migrate from Mexico and Central America and also to how it punctuates the experiences of Mexican and Central American women in the United States.

An emerging literature underscores the politics of deservingness particularly as it relates to a moral economy of migration (Sargent 2012; Sargent and Larchanche 2011; Willen 2012). Resistance on the part of nation-states toward creating a category of "economic refugees" alongside "political refugees," as well as the disavowal of many nation-states to recognize the impact of free trade agreements on livelihoods elsewhere, attest to how the political and the economic are often imagined as separate and distinct spheres. Certain conditions impelling people to migrate, such as war, religious persecution, or severe illness, tend to elicit more moral sympathy than do poverty, hunger, or unemployment. With moral logics shaping conceptualizations of deservingness, not everyone who migrates is deemed worthy of entry. In her research with the *sans papiers* in France for instance, Miriam Ticktin (2011) analyzes the social consequences of France's "illness clause" through which the state delineates the terms of "morally legitimate suffering" and inclusion of those who are then eligible for legal authorization while excluding all others who do not fit these criteria, noting, "A politics of immigration based on this type of care and compassion gives papers to an HIV+ Malian woman, an Algerian child with cancer, and a gay Moroccan man gang-raped by Moroccan policemen and closes doors to most others, making these strangely desirable conditions for immigrants" (4). In asking, "Why is it that illness can cross borders while poverty cannot?" (95) Ticktin highlights the contradictions of a moral economy of suffering that prescribes deservingness differentially. Missing from this maneuvering by nation-states however, is a rec-ognition of how disparate forms of suffering are imbricated with one another: poverty produces sickness just as sickness may also compound poverty. Food insecurity serves as one example, for despite being intimately connected with health status it has not been recognized as a legitimate basis for seeking authorized entry into countries such as the United States.

Several researchers have highlighted the importance of food for the process of resettlement, specifically in terms of women's social and cultural identities. Purnima Mankekar (2002) suggests that the inability of diasporic populations to re-create the culinary tradi-tions of their homeland poses hindrances to the linked process of social and cultural reproduction. Mares notes that, "In the midst of dislocation, sustaining and re-creating the cultural and mate-rial practices connected to food are powerful ways to enact one's cultural identity and sustain connections with families and com-munities who remain on the other side of the border" (2012, 335).

Women's food preparation in the context of migration, Sukovic and colleagues (2011) argue, "serves as one of the few connections between new life in the United States and the old way of life and culture in Mexico" (237). Moreover, Van Esterik suggests, "The power women have includes the power to feed," (1999, 230).

As Mexican and Central American women encounter the "everyday violence of imposed scarcity, insecurity, and fear" (Quesada et al. 2011, 393) associated with unauthorized status in the United States, they find it increasingly difficult to meet the basic nutritional needs of their families, much less to re-create traditional foods, sociability around mealtimes, and other important food traditions. As women respond to the unevenness in food access and distribution that often translates to heightened health and nutritional vulnerabilities, they invoke a "subjective transnationalism" (Segura and Zavella 2007)—in other words, an agentive negotiation of what it means to be a gendered subject in *borderlands*—a space located in between different places and cultures. These women also actively contest the limited means of survival afforded them in these spaces of in-betweenness (Counihan 2005). While the women I interviewed often associated migration with improved capacity to nourish others through food, they also described impediments to everyday nutritional needs and thus to the long-term demands of social reproduction. In chapter 2, I examine more closely migrant women's conceptualizations of motherhood and how they navigate everyday constraints to "nourishing bodies and social ties" (Pérez and Abarca 2007, 141) while living in the United States.

CHAPTER TWO

Caring through Food

La Lucha Diaria

A BASIC NECESSITY OF LIFE

"I think that every person must have the ambition to get ahead, more than anything to ensure what is necessary," comments Yolanda. "That is food. Food comes first, before material things. Material things come and go; it's food that comes first and is the thing that is needed."

As so many migrants before her who have associated coming to the United States with the prospect of "getting ahead," Yolanda's words are a subtle reminder that getting enough to eat represents, above all else, the most important means of survival. Yolanda alludes to the set of personal obligations that inform one's fulfillment of this basic need in spite of precarious circumstances that may impede efforts to put food on the table. As such, she insists that individuals must summon an unrelenting ambition from within to overcome the circumstances imposed on them. In Yolanda's formulation, food does not belong in the realm of "lo material" because, unlike the fleeting importance of material things, food has life-sustaining properties.

As something that is ingested into the body and animates us as living beings, food is a basic substance of life, but its exchange and communion are also embedded in relations of social reproduction. Consequently, food is pivotal in the production of people as cultural, social, and physical beings. Yet, in stratified societies the parameters of social reproduction are profoundly uneven and vary along lines of gender, race, class, ethnicity, and citizenship. These hierarchies also prevail within the realm of socially reproductive *labor*, which includes the work of providing care, or what I will interchangeably refer to as *caring labor*. In discussing *care* I seek to operationalize the definition provided by Mary Zimmerman, Jacquelyn Litt and Christine Bose: "the multifaceted labor that produces the daily living conditions that make basic human health and well-being possible" (2006, 3). As I mentioned in the introduction to the present volume, women throughout the world have been charged with the bulk of responsibility for overseeing social reproduction, but doing so often requires navigation of complex material, institutional, and ideological constraints (Barker 2005; Hondagneu-Sotelo and Avila 2007; Narotzky 1997; Rae 2008; Segura 1993; Van Esterik 1999a, 1999b). These constraints imply that the means to enacting care, and the forms of labor such an enactment requires, are not equally available to all women.

CARING AS A "LUCHA DIARIA"

In March 2010 I visit Tina at her home in one of Santa Barbara's lower-income neighborhoods. The building in which Tina makes her home has sunk into the ground in several sections, reeks of mildew, and has large sections of paint peeling off its exterior wood panels. As Tina prepares a *caldo de pollo* (chicken soup) for lunch, she recounts the difficulties of having been a single mother for so many years. Although all of Tina's children are now grown and have moved out of her household, she recalls with vividness what she terms *la lucha diaria* (the daily struggle): a combination of institutional arrangements, social relations, and material insecurities that characterize her daily milieu and threaten to jeopardize at any time her ability to care for her children.

Tina migrated to the United States as a teenager with her mother and two sisters from the Mexican state of Sinaloa in 1981. Because she had limited knowledge of English, she attended high school for a very short period of time and instead pursued a series of clerical and factory jobs before marrying and having three children. When I meet Tina she has been divorced for several years, her ex-husband having already returned to Mexico when their children were still young and living at home. Although Tina laments the hardships of her youth, she also exhibits pride in having fought so hard years ago to ensure her children's well-being. She coats the discourse with which she speaks of this *lucha diaria* in a sort of twisted nostalgia, relaying graciously how her former struggles precipitated the level of self-confidence she claims today.

Feminist scholars have underlined the intrinsic inequalities that give caring labor its structure and meaning as it traverses the spectrum of women's lived experiences. As JaneMaree Maher notes, "Women's work in unpaid care is crucial to functioning societies, but the requirement to give this care and the conditions for it affect differently located women in different ways" (2012, 21). In the United States, the reproductive labors of low-income women have historically been constrained by low-wage labor and other structural disadvantages that create serious tensions around maintaining employment, caring for children, balancing household resources, seeking social services, and enduring discrimination (Dodson 2007). While shrinking welfare states have implied additional reproductive burdens for women of various social classes, much of this burden has been transferred to women of lower socioeconomic status or foreign origin (Narotzky 1997). Increasingly, "the physical and social elements of mothering" (Maher 2010, 16) are sought after as transnational commodities.

In a global context, the work of caring across borders reveals a rearranging of the social organization of caring labor as it also speaks to changes in what is required for economic survival. Migrant women may find themselves doing the work of social reproduction for others' children while simultaneously enduring long-term physical separations from their own (Hondagneu-Sotelo and Avila 2007; Nicholson 2006; Parreñas 2001; Segura 1993). This demand for a particularly mobile and flexible labor force has followed the emergence of care "deficits"—the loss of workers to other sectors of the economy—resulting from the low wages and overall low prestige assigned to care work. Observing trends among foreign-born women toward increasingly filling positions for which emotional as well as physical labor are core requirements, feminist scholars critique a transnational transferring of the burden of care from those within the family sphere to foreign others (Cheng 2006; Glenn 2012).

Some social scientists have suggested that by entering transnational spaces of care, women forge "new arrangements and meanings of motherhood" in terms of relating to children who have been left behind (Hondagneu-Sotelo and Avila 2007, 389). Remittances, letters, and phone calls become important channels of communication for sustaining these transnational mother-child relationships (Hondagneu-Sotelo and Avila 2007; Nicholson 2006). Notably, these less-conventional parenting strategies do not make women any less fit for motherhood; rather, as poignantly asserted by Nancy Scheper-Hughes, motherhood is always "grounded in specific historical and cultural realities and bounded by different economic and demographic constraints" (1992, 356). In the case of many Latin American women living and working in the United States, meeting the demand for caring labor across borders has helped in fulfilling their own goals of economic advancement. Indeed, partaking in transnational economies of care may enhance women's capacities for social reproduction both in the United States and/or abroad. Yet these transnational economies of care also act as a form of stratified reproduction that may actually detract from women's desired efforts to improve the well-being of their own children.

In this chapter I describe what it means for Mexican or Central American women in the United States to struggle with the everyday demands of care and motherhood, particularly as these relate to the realm of feeding. I foreshadowed some of the themes of this chapter in Tina's description of *la lucha diaria* because of how much her experience overlapped with that of other women in my research, especially in terms of feelings of obligation and devotion to motherhood. However, rather than strictly focusing on the ways that care contributed to women's subordination in the household (Rae 2008; Van Esterik 1999b), several of my key informants upheld the practice of care—and specifically care enacted through foodwork—as a site of social empowerment. I examine the complex concerns of women in overseeing this practice, and how these concerns relate to a gendered division of labor that is transnational in scope. I argue that feeding—perhaps the most basic form of caring labor—is significantly constrained by the circumstances of living as a racialized, undocumented, or speciously perceived-to-be undocumented immigrant woman in the United

States. This argument requires engaging an intersectional analytic lens that attends to the matrix of "overlapping structures of subordination" such as transnational dynamics and processes of racialization as well as gendering that shape and render uneven life chances (Cho, Crenshaw, and McCall 2013, 797; Patil 2013).

While it is not my objective to downplay how the experiences of foreign-born Mexican and Central American women resemble the historical experiences of other marginalized groups of women in the United States, as this would undermine the purpose of an intersectional analysis, I also think it is important to acknowledge how immigration status (or lack thereof) compounds the struggles of the former group. Responding to the ways that US immigration policy as well as public attitudes toward those who are foreign born have fluctuated with economic conditions, so that welcoming policies characterize periods of economic expansion and punitive policies during recession, Carlos Vélez-Ibáñez contends that migrants have struggled to "defend themselves against repeated attempts by the state and/or 'market' to exert complete control over their labor and productive capacities" (1996, 135). And while generational advancement and socioeconomic mobility may help to strengthen migrants' social networks in the United States, not all migrants have equal access to these forms of social support. These "buffers" are also not sufficient to undo the historical trauma of repeated displacement and exploitation, as I mention below through a brief history of Anglo settlement in Santa Barbara County.

From "Barriorization" to "Illegality"

Prior to the US annexation of California from Mexico in 1848, the region of Santa Barbara had belonged to the area known as Mexico and its population primarily comprised Hispanos. Less than thirty years after the annexation, the city of Santa Barbara had become dominated by its Anglo settlers, who viewed Mexican society as "an impediment to the development of the city as a desirous home for Anglos" (Camarillo 1979, 16). Discrimination of and hostility toward Mexican society characterized this early period following annexation and later became institutionalized (Camarillo 1979; Irazabal and Farhat 2008).

In *Chicanos in a Changing Society*, a book that documents historical shifts in the Chicano population of the American Southwest, and particularly that of Southern California, Albert Camarillo focuses most of his attention on Santa Barbara, which he deems "the stronghold of Mexican socioeconomic and political influence in nineteenth-century southern California" (1979, 3) and thus witness to some of the most drastic changes resulting from Anglo-American expansion. He argues that the present-day subordinate socioeconomic and political status of Chicanos and Latinos "emanated from the establishment of the dominant Anglo society in southern California and the corresponding growth of the capitalist economic system during the late nineteenth century" (1979, 4). The incorporation of Chicanos into the capitalist system during the late 1800s and early 1900s, Camarillo explains "locked them into the status of a predominantly unskilled/semiskilled working class at the bottom of the occupational structure" (5).

Camarillo notes that by the end of 1873 Santa Barbara was "undeniably more 'American' than 'Mexican'" (33), having undergone the gradual transition from Mexican "pueblos" to American "barrios," the former characterized by political influence and considerable wealth from a pastoral economy and the latter by impoverishment and marginalization. Chicano families were relocated to remote areas of the city, thus initiating a process of "barriorization," defined by Camarillo as "the formation of residentially and socially segregated Chicano barrios or neighborhoods" (52). The barrio, Camarillo notes, quickly developed into an area of concentrated poverty as the city neglected to provide resources and denied representation to Chicanos in city politics.

As the Anglo-American capitalist industry in the areas of tourism, urban development, and agricultural production gradually replaced the traditional Mexican pastoral economy, Chicanos were restricted "to the most menial, unskilled, and semiskilled occupations" (Camarillo 1979, 79). With persistent unemployment in these industries, women assumed "a triple responsibility of head of household, mother, and wage earner" (91). Chicanas worked low-wage jobs as domestics, laundresses, cooks, ironers, and seamstresses. While female employment challenged notions of women's traditional roles within the Chicano community, there were still "some prejudices against married women working in jobs which would take them away from their household obligations" (Griswold del Castillo 1984, 38).

A period of renewed economic migration from 1890 to 1920 led to an expansion of the Chicano community in Santa Barbara (Camarillo 1979). Close to 50,000 Mexicans entered the United States during this time (Irazabal and Farhat 2008). As Camarillo explains, patterns of the familial migration network were initiated: "After one family situated itself, it would attract relatives and friends from the original home in Mexico" (1979, 144). This trend continued into the 1920s, with more than 410,000 Mexicans entering the United States during this decade, but it curtailed significantly during the Great Depression (Irazabal and Farhat 2008). The US government initiated deportations, arguing that assimilationist "Americanization" programs failed to improve the lives of Mexicans (Camarillo 1979). Deportations of some 500,000 Mexicans ruptured the social fabric of the barrio community, estranging family members and spatially disaggregating social networks (Camarillo 1979; Irazabal and Farhat 2008). It was not until World War II and the establishment of the *bracero* program that migration from Mexico to the United States resumed with some measurable significance, as more than four million men were granted temporary work contracts amid the labor shortage.[1] Many of the *bracero* workers later resettled with their families in the United States and were granted amnesty through the passage of the Immigration and Reform Control Act of 1986 (Plascencia 2012).

Although the US government has intermittently waged deterrence and deportation measures against unauthorized migrants throughout the nation's history, today's policies and practices of immigration enforcement reflect an amplified "immigration regime" (Ferreti-Majarrez 2012; Menjívar 2013; Zavella 2011). State disciplining and surveillance of "noncitizen" bodies characterizes a variety of settings that operate in tandem with the militarization and enforcement of geopolitical borders (Boehm 2012; Fassin 2011; Ong 2006; Zavella 2011). Particularly since the establishment of the Department of Homeland Security and the recent onset of economic recession, unauthorized migrants have been living in heightened fear of criminalization by the state (Bank Muñoz 2008; Hacker et al. 2011). There have been more than 400,000 deportations annually since 2009, representing about double the annual average during George W. Bush's first term (Lopez, Gonzalez-Barrera, and Motel 2011). State-level forms of legislation around immigration, including Alabama House Bill 56, Arizona Senate Bill 1070, Georgia House Bill 87, and South Carolina Act 69, attempt to achieve attrition through enforcement, criminalize the existence of unauthorized migrants within state boundaries, and deny migrants access to employment, housing, education, and forms of public and private assistance (Ferreti-Majarrez 2012; Menjívar 2013; Plascencia 2013). The US government has also substantially increased funding to further militarize its borders; notably, recent proposals for immigration reform reviewed by Congress have consistently included more robust funding for border militarization alongside future pathways to citizenship for people already in the United States.

Nicholas de Genova contends that migrant "illegality" is predicated on the erasure of legal personhood, marooning the individual into "a space of forced invisibility, exclusion, subjugation, and repression" (2002, 427). Simultaneously a juridical status, sociopolitical condition, and way of being in the world (Plascencia 2012; Willen 2007), "illegality" renders an individual "physically present but legally absent, existing in a space outside of society, a space of 'nonexistence,' a space that is not actually 'elsewhere' or beyond borders but that is rather a hidden dimension of social reality" (Coutin 2007, 9). Roberto Gonzales and Leo Chavez offer a revision to this definition by suggesting that "to be illegally present is not to be 'outside of society' but to be allowed to participate in some aspects of society (e.g., schooling) but not others (e.g., work)" (2012, 258). The precarious state of "illegality" experienced by many unauthorized migrants also makes it increasingly difficult to avoid food insecurity once living in the United States, a condition that precipitates a decline in health (Fitzgerald et al. 2011; Weigel et al. 2007). Forms of discrimination and social exclusion enacted through the frame of "illegality" should not be misinterpreted as separate or distinct from the discrimination and hostility toward Chicanos that characterized early Anglo settlement in the American Southwest; indeed, these newer oppressive regimes are a continuation of settler colonial dynamics.

Women's immigration status was always in the backdrop of this research, posing new anxieties for the *lucha diaria* and also framing interactions within the research itself. Undocumented women feared the consequences of bringing attention to their circumstances, but also suffered from feeling confined within these circumstances: "Here one does not suffer from not having shoes—or other material items—but rather from not being able to go out freely because we are like little caged animals," commented Luisa. Women without documented status were extremely cautious in interacting with others beyond kin, as rumors circulated about Immigration and Customs Enforcement (ICE) informants living among them in the community. There were also fears about being approached by ICE with bribes to serve as informants; staff members from Casa de la Raza—a local nonprofit that strives "to empower the Latino community"—mentioned to me on several occasions how they were protecting people who had been the targets of these bribes. Women with access to cars avoided driving for fear of being caught without a license and subsequently detained or deported. (At the time of this research, California would not grant driver licenses to undocumented persons. State legislation has since changed.) They canceled plans to visit family on *el otro lado* (the other side—i.e., the other side of the US-Mexico border) and they postponed plans to bring family members in need of care—such as older relatives or younger children—to the United States for fear of being intercepted by *la migra* (border patrol and ICE). My findings also corroborated research that has identified similar fears and anxieties about immigration enforcement and local authorities existing among even documented persons, especially when language proficiency was lacking. Women with formal status were also anxious about potentially having to furnish documents or encountering language barriers with ICE officials or police, or they were protective of others in their mixed-status families and social networks who lacked documents.

In the following pages I describe the ways that women negotiate changes to diet and to the forms of caring labor that they provide in the context of the migration experience. Although the language of illegality is not explicit here, there are certainly implications for the prospects available to these women according to the lasting effects of illegality in structuring their lives. In other words, these everyday negotiations and behaviors permeate one another as they are also in constant flux and always occurring within the broader context of intersecting political and economic barriers.

CUIDARNOS EN LA COMIDA: CARING THROUGH FOOD

An abundance of fresh, nutritious foods were part of Natalia's upbringing in rural Oaxaca. Her family also enjoyed a regular supply of seafood from her father's exploits as a fisherman. They exchanged much of this seafood for fresh produce from relatives who practiced subsistence farming. As she noted to me on several occasions, Natalia believed that eating healthfully played a central role in maintaining one's health: "One should know how to eat as a way to prevent obesity, diabetes, high cholesterol; all of this [eating] should be a means of prevention. Eating well, eating more fruits and vegetables than tortillas, than bread, than pizza, this should be a practice." Indeed Natalia abided by this practice on a daily basis, even though she encountered some resistance from those around her. Her son, for instance, who had suffered from a rare form of cancer at the early age of five, consumed the lunches of pizza and burgers supplied everyday at his school, much to the dismay of his especially vigilant mother: "I don't like junk food. I fight with [my son] because I prefer that he'd eat a plate of lentils, [for example], rather than a burger. The school only gives burgers or pizza to the children. So I prefer that in my house, [he eats] rice with chicken, lentils, or a piece of fish with salad." Like Natalia, many of my key informants perceived the abundance of readily available *comida chatarra* (junk food) in the United States— burgers, pizza, processed bread, fast food, and the like—that was often served at school lunch as jeopardizing attempts to establish a healthy diet among family members. Mothers found it difficult to regulate children's consumption of *comida chatarra* as they sometimes could not avoid purchasing it for the reasons that it was cheap and easy to prepare.

Such everyday disruptions to the work of healthy feeding were particularly disheartening amid social expectations that competency for motherhood necessitated efficacy in foodwork. Stated otherwise, many women despised children's consumption of *comida chatarra* for making them look like bad mothers, when indeed they hoped to prove themselves to the contrary. One revealing example could be found in women's modesty in discussing modes of self-care, preferring instead to boast of the ways that they cared for their children. For instance, Luisa, who was discussed more fully in chapter 1, often deflected my questions about her own food habits by redirecting me to a discussion about how she fed others. She wanted to tell me about how she refused to buy juice from the store and opted to make *aguas frescas* such as *horchata* (a traditional beverage made from seeds, nuts, and/or herbs) and *agua de Jamaica* (hibiscus tea) as a way to limit the amount of sugar consumed by her children. She also wanted me to know that although she never actually enjoyed cooking, she knew that she had to learn from her *cuñadas* (sisters-in-law) prior to becoming a mother. As a mother, she said, "tengo que cocinar" (I have to cook).

Women's concerns about how control over household diets had been undermined related back to a practice identified by many in my research as *cuidarnos en la comida*. Translated from Spanish as "we care for ourselves through food," this practice adhered to the idea that one's health hinged foremost on diet. Yet it was not just any variety of food that facilitated this practice, but specifically *comida saludable* (healthy food).

"Junk Food Is What Makes Us Sick"

Belen, age twenty-three and diagnosed with gestational diabetes during her first pregnancy, attributed her ability to manage her disease precisely through relinquishment of *comida chatarra* and better adherence to a diet of *comida saludable*. "It's healthier to eat at home," she remarked. "My husband, my first child indulged me. I'd tell them, 'I feel like this, I feel like that [food].' I'd buy fast food. Since [the birth of] my daughter I didn't try to buy any [junk food]. As I said, this does harm to a person. My *comadre* told me [eating in the mode of *chatarra*] did me harm during my pregnancy and so I didn't buy it.[2] Since I've stopped [eating *chatarra*], I've overcome my diabetes." Belen elaborated on the health behaviors she had cultivated since her most recent pregnancy; she heralded her own success with losing weight, which she was able to accomplish through reducing the quantity of bread and oil in her diet and by eating more fruits and vegetables:

> I can't eat things like this, like pizza, for the reason that I'll develop diabetes and I don't want this [disease]. Integrating more fruits and vegetables into the diet is what helps one most, and helps to get rid of diabetes. It can be hard but you have to avoid [these foods] in order

to avoid diabetes. You can avoid sickness by eating healthier food. This is what I've tried to do, so when I think, "I want a piece of bread, I want a piece of pizza," I think first of my children. I say no, for my children's sake. Or else I'll get sick ... and then what will happen to my children? They live because of me, they are nourished by me. I'm the one who makes their food, who makes little changes to keep them healthy. Yes, their father [helps] also, but not like a mother. Their father leaves the whole day working to have a little more money for food.

As Belen explained to me on this occasion, the well-being of her children depended first and foremost on her own health, and specifically on her ability to regulate her own health behaviors. Thus, her words suggest that she is not committed to eating *saludable* simply for the sake of her own health but really does so out of interest for her children. Without this self-discipline Belen believes that her ability to adequately provide for her children would be compromised. *Comida chatarra*, once a symbol of indulgence, has become her nemesis. While her adherence to a diet of *comida saludable* reflects her own feelings of obligation as a mother, she also extends her thinking to the realm of motherhood more generally. Her outlining of how a father's provisioning of financial resources helps to ensure the continuation of a mother's caring labors highlights her own subscription to the notion that care comprises a gendered labor.

In seeking to avoid *comida chatarra* my informants employed a variety of strategies such as preparing foods at home instead of purchasing premade foods and cooking meals from scratch instead of relying on heavily processed foods. Dora, for instance, contrasted her insistence on cooking meals at home and from scratch with her initial experience of coming to the United States and consuming a diet of fast and junk foods. Describing her eating habits while working long hours as a hotel housekeeper, she noted, "At night I'd go to work, and when I got hungry, I'd go out and buy something to eat. But yes, I feel that it did me a lot of harm because I got really fat. When I came [to the United States] I got very fat, overweight, I think 180 pounds [standing at five feet tall], but I was also eating all of this prepared food." Dora credits her own mother for having helped her to overcome these eating habits. One afternoon at her home, Dora tells me about how she had phoned her mother in Honduras as soon as she had noticed the extent of her weight gain. She recounts what for her had been a life-altering conversation: "My mother said to me, 'You have *to cook* for your family, you shouldn't have to buy or eat food from the street. You have to *know* how to cook.'" Since then Dora has always strived to follow her mother's advice of *cuidarnos en la comida* through nourishing her children and her own body with food that she prepares at home, even though doing so presents its own set of challenges.

As demonstrated through the experiences of Belen and Dora, management of the *comida* (meal) required careful discrimination between "healthy" and "unhealthy" foods. *Comida chatarra* was seen as inducing harm on the body in the form of *enfermedades* (illnesses). "The junk food.... This is what makes us sick," commented Olivia. Thus, many of my informants perceived *comida saludable* to play an important role in preventing illness and enabling the process of healing. For a variety of health problems, food could thus serve either as the culprit in the form of *comida chatarra* or the remedy in the form of *comida saludable*.

"The Barriers Begin in Your Own Home"

Juliana had migrated without papers to the United States in 1999. Her family of five shared a home with another family in the Eastside neighborhood of Santa Barbara. Given that her husband was the sole breadwinner in her family, and given his own tendencies to spend frivolously on his drinking habit, Juliana faced major economic constraints in managing household resources. In addition to these monetary barriers she alluded to the ways that actions by male household members sometimes interfere with a woman's efforts toward providing food that is *saludable*. In her opinion, disregard for women's management of the *comida*, displayed in men's provisioning of junk food to children, compromised a mother's efficacy in foodwork and her ability to provide healthy food. To illustrate her conviction, Juliana cited an incident with her husband that had occurred recently:

> There are barriers... I'm referring to the food that I know [my husband] gives to [my children]: sweets, Cheetos. I would never give them Cheetos. Truthfully, I prefer to buy some peanuts, something that is going to nourish them, rather than give them some chips, so I always have this problem with my husband. He is the first obstacle because he thinks differently, I think differently. For example, this Mother's Day I was making a chicken soup that I was going to feed [my family], but [my husband] wanted to take us out, he wanted to eat out with us. I declined, so he brought us a pizza, which made me angry because I had something nutritious ready for my kids, and he brings pizza! Also these people that go selling corn nuts... Cheetos, chips. [My husband] buys it for [my children] and it makes me mad because it is so unhealthy. These are the barriers. They are not far away; they are right here, with my husband. You don't have to look far, they are right there in your home, right?

Here Juliana speaks to the power dynamics within her household that are counterproductive to efforts in support of *comida saludable*. On this particular occasion, Juliana perceived her husband as attempting to undermine these efforts. Although this incident is by no means isolated, that it happened on Mother's Day reveals an extra layer of significance. Specifically, the undercurrent of sentimentality marking this day as a holiday in honor of women amplifies the degree to which Juliana feels dishonored by her husband's defiant behavior. This display of defiance also detracts from the means Juliana has available to her for feeling like a good mother.

Contrary to romanticized notions of solidarity, empirical research shows that members of migrant and mixed-status households are not always united against the exploitative prowess of the state and markets (Quesada 2011; Zlolniski 2006). Dissonance and conflict along lines of gender, generation, and legal status translate to differential access to resources and negative repercussions for care: "along with cooperation and mutual help, there is also inequality, conflict, and exploitation" (Zlolniski 2006, 140). Conflict is particularly pronounced in the context of scarcity (Narotzky 1997) arising between primary breadwinners who control financial resources by allocating money for specific expenditures to different household members and secondary income earners or the unemployed who manage and implement financial decisions on their behalf (Graham 1987). Discrepancies in the control of financial and in-kind resources, and inequalities in resource management and distribution, may foster tensions among household members (Narotzky 1997). There is sometimes also resistance to women gaining more equal status with men in what have previously been traditional, or patriarchal households.

Immigrant women may "contest patriarchal ways of being" (Segura and Zavella 2007, 3) as they integrate with the global economy. Vélez-Ibáñez describes patriarchy as "male-centered strategies of familial development" that "define women subtly ... whose labor and work within the household or outside of it are valued less than that of men" (1996, 138). In patriarchal household configurations, the mother/wife assumes "management of the *casa*" while the husband manages relations outside the home through serving as the "protector and breadwinner" (Griswold del Castillo 1984, 29).

Rather than try to explain disparities within the household by employing the tropes of patriarchy, machismo, or hypermasculinity, however, I suggest that we entertain a broader conceptualization of power. That is not to dismiss the palpable effects of a patriarchal ideology for both the expectations that women impose on themselves and how they evaluate other women's performances of motherhood. Rather, it is to say that the provision of care is not merely a question of gendered power dynamics but also of other forms of inequality.

The Problem of a Mother?

In comprising a gendered labor, the practice of caring through food demands women's physical and emotional labors (DeVault 1991). As the accounts in this chapter illustrate, women in my research strived to oversee this practice through the provision of healthy foods. Yet these healthier foods were usually more time-intensive. Despite the demands of wage-earning activities that limited the amount of time women could devote to meal preparation, working mothers absorbed a litany of purported "failures" in the realm of food provisioning as they were targets of intense social scrutiny.

Gloria, who much to her dismay had migrated with her husband and their children to the United States in 1998, believed that a woman's place was in the household. She engaged in some income-generating activities such as offering laundry services, selling prepared foods, and providing child care, all from

Figure 9. Gloria trimming nopales to prepare for sale to her neighbors.
Photo by the author.

the comfort of her own home. Being a mother, she explained, required such arrangements: "I've never worked because I had three little girls. My husband also never wanted [me to work]; he said, 'You're going to work and what is going to become of these girls?'"

Linda, who was discussed more fully in chapter 1, also pursued income-generating activities but described herself as unemployed. In addition to offering laundry services from her home she left the house once every week for a housecleaning job. Linda deemed these income-generating activities as worthy of pursuing only if they melded easily into her routine, which she elaborated as follows:

I get up and take my husband to work. I come back and wake up the kids to take them to school. I feed them breakfast, make them a snack for the day, usually fruit. I return from school and clean the house. I go to the store if I need something for the *comida*. Afterward, I wash the clothes if they need washing. At one o'clock I pick up the little one from kindergarten. I pick up my other child at 4:30. My husband comes home and I feed everyone dinner. I wash the dishes, clean the kitchen, bathe my children and read them a book, and then go to sleep.

Instead of portraying themselves as fully employed, I found that these women framed their income-generating activities through less explicit terms, aligning with what Patricia Zavella has described as *informal work*: "Informal work allows women to combine domestic and wage labor by keeping an eye on children... or organize their tasks so they can perform household chores in between work for wages" (2011, 99). Married women like Gloria and Linda, perhaps privileged by their partners' incomes, were more inclined to view staying at home as a mother's duty.

Among women who benefited from the financial support of a spouse there were concerns about the possibility of children of working mothers being deprived of adequate care, which was frequently framed in terms of food. Olivia, for instance, described working mothers as too relaxed about their children's diets. "The problem that children eat junk food is the problem of [a mother]," she commented. "We have to find options to buy better food or to make food at home. Because here, in this country, as mothers work, it is easier to buy prepared food or to take your kids to McDonald's. But it depends on how you, as a mother, provide them healthy food." In attributing the absence of a mother to more regular consumption of unhealthy food among children, Olivia aligned with other women who viewed caring for children as a woman's responsibility, thereby directing blame at women when such care was not available.

These sorts of moral discourses speculating on a working mother's absence even extended into accusations around gang violence, as some women alluded to antisocial or violent behavior among youth as a product of so-called neglectful mothers. Belen referred to one of her husband's coworkers, whom she believed did not have time to provide adequate care—particularly with respect to meals—and suggested that this could steer children toward gang culture. She then evaluated this woman's performance as a mother against her own:

> My husband says that this woman he knows at work has two jobs, she leaves the nursery at 4:30 p.m. and goes to the other job at 5:15 p.m. I tell him it's fine but that she doesn't have time for her children. I see her husband with their son, in the street or in the store buying something to eat, because the mother doesn't have time to feed him. This is what they say affects children when they're older. When they go to school they join gangs, this is what happens. I say that I hope my son has other ideas for the future but I'm giving him all of my time.

Belen's description bestows the impression that her husband's coworker had the privilege of choosing to work two jobs. She also does not indicate whether this woman was a single mother. Despite the omission of specific details relating to the coworker's circumstances, however, the woman is still held accountable for apparently failing to provide her child with adequate meals.

In reflecting on her own need to work, Dora expressed doubts about being away from her children. She described coordinating her work schedule with her husband so that one of them was always at home:

> Many people—you know what they do?—they leave their children, and to me this is not good. My husband works in the day and I don't want to leave my children on their own. They are with me during

the day and my husband arrives in the evening and is in charge of them so that they are always with us. I leave for a little while in the evening to go to work. There are gangs because many mothers leave their children alone all day in school, or at a nursery and then they make little friends and they form gangs because their mothers were gone all day.

While Dora and Belen were not completely isolated in their thinking, youth involvement with gangs hardly stems from any single factor alone (Cammarota 2008; Vélez-Ibáñez 1996; Zavella 2011). Notably, the women in my research did not vilify alcoholism in the home or connect it to antisocial behaviors among youth, despite women's complaints that men regularly engaged in *el tomar* (drinking). Instead, I found that these women embraced a discourse of blame that held working mothers accountable for antisocial behavior and gang violence. This does not necessarily suggest that women from these communities actually harness negative sentiment toward working mothers. A more likely explanation for the women's participation in this discourse is that they wished to distance themselves from the category of "bad mothers," thereby exhibiting their own competency for motherhood and seeking the means to legitimize their own acceptance into mainstream society.

On the one hand, the preoccupations of these mothers were not entirely unfounded; when coping with food insecurity on a daily basis, the practice of *cuidarnos en la comida* and associated foodwork demanded a significant investment of time by women, practically comprising a full-time job. On the other hand, the working mothers I encountered were no different from women who were married and informally employed in expressing aversion to *comida chatarra* and conveying concern about and commitment to providing children with healthy food. Consider, for example the following account from Malena, who was discussed more fully in chapter 1; she was working almost seventy hours per week as a hotel housekeeper to provide for her four-year-old daughter. Malena explained, "I'll think to make this meal and then suddenly the time has flown by and I have to make something else, or I have to leave, to call my children or my mom [in Mexico], and when I have to do something, like bathe my daughter, change her, go to the store, I take her on a walk and we go for something quick to eat. But in general we try not to eat out because it is expensive, and it is healthier to eat at home."

RETHINKING CARE IN THE CONTEXT
OF RECESSION

It is important to note that low wages earned through Santa Barbara County's service economy do not adequately cover the exorbitantly high cost of living, and despite the negative effects economic recession had imposed for *earning* a living during the period of my research, expenses such as housing, utilities, food, and fuel had actually increased: "Many families complain that the money doesn't accumulate," commented Serena, "especially now that work has dropped, and meanwhile the rent and other bills do not go down. My husband works but he is only able to save for the rent."

Celina, who is thirty-six, from Veracruz, and working as a hotel housekeeper, perceived contradictions in an economy that relies on tourism: "Right now we are in a situation, a crisis [of fewer tourists and] of no work. Santa Barbara is a beautiful city, but as a tourist destination it is very expensive to live here."

Although the housing market suffered a severe blow following the recession that began in 2008—so much so that the county was ranked third out of nine in the article "The Nine American Cities Nearly Destroyed by the Recession" (Sauter, Allen, and Stockdale 2012)—the cost of living in Santa Barbara County remains high in comparison with the rest of the state and nation. Affordable housing prevails as a limited good, in part because of constraints on urban development. Much of the surrounding open space is allotted to agriculture and recreation, and Santa Barbara city government has passed measures prohibiting developers from building vertically. During my time as a resident of Santa Barbara, I frequently encountered petitioners at the farmer's market each Saturday who were looking to collect signatures against the development of buildings above a certain height.

Securing stable housing proved a perpetual challenge for many of my research participants. Malena, for instance, had been living in a small apartment with two other families close to the train station when I made my first visit to her home. On one of my visits to this residence, I learned that Malena had been evicted by one of the families the night before. Confused, I called Malena on her cell phone. She explained that the manager's brother had wanted the room that she and her daughter were occupying. He offered to move their things to another room in the downtown area, some miles away. Malena was somewhat relieved to move because one of the men in the house regularly arrived home inebriated and with friends, and he played music at all hours of the night. Yet only a few months following her relocation Malena was again distressed about her living situation, citing issues with the "señora" with whom she shared an apartment. This woman complained to Malena about her daughter being a nuisance, so Malena was looking for an alternative. Sudden disturbances to one's living situation, such as those encountered by Malena, require making constant adjustments to one's means and routes of transportation, to items allocated in household budgets, and to daily routines more generally.

My informants' outlook on employment and overall economic conditions varied with length of residency; women with fewer years living in the United States were surprised by the lack of employment opportunities and expressed much disappointment in discovering the unfortunate state of the economy. These women described feeling cheated of what they had been promised by those in their home countries who had benefited from lucrative experiences abroad. Women who had lived in the United States for more than five years recalled better economic times. Tina, whose reflections on being a single mother were featured at the opening of this chapter, reflected on economic conditions in California over the past few decades: "Before I think there was much more work and it was better than today. Others say it is very difficult to find work. My son, for instance, has been without work for four months." Juliana, having resided in the United States for twelve years, shared similar observations. "Before, there was more work," she explained. "It was easier to find work in those times, when the economy was still good. Now it is difficult. Many people cannot find work. I stopped working when I was pregnant. But after my pregnancy, to earn something I had to. I started to babysit, and that was going well. Babysitting for people I knew, but now there aren't even babysitting jobs. Sometimes I watch this girl, once in a while, but today for instance the woman was called off from work [so she didn't need me]." Juliana interpreted declines in the demand for service work in tourism and hospitality (i.e., housecleaning, child care, janitorial work) as a result of the market becoming increasingly saturated with people in search of these jobs.

Similarly, Natalia lamented reductions in her work schedule, explaining, "There is a lot of competition in housecleaning. Many women want to clean houses. And there isn't a lot of work [for them]." Competition in the market sometimes translated to a reduction in work hours. Celina, for instance, working as a hotel housekeeper, reported changes to her work schedule: "Before, I was given eighty hours [every two weeks] and now I only have seventy, and this is less money for me. There are people who only work two days a week and this adds up to very few hours every two weeks [when one is paid]." The pressure to manage expenses required women to seek multiple part-time jobs, translating to a life consumed, as Margarita described it, "Only work and work. It's a hard life because one needs to work, work, work always."

Caring for a Family "Split in Two Places"

Dora began each day praying for the opportunity to acquire formal residency status because it would mean she could bring to the United States her two children, ages ten and twelve, who were still living with her mother in Honduras. She arrived from Honduras as an unauthorized migrant in 2005 and met her Mexican-born husband while working part-time as a housecleaner in Santa Barbara. Since living in the United States, Dora and her husband had two more children, ages two and five. She clung to the hope that her husband would be able to obtain papers for the both of them through his employer, who had supposedly broached the subject on several occasions. With these papers she could feasibly end the six years of separation from her children in Honduras.

My conversations with Dora about her children in Honduras were always very emotional. She meditated on her present feelings

Figure 10. Dora with her two US-born children at their home in Santa Barbara. Photo courtesy of Dora.

of isolation and she grieved intensely for the children she left behind. She explained the trade-offs of providing care to her US-born children versus mothering from across borders:

> I'm here with them [my US-born children] so that I am not a disgrace to them; it hurts. It would hurt so much if one day [my children in Honduras] said to me "this and this [bad thing] happened"...it would hurt me very much. I don't want to hear bad things from them; I think to remind myself to look after them all equally. Here I miss everyone...I miss them all because I'm here. And I tell them, "I can't send much money, we are in a very ugly situation," but even if I send them only a little each month, I know that my children are safe and fed because my mother is taking care of them.

Dora's words echoed the sentiments of other mothers in my research who experienced guilt in trying to reconcile the disparities in quality of life and care dictated by the presence of geopolitical borders. Dora regretted being unable to send much money to her children in Honduras, but she found some solace in knowing that her mother was looking after them and feeding them.

Although she feared that her children there could grow up to resent her, she was hopeful that she could unite everyone in her family through the documentation process. As we hugged good-bye on the day before Christmas Eve, Dora reminded me to cherish time with my family stating as she wiped tears from her eyes, "It is not a life to have your family split in two places." Dora remained optimistic about the possibility of formal status, even forgoing forms of assistance that her US-born children qualified for, such as food stamps; she feared that asking for help would jeopardize her prospective application for legal residence and thus her ability to bring her other children over safely. In such a way the well-being of her US-born children was tethered to her own undocumented residency status and to the uncertain future of her children in Honduras.

CARE FOR WHOM?

Undocumented and mixed-status households in the United States straddle the precarious boundary between what the US Department of Agriculture defines as food security and food insecurity. This chapter has highlighted how overseeing management of food in these households, and furthermore ensuring provision of healthy food, requires significant daily investment, at times even resembling the demands of a full-time job. Moreover, at risk in striving for a diet of *comida saludable* is the entire process of social reproduction. Part of the *lucha diaria* for women from these households thus relates to lacking the time required for feeding others. Alternatively, women who are unable to devote their entire day to this activity because of needing to work for a wage become targets of derision; because working outside of the household is believed to detract from a woman's ability to perform foodwork, women who are employed face social scrutiny regarding their competence for motherhood. Olivia's assertion that junk food was "the problem of a mother" suggests that working mothers are too relaxed about their children's diets. Such negative forms of social capital have operated historically to devalue and demoralize certain social groups, particularly low-income women (Glenn 2012). In facing myriad constraints such as limited economic resources and social networks, low-income immigrant women, particularly single mothers, are challenged to resist their own further marginalization into the class of those considered by society as always already less deserving.

The binary quality of the caring labor that goes into feeding, at once enabling women to appropriate kitchen space while also relegating them to a particular place within the household, stands as evidence of the need for feminist critique alongside recognition of women's expressions of agency (Abarca 2006; Counihan 2009). By presenting themselves as engaged rather than withdrawn from the *lucha diaria*, the women in this chapter convey a desire to resist everyday structures of power that both constrain their capacities for care and undermine efforts toward social reproduction.

Alicia Schmidt-Camacho (2008) questions the extent to which the state's holding out on an end to the condition of "illegality" represents a form of governmentality predicated on the social death of Latino immigrants. I argue that we need to extend this thinking to looking at how impediments to eating and feeding are also causes for social death, and recognize how—through the privatization of welfare—the state reorganizes caring labor. I suggest that much of the state's interest in embedding itself in the intimate relations of transnational families and mixed-status households (Boehm 2012) stems from contemporary biopolitics that seek to govern populations differentially, and in the case of unauthorized migrants, to maintain them as a highly exploitable source of cheap labor (Carney 2013).

Chapter 3 examines the repercussions of this marginalization particularly for Mexican and Central American women's subjectivities and self-perceptions of health. Following accusations of Latino immigrants draining the state of health resources (Chavez 2008), anti-immigration and antiwelfare proponents often strategically invoke discourses tethering migration to health to rally support for denying people (specifically Mexicans and Central Americans) authorized entry to the United States and, relatedly, access to state services (Chavez 2012; Park 2011; Sargent and Larchanche 2011). Similarly, in the context of western Europe, Stephanie Larchanche finds that "the visa for medical reason is perceived as providing a strategy for dishonest individuals to gain legal status by 'faking' their illness" (2012, 861). Yet, contrary to these accusations, research shows that undocumented migrants in the United States are significantly less likely than those with formal status to seek medical care (Chavez 2012).

Despite the extent to which people are motivated to migrate out of concerns for health, emerging research suggests that migration is actually harmful to one's health. As Carolyn Sargent and Stephanie Larchanche argue, "Immigration status—documented or undocumented—has significant implications for migrant health and access to health services" (2011, 347). Instead of finding improved access to more affordable and adequate health services, Sarah Willen, Jessica Mulligan, and Heide Castañeda emphasize the ways that "'illegality' often places im/migrants in positions of considerable health risk" (2011, 336). As an aspect of their "illegality," unauthorized migrants are viewed as undeserving, and "it is their construction as an illegitimate social group which in fact hinders their access to health care and produces ill health" (Larchanche 2012, 858). Chapter 3 explores some of these health risks for (im)migrant women by turning to the collective narratives that marginalized groups sometimes deploy in attempting to reflect on and reconcile the conditions of social suffering.

CHAPTER THREE

Nourishing Neoliberalism?

Narratives of Sufrimiento

> One knows that yes, it is true about all that we suffered
> [*sufrimos*] in Mexico. Right now, here, we don't suffer
> from the same things we did in Mexico, but from
> others, yes. Because here, they do not suffer [*sufren*]
> from [a lack of] shoes, but they suffer from going out
> freely because all the time they have to live like little
> caged animals. It was better in Mexico. One wanted to
> live in Mexico, to relive the time there, but when?

In the above account, Luisa alludes to the collective experience
of suffering both in Mexico and in the United States (using the
form "we") while also noting how the parameters of suffering have
shifted. Present in her account is a reference to the coproduction
of these new forms of suffering associated with the process of
resettlement and a feeling of nostalgia for what existed before.
Moreover, part of the collective experience of suffering stems from
the desire for what represents an impossible return ("One
wanted . . . to relive the time there, but when?").

Feelings of loss and nostalgia as endemic to the migration
experience are by no means unfamiliar to scholars of migration,

especially in cases of forced displacement. A rich body of literature documents how people in diaspora are constantly negotiating the pragmatic aspects of adjusting to life in a new country as they also attempt to reconcile the conditions of their dislocation and to mourn that which has been lost (Appadurai 1996; Das et al. 2001; Ricoeur 2004). As such, the experience of being "in between" places and cultures characterizes many diasporic and borderlands communities (Boehm 2012; Zavella 2011). There is much to be read through individuals' experiences with these transborder processes with regard to subjectivity and agency, specifically in the ways that people come to understand and respond to the conditions of their existence. Narrative in particular offers a powerful medium for interpreting one's own subjectivity, whereby memory and language lend narrative its form (Seremetakis 1996). This is perhaps especially pronounced for people in a state of diaspora for whom narrative is a way of memorializing or, as C. Nadia Seremetakis notes, "the absent becomes narrative" (1996, 2).

My research participants often invoked narratives of *sufrimiento* (suffering) in reflecting on the conditions of their migration and everyday struggles for survival in the United States. As illustrated with Luisa's statement in the epigraph above, several women indexed these narratives with variegated use of the Spanish verb *sufrir* (to suffer). In the following pages I explore patterns of social suffering as they emerged across my informants' individual narratives, including imbricated woes of material scarcity, social isolation in the United States, nostalgia and longing for "home," and encounters with violence. Couched within these narratives of suffering were also allusions to what women understood as the embodied effects of this suffering: struggles with weight, diabetes, and depression. Above all recurring themes, however, food received special attention in these narratives, functioning as a tangible medium through which women reinterpreted the past as a means to situate the present.

IMPOVERISHED EMBODIMENTS

Economic marginalization of Latinos in the United States has produced significant health disparities, particularly among women (Quesada, Hart, and Bourgois 2011). Participation in the secondary job market has translated to no benefits or health insurance for Latinos, subsequently perpetuating a long list of unmet health care needs (Zambrana, Dorrington, and Hayes-Bautista 1995; Zlolniski 2006). Stress (*el estrés*) that migrants associate with the angst to acquire work and to work longer hours may negatively affect health while also preventing sick or injured workers from seeking medical attention (Gleeson 2010). Reported rates of depression and mental illness are also comparatively higher among Latinos than other ethnic groups in the United States, especially for women and those whose dominant language is Spanish (Vélez-Ibáñez 1996). In reviewing the disproportionately lower health status of Latinas, researchers highlight the multiple responsibilities both within and outside the home, largely assumed by women, that contribute to stress: "Health data would suggest that women pay a high price for this balancing act, given their increasing rates of heart disease, hypertension, stroke, and substance abuse," (Flores-Ortiz 2000, 212).

The research findings that I have presented thus far in this book have demonstrated how chronic food insecurity impels many women to migrate but then persists in the United States. This is one dimension of migrants' structural vulnerability, especially in terms of the constraints shaped by the conditions of "illegality" that limit the range of possibilities for women in overseeing caring labors. Yet what are the broader repercussions of women's struggles with scarcity—particularly food—and obstructions to overseeing the process of social reproduction? The claim by Yvette Flores-Ortiz (2000) that "[t]he psychological well-being of women is determined on the basis of their ability to perform socially expected and mandated roles" (212) suggests that the daily challenges of food insecurity experienced by these women, insofar as these challenges interfere with the ability to provide care, have profound effects for women's subjectivities and overall health status. Meanwhile, policies and configurations of "illegality" threaten (im)migrant health status, limit access to health care, and constrain positive health behaviors (Castañeda 2012; Holmes 2012; Larchanche 2012; Sargent and Larchanche 2011; Willen 2007). Taking these factors into consideration, I now turn to exploring how the stress of food insecurity interacts with and possibly compounds extant health disparities and social malaise in low-income, immigrant communities. I resume the discussion from chapter 2 on impediments to women's caring labors for the purposes of illustrating how these articulate with the feelings of loss and dislocation so common to the migration experience.

Ethnographic research demonstrates that suffering from such health problems as diabetes, hypertension, and depression has an exacerbating effect on women's anxiety. Yet many mental health problems, such as anxiety disorders or depression, often remain undiagnosed and untreated, thereby undermining the health of those afflicted and inhibiting them from seeking and adhering to treatment. Emily Mendenhall (2012) has argued that the structural vulnerability of Mexican women in the United States, and the psychosocial stress linked to their own marginality, puts them at higher risk for certain diseases and thus serves as a form of neg-

ative feedback for women's psychology. She terms this phenomenon "syndemic suffering," borrowing from Merrill Singer's (2009)
theory of *syndemics*, the idea that interactions among diseases,
social problems, and pathogenic environments compound the
effects of disease and yield to more negative health outcomes. In
"conceptualizing the syndemic," Merrill Singer and Scott Clair
(2003) offer a departure from a traditional biomedical approach
that has interpreted disease as a distinct entity in nature. This conceptualization was founded on three basic tenets: (1) infections and
noncommunicable diseases co-occur among certain populations,
specifically those systematically marginalized; (2) the interactions
of two or more diseases must be accounted for (biological syner-
gism); and (3) poor health is associated with social, cultural, economic, and physical environmental factors (social context; Singer
and Clair 2003; Singer et al. 2006). Thus, syndemics represents "a
holistic approach that emphasizes interrelationships and the influence of contexts" in unveiling the "deleterious conditions among
populations from the structural violence of social inequality"
(Singer and Clair 2003, 434). While borrowing this framework, I
argue that food insecurity and the conditions of "illegality" both
compound the structural vulnerability of Mexican and Central
American women in the United States and operate syndemically
with women's predispositions for particular health problems.

    We cannot begin to understand the structural vulnerabilities
experienced by the women at the heart of this book without
accounting for the ostensible banality and ordinariness of everyday life that indeed harnesses political significance (Stewart 2007).
As captured through migrant women's narratives of suffering,
these composite layers of everyday life have a profound influence
on the formation of women's subjectivities and self-perceptions of
health. Narratives of *sufrimiento* thus contain political value that

requires more critical engagement on the part of social scientists. Specifically, these narratives bring attention to the affective, human dimensions of structural violence condoned by states and enacted in transnational processes.

Arguably one of the most profound effects of neoliberal ideology as it has infiltrated policy circles and the social imaginary has been a suppression of social suffering whereby individuals come to internalize and accept the conditions of their existence as "natural" and deserved (Holmes 2013). In her ethnographic account of Latina women's experiences with everyday violence in the highlands of Guatemala, Cecilia Menjívar (2011) illustrates how everyday acts of violence and the ways in which women are afflicted by them do not occur randomly but unfold as part of a continuum of structural violence that extends from neoliberal economic policies and structural adjustment programs to individual bodies. Anthropologists underscore the health failures of structural adjustment programs whose repercussions are never gender-neutral (Farmer 2005; Pfeiffer and Chapman 2010). James Pfeiffer and Rachel Chapman (2010) argue that structural adjustment programs harm society as they involve cuts to basic public health and welfare services, higher charges for basic health services, dramatic price increases for basic commodities, wage cuts, and job losses.

Noting the ways that women shoulder the bulk of negative consequences linked to neoliberal economic development, critical scholars invoke the phrase "invisible adjustment" to refer to the changes in behavior and survival strategies overseen by women that make adjustment policies socially possible (Beneria and Feldman 1992; Wamala and Kawachi 2007). Forms of invisible adjustment enacted by women include increasing their own economic activity, working harder, and suppressing their own basic needs

(Beneria and Feldman 1992). Menjívar (2011) suggests that women especially come to believe that they deserve this suffering, leading to its naturalization and normalization whereby gender disparities are concealed in differential health outcomes.

What emerges in the following pages is a collective narrative of embodied suffering that reveals how the conditions of women's transnational migration from Mexico and Central America to the United States, connected as they are to neoliberal policies, attest to an impoverishment of migrant women's subjectivities and subsequent life chances.

WOMEN'S NARRATIVES OF *SUFRIMIENTO*

Malena's description of adjusting to life in the United States and negotiating her role as a mother highlighted some of the layers of suffering that confront recent migrants. She found adjustments at first as "doloroso" (painful), and described how life was "puro llorar" (full of crying) for the entire first year: "I suffered [*pasé tanto sufrimiento*] so much at first. For me it was a very painful situation as I found myself far from my three children." Her husband, whom she had been inclined to reunite with in the United States after he had severed ties with the family, did not help to ease her arrival; he was verbally abusive and slandered her in front of others with whom they were sharing a residence. While he complained of her being a drain on household resources, he also tried to disparage her hopes of finding work. Malena described living her first few months in total "desesperación" (desperation), afraid of revealing her undocumented status to authorities and of being unable to communicate with others for a lack of knowledge of English. Overcome by feelings of fear, grief, and shame, she confined herself to the room she shared with her husband:

I was in despair; all I did was mourn because in truth, I could not communicate with anyone. I was so afraid because I saw the authorities everywhere. I was so afraid to go outside . . . so I came to lock myself away in this house. Telling myself "I'm not going out," and wondering about what I was going to do made me cry. It didn't bother me if my brother-in-law or my sister saw me crying, or if my cousins noticed me crying, because it was very difficult for me. And later, I cried a lot because I left my children [in Mexico] and even now it pains me very much to see them left [behind].

Malena's reflections on her initial period of adjustment to life in the United States underscore multiple phases of grief. At first she felt isolated and unable to communicate. She was then overcome by fear of being caught because of her undocumented residency status. As this fear subsided somewhat, she was then haunted by grief for the three children she had left behind.

Unlike the fear that had stifled Malena in her quest for seeking employment, but which eventually leveled off, this mourning over the separation from her children never dissipated: "How do I tell them that I am not drawn to return home?" she asked. "I hope to do something better for them because they are young and they still need me." Malena could not justify a return to Mexico because she relied on the wages she earned in the United States to support both her young daughter who lived with her and her children back home. Alternatively, she pondered bringing her other children to the United States, but she worried that they may not succeed in the way that she had hoped for them and that they would have to abandon all that was familiar to them in Mexico. She did not want them to suffer coming across the border—"como yo" (like me), she said. Rather, she hoped to spare them this unnecessary suffering.

While many of my research participants affirmed Malena's sentiment about the initial period of adjustment to life in the United

States being the most difficult and ridden with grief, they also noted that the process of grieving is an ongoing, relentless one. In familiarizing themselves with life in a new country, these women fought against the persistent social exclusion and structural marginalization that together amplify women's extant feelings of social isolation and heightened awareness of the intractability of things that had been lost (and would likely never be recovered).

Missing from the Table: Accounts of Loss and Social Isolation

Gloria described her former life in Guanajuato as "bonita" (beautiful); life on the *ranchito* consisted of bathing her children, tending to the cows, taking her kids to school, cooking and sewing with her mother, and spending time with family. When she arrived in the United States in 1998, her family depended on the generosity of others; a cousin was able to offer sleeping space on his floor for Gloria, her husband, and their three daughters. Meanwhile Gloria and her husband did whatever they could to save money; she offered child care services to neighbors to supplement her husband's meager income, but the family still struggled financially: "It made me very sad because my husband earned hardly any money and sometimes we didn't even have enough to feed my daughters." Eventually Gloria's family saved enough money to move into their own place.

No longer distracted as much by the pressure to establish a more comfortable living situation, Gloria now faced a difficult battle with loneliness: "I was accustomed to being with my family in Mexico and it was difficult and sad for me here." Her husband worked long hours that prevented him from arriving home in time to share and socialize with Gloria over meals. Her three daughters, ages twenty-four, twenty, and sixteen, had all been very young when they migrated to the United States from Michoacán. They now showed no interest in spending time with her in the preparation of meals because, unlike Gloria, they had relatively fewer memories of sharing meals with family in Mexico. Although Gloria was upset by her daughters' lack of interest in cooking, primarily because the practice of cooking with other women was a tradition that she associated with nurturing family ties in Mexico, she also appreciated her daughters' school and career ambitions.

As we sit together in the quiet of her empty house, Gloria declares with much conviction that she strongly opposed her family's migration to the United States. Even today she longs for life on the ranch, "where we had everything," despite not having any plans to ever return. Her experience as an immigrant to the United States and being the bridge between one generation (subsistence farmers) and another (wage workers) holds much significance for understanding some of the practical consequences of her family's proletarianization such as changes to the social relations within her household.

Others in Gloria's family and social network with whom I spoke, including a couple of her daughters and closest female friends, discounted Gloria's nostalgia for home and accused her of overly romanticizing the conditions of her former life in Mexico. They alluded to her tendencies to rarely leave the house and to impose certain expectations of womanhood on her daughters as indicative of her own refusal to socially integrate herself in the United States. In some cases, these others' perspectives could be ascribed to generational differences.

In interviews with women of Gloria's generation, feelings of loss and social isolation were frequently articulated through describing changes to the social aspects of eating and feeding. Car-

Figure 11. Gloria in her kitchen. Photo courtesy of Gloria.

olina, a mother and grandmother, lamented that life in the United
States afforded fewer opportunities for gathering around meals.
She attributed this change to the attrition of the *comida* (meal) both
in frequency of occurrence and degree of sociality. Prior to arriving to the United States, Carolina had worked thirteen-hour days,
seven days a week, at a Levi's jeans factory in Guerrero. Although
her earnings allowed her to acquire sufficient food, she struggled
to pay for much else, including medical expenses. When one day
she noticed her infant daughter showing symptoms of a serious illness, Carolina was compelled to consider other options as the visit
to the doctor alone could cost her an entire paycheck from two
weeks of work. Fearing that she could not afford medical care in
the future if necessary, she decided to reunite with her husband,
who was already working in the United States. Despite realizing
certain material gains since migrating from Mexico, Carolina

described how people who migrate to the United States must adapt
to consuming fewer meals: "In Mexico we had three meals per day.
You had a little milk with tortillas that could be for breakfast or
lunch. In the afternoon, [you had] your *comida*, and in the evening
[you had] your dinner. Here [in the United States], no more than
one meal and no more than bread and milk in the morning. I think
it is because of how busy people are, because one is always out and
not at home. In Mexico it's nice because even if you are poor you
eat well with three meals." In Mexico and much of Central America, the *comida* is the main event of the day, consumed in the presence of others and usually over a long duration. Aside from offering necessary nourishment, the *comida* exists for the purposes of
socializing and sustaining social ties. Catalina, however, faced
many hurdles in continuing and passing on this tradition; she
lacked the time to invest in meal preparation and her family members had limited authority in being able to arrange schedules that
would allow them to be at home to share these meals. As a result
of these changes, Catalina perceived herself becoming more
socially isolated.

Betanía, also both a mother and grandmother, articulated similar feelings of loss while remembering her own role in orchestrat-
ing meals around the dining table in her former home. "There [in
Guerrero] I remember a large table in my house, large because I
had eight children," she remarked. "Today [all of my children] are
still alive, thank God. I used to cook for all of them. They sat
around the very large table, with chairs and more chairs. I would
cook mole verde, mole rojo, rice, and salsa with eggs that we would
call birría. Chicken birriado. I know how to cook it all. There I
would sit, socializing for the duration of the comida." Betanía contrasted the practical role of meals that had once nourished family relations with the desolation and disease that she and her hus-

Figure 12. Betanía warming tortillas. Photo courtesy of Betanía.

band now associated with the act of eating. Since living in the
United States, both Betanía and her husband had developed type 2
diabetes, a disease previously unfamiliar to either one's family.
In addition, she described with some remorse how she usually
dined alone, even though she was sharing a small home with several of her own children and grandchildren in the Eastside
neighborhood of Santa Barbara. As she explained, many of her
relatives—including her own husband—were coerced into working long hours, and her grandchildren had minimal interest in
sharing meals with her.

Work-life demands foreclosed many traditions around food
and mealtimes for these women. The discontinuation of traditions around commensality and meal preparation subsequently
amplified my informants' feelings of social isolation. Juliana, for
instance, perceived demands of employment and financial constraints as undermining her family's ability to gather together

during the holidays. She contrasted the spatial separation of her own family with the spatial proximity of families in Mexico. "[In Mexico] families get together more often," she explained. "I saw when there were times, special times—Christmas, for example—everyone, my aunt from [Cuernavaca], or from Morelos, or from [the state of] Mexico, everyone traveled and came [to visit]. There nobody asked where you were running to, no, because everyone was free and happy. Here, sadly, one cannot [do this] even when one wants to. I have a sister in San Diego, another in Anaheim. If it's not one, it's another that we miss. Someone is always missing when we get together.[11]

In the absence of family with whom to socialize around meals, I wondered if my informants pursued social ties or engaged in reciprocal relations with others beyond family, given the precedence for this practice as documented by other ethnographers. Yet when I asked about occasions for socializing with others outside the immediate family or household, many of these women claimed to abstain from forming such alliances. Some provided more specificity in explaining that a lack of *confianza* (trust)—reinforced by gossip (*chisme*) among neighbors—required a certain level of discernment in community interactions. In desiring vindication from such gossip, and to avoid possible encounters with *la migra* (border patrol authorities), they withheld much of their personal biographical information from others. Thus, instead of benefiting from social networks and social support that may have helped to buffer them from feelings of loneliness, or even to prevent negative health outcomes associated with lower socioeconomic status more generally (Fitzgerald 2010; Osypuk et al. 2009), my informants reported much the opposite. They longed for quality time with family (similar to the findings, for instance, in Himmelgreen et al. 2007) and alluded to an overall unwillingness or failure to cultivate a practice of mutual aid with others in the community.

The Taste of Nostalgia

Since coming to the United States, Dora had longed for the "muy fresco" (very fresh) foods in her memories of Honduras. Despite evidence that much of Central America, including Dora's native country of Honduras, has experienced a nutrition transition and wider adoption of processed foods (Hawkes 2007), Dora was convinced that processed foods were really only a feature of life in the United States. Undoubtedly her perspective had been shaped by her transition from being more connected to the land, as she was with family in Honduras, to having no such connection in the United States. Coming from a family of *campesinos* (farmers), Dora reflected on participating in harvests and how she missed the social aspects of this pastime:

> My father is a farmer. He grows beans and corn. Corn, beans, coffee, and rice—he grows them all. He also grows vegetables such as radishes, onions, green beans; he has his plot of land where he grows all of this. I like going out onto the land. My father had me put on my shirt with the long sleeves, a hat, and my rubber boots. I liked helping my father to harvest the beans, collecting bunches of beans. When you pull out the plant, you can see the beans sprouting, which is the part you take. I liked this about harvesting the beans. My father loves this [work]. He loves growing and harvesting everything. And I love it too.

To illustrate her longing for "fresh" foods, Dora alluded to differences in tortillas between the two countries. Dora found food in the United States to be too far removed from its site of origin and from the social relations that allowed for its cultivation.

Recalling how she used to harvest corn straight from the field, she described feeling less satisfied by factory-manufactured tortillas. "In Honduras," she explained, "I cooked everything from scratch: corn to make tortillas was always very fresh, I had never even tried tortillas from [factory, machine-processed] corn flour. I'd say 'tortillas made with corn flour do not fill you.' I was always used to eating really thick, fresh tortillas ... there [in Honduras] tortillas are always made by hand. I miss these things. the food here is all processed and there it is all fresh. Here I'm left feeling so dissatisfied with all this food that has no taste [*sabor*]." Despite evidence of the rapid spread of supermarkets in Central America, Dora's claims about tortillas being "always made by hand," Honduran food in general being "all fresh," and her "feeling so dissatisfied" with food in the United States all reflect the nostalgia that she feels for her homeland and the physical discomfort she associates with being in the United States.

Also from a family of *campesinos*, Yolanda missed the freshness of foods that she consumed in her hometown of coastal Acapulco, Mexico. Her family had raised pigs, chickens, and cows, maintained a small garden, and harvested local fish. While we conversed in her kitchen one evening, Yolanda described longing for the *sabor* of these foods. "The food is fresher there [in Acapulco]. So much of the time here you have frozen food, like chicken. There one goes and kills [the animal] for fresh meat; everything is fresher. Here the food is frozen: frozen chicken, meat. There it is completely fresh. The tomatoes, chilies, vegetables; all of it is fresh. One has one's own little garden in which to grow tomatoes, chilis, and bananas. For someone who is used to it, food tastes better [*es mas sabroso*] when it is fresh."

For both Dora and Yolanda, *sabor* was connected to the experience of feeling full (*lleno*) and satisfied, while foods without *sabor* could induce a loss of appetite. These women perceived many foods in the United States to lack the *sabor* and freshness associated with the foods of one's homeland (Abarca 2006; Bank Muñoz 2008), a perception perhaps exaggerated by feelings of homesickness. For Angela, even the taste of water provoked feelings of nostalgia; "the taste of the water was very weak [*delgada*] and it did not quench me," she said.

Narratives that reserved a place for nostalgia, such as those presented above, arguably helped many of my research participants to manage their memories, as food facilitates a tangible "anchor" that connects the past with the present (Mannur 2007). In contemplating nostalgia as a practice, Kathleen Stewart notes that, in narrative, "the search for the past and a place leads [people] to reconstitute their lives in narrative form, a story designed to reassemble a broken history into a new whole" (1992, 261). Yet while this narration of nostalgia may offer stability through restoring a sense of identity and lending comfort to those who have been physically displaced, Anita Mannur notes that "it becomes apparent that these homelands, both phantasmatic and contradictory, become spaces that are limiting or emancipatory, and typically both at once" (2007, 28). Thus these performances of nostalgia, actualized in my informants' narratives, contrast sharply with the memories of scarcity and suffering in their homelands that had ultimately provoked displacement.

Violence in a Lawless Space

Juliana had migrated to the United States on two separate occasions, first to flee from her alcoholic father and later from her alcoholic husband. Both times her sister, who was already settled and living in the United States, offered Juliana a place to stay until she found a job. In explaining how authorizes in Mexico did not intervene in cases of domestic violence, Juliana stated that "las leyes son diferentes allá" (the laws are different there). To her dismay, Juliana did not feel any more protected from violence in her new home in the United States.

Juliana's husband had followed her to the United States, seeking reconciliation and vowing to alter his behavior. In the twelve years that they had been reunited, together with their three children, Juliana regretted that he had not since upheld his promise. Abuse from her husband triggered painful memories for Juliana of her own father's alcoholism. She explained how her own mother had committed suicide as a means of escape from her marriage when Juliana was only five years old:

> I had a very hard, very difficult childhood. My father was an alcoholic and I suffered very much [*sufrí bastante*]. I didn't know my mother. My mother took her life due to the life she had. Because my father was very rough with us, he beat us often, so the reason my mother took her life is because she couldn't continue with the life she had. She could not bear it anymore. In reality I didn't know my mom. This is what I've come to say. I suffered [*sufrí*], for my father who rests in peace, he also took his life. They both chose this path instead of facing problems or continuing to live under those conditions, but I respect their decision, yes. I don't judge them, but at times I hurt; because of alcohol I lost my parents. So I say to my husband, "I don't want to lose you to alcohol." So this is the problem. He is in charge of everything, but the only thing he has is alcohol destroying our home. Apart from this, infidelity, so there are two things. Apparently insignificant, but difficult to address. Because when one loses trust it is difficult to resolve the situation.

While Juliana wished that her husband had not been the sole breadwinner for the family, she could not seek formal employment for the reason that she had endured a hip injury during her most recent pregnancy. Yet because her husband was the breadwinner, he exercised control over household finances, often siphoning off much of his earnings for alcohol. Conflicts frequently surfaced between the two of them, with Juliana often pleading that he allot more of his earnings to meeting the needs of their children. He sometimes reacted to her pleas with violence, compelling Juliana to seek refuge at local women's shelters. During one of our conversations at her home she recounted the guilt that ensued following a recent decision to stay at one of these shelters, despite her own desperation at the time:

> It hurt me most to see my children [hurt by my absence], to have let this pass. It is difficult for me, because I see, I see how my children love [my husband] and this is difficult for me. How I want to move on—I say, "I'm going to move on,"—but as I was raised without my mother, you could also say without a father, because he had to leave us with some of our aunts while he went to work. As I say, I want to form a family where my children have a father, a mother, and at times this costs me, I already can't bear anymore—I can't—and I say, "I'm only waiting two more years, until my daughter goes to kindergarten." But others tell me, "You're going to put up with this until you get sick. It won't serve you or your children to be sick, this is certain." I'm overwhelmed with stress because I hurt so much.

Although Juliana desired to leave her husband, she feared that he would refuse to support the children financially. On the one hand, she wanted to keep the family together for the children's sake. On the other hand, she had come to identify her marriage as a source of suffering and worried that her children were already suffering in a manner similar to how she had as a child. Yet just as Juliana could not seek recompense through the legal system in the form of child support if she were to terminate her marriage, her undocumented status prevented her from notifying authorities when he was abusive. Although she understood that authorities in the United States generally responded to calls about domestic violence, she perceived her own undocumented status as relegating her into a lawless space, one deprived of the right to be protected from violence.

HEALTH AT THE MARGINS

Intertwined with these women's narratives of suffering were references to what some conveyed more explicitly as the embodied effects of this suffering, such as struggles with weight, diabetes, and depression. When reflecting on self-perceived poor health status, my informants couched health problems in the broader contexts of migration, *la lucha diaria* (the daily struggle) for survival, and gendered forms of suffering. In some ways, these women's perceptions of self resonated with what Lauren Berlant has called *slow death*, "a condition of being worn out by the activity of reproducing life" (2007, 759). Berlant elaborates, "At the same time that one builds a life the pressures of its reproduction can be exhausting" (778). As noted in previous chapters, structural vulnerability constrains low-income, immigrant women in the United States to reproducing life at the social margins; the specter of slow death thus unfolds through the various ways that these women are then predisposed to health problems.

Relatedly, Sarah Willen (2007) proposes the notion of "abjectivity" in considering the experience of nonbelonging endured by those pushed into a position of "illegality." As lived experiences, abjectivity and illegality "constrain daily life, create internalized fears, in some ways immobilize their victims, and in other ways motivate them to engage politically to resist the dire conditions of their lives" (Gonzales and Chavez 2012, 255). Among its many undesirable effects, abjectivity imposes a sense of "discomfort in one's own physical body" (Kenworthy 2012, 127). The despair that comes with the uncertainty and liminality around one's experience of "illegality" is part and parcel of abjectivity, and the means through which the state "[holds] out of the possibility of an end to that condition" (Gonzales and Chavez 2012, 258). Accordingly, the conditions of abjectivity also preclude many of the possibilities of these women seeking preventative care.

In the accounts that follow there is an aura of ordinariness that surrounds the women's descriptions of the embodied effects of social suffering. By *ordinariness* I mean to suggest that there is a high prevalence of health problems but a lack of coordinated response that views this prevalence as exceptional.

Stress in the Body: Linking Weight, Diabetes, and Depression

[I would blame my being] a bit overweight on my husband's being fat. He keeps gaining and gaining. But he drinks and I think this makes him fat and he likes to drink a lot—*a lot*—everyday. I've gained eight pounds and I think it's because I'm not eating well, because I'm not keeping to a schedule. I think that now my weight is really affecting me, because I have back pain. I'm stressed because my back hurts me so much— three months ago I was at a normal weight. I feel bad, I need to lose weight. [Maybe] stress makes one gain weight? Because I'm really stressed. I stress all the time and I think that is what this is. I get nervous, but in the form of hunger. Anything I put into my mouth, bread, a cookie, makes me gain weight when I'm stressed. The stress also comes from driving without a license all the way to my job. It comes from needing to pick up my kids quickly, to get home to make the meals. Now

> my husband is getting home from work very late,
> like at eight o'clock at night, so every responsibil-
> ity falls on me: go to work, leave the kids at
> school, return, get them from school, make
> dinner, do the laundry; everything is for me to do,
> and for this reason I feel so much stress. But I can't
> stop working because when I do I feel stressed
> again because there is no money to pay the rent,
> the bills, for things we need. If it is not one thing,
> it is another.

The above reflection from Linda illustrates how the combination of stressors related to working for a wage, managing a
household, being an undocumented resident of the United States,
and dealing with a spouse's alcoholism translates to her own physical and psychological deterioration, particularly manifest in self-
deprecating thoughts about her weight. This type of thinking
among my key informants was not only directed at themselves but
in many instances also referred to depreciating health status
among family members, friends, and acquaintances to highlight
how chronic anxiety could transform the body or even progress to
give into various pathologies, including diabetes and depression.

Brenda attributed the onset of her diabetes to her struggles with
weight that had persisted during the past twenty years of living
in the United States. She talked about needing to adopt different
eating habits as a result of juggling two full-time jobs, one at the
fast food restaurant Wendy's and the other at a clothing factory.
Although she worked mostly on her feet at the restaurant for eight
hours each morning, her evening factory job required her to be
more sedentary. After many years of balancing this work schedule, Brenda had gained eighty pounds (topping out at over two
hundred pounds on her four-foot, eleven-inch frame) and had
been diagnosed with diabetes. Concerned about her diabetes but
unhappy with the mood-altering side effects she experienced from

prescribed medications, Brenda decided to pursue gastric-band surgery. Since she could not find a physician who would approve her for the procedure, she followed a friend's advice and traveled south of the border to Tijuana, where indeed a physician from the clinic in Tijuana was willing to authorize her for the surgery. Brenda eventually paid more than $10,000 in combined medical and travel expenses, even though she had to borrow from friends and take out loans to do so. Although the surgery enabled her to lose weight, her desired results proved only temporary, as she also encountered some complications:

> I have everything: high blood pressure, diabetes, high cholesterol, et cetera. I weighed 212 pounds so I got a gastric band. The truth is I had to do it because I'm a compulsive eater; I'm one of those people for whom everything revolves around food. The truth is that I love food. I don't have diabetes for just any reason—I love sweets. At last, I try not to have sweets in our home because the sugar makes me feel bad. For twelve years I've suffered from diabetes. Recently, when I had my surgery I went from 200 pounds to 135 pounds. But the truth is that I started to feel that my [gastric] band was opening up. Here they told me that you had to be at least 100 pounds overweight [to qualify for the surgery] but I explained to them that I have diabetes, high blood pressure, but they still told me no. So my husband and I made the sacrifice of going to Tijuana for the surgery. When I reached 135 pounds I started to eat and I realized that the food was passing through too quickly. In less than three months I had gained twenty-five pounds. I felt that the band had opened. The last time that I visited my doctor in Tijuana I was at 185 pounds. I need them to adjust the band. Yes, I've had to take radical measures because the truth is I'm not like most people. I cannot stop [eating]. I always start to eat [too much].

Aside from her ongoing struggles with weight and diabetes, Brenda notes other ways in which her health is compromised (high blood

Figure 13. Brenda's self-portrait. Photo courtesy of Brenda.

pressure, high cholesterol). She also makes several references to her compulsive eating habits. Arguably, Brenda's efforts to lose weight via elective surgery were not successful because they did nothing to address her tendency toward compulsive eating, a behavior she had developed because of working nonstop, living estranged from much of her family in Mexico, and spending the bulk of her limited leisure time alone.

While only five of the women I formally interviewed had actually been diagnosed with diabetes since living in the United States, all of them reported knowing someone with the disease—often a relative. Yet even without a formal diagnosis, many women worried about the possible onset of the disease and lacking the means to obtain a diagnosis. The prevalence of this concern among women contrasts significantly with the stance assumed by many public health practitioners—basically, that economically disadvantaged populations develop diabetes because of a lack of awareness about the disease, thus signaling a need for more education (an issue that I will revisit in chapter 4).

Pilar, for instance, agonized about her potential for developing diabetes as her own father had died of complications related to the disease. She worried incessantly about her weight despite recently having come to term in her pregnancy:

> PILAR: I feel bad because I've gained weight. I feel a lot of pressure, anxiety. I feel very bad.
>
> M [MODERATOR OF FOCUS GROUP]: Why do you feel pressure?
>
> PILAR: Because I've gained a lot of weight and I don't like it. I don't feel well, because it does me harm. I run the risk of my blood sugar rising, my father died from this.
>
> M: He died from diabetes?
>
> PILAR: Yes. My problem is with my health.
>
> M: So you see everything as being connected to your health?
>
> PILAR: Everything is connected to my health.

Pilar had arrived in the United States only recently, having spent several months in an immigrant detention center while pregnant. She had migrated from Honduras because she feared for her life there. However, she had also left behind two children with her own mother. She was anxious about her children's well-being, and having recently obtained asylum status she hoped to send for them soon. Yet she was also adjusting to her new life in the United States, and to becoming the mother of another child. Although Pilar benefited from support through her friends and boyfriend, she was dealing with multiple sources of anxiety that no doubt had an imprint on how she perceived her own health.

Several of the women I interviewed often connected concerns about weight or diabetes to feelings of depression. Paloma, who had been struggling to find work for several months and whose husband had endured a work injury (thus putting him out of a job), relayed her memories of being diagnosed with diabetes: "When I realized I had [this disease], I went into a depression. I said, 'I'm going to die,' but [the doctors] said, 'No, you can control this.' However, I still went into a depression." Since her diagnosis, she had been taking nutrition classes and was "trying to eat healthy" through the practice of *cuidarse en la comida* (caring for herself through food). Considering her broader circumstances, Paloma's depression may have also been brought on by the stress of no income between her and her husband as well as the shame she associated with being part of a childless couple. Paloma was hoping to adopt through familial networks in Mexico.

Camila, a woman in her mid-fifties and originally from Acapulco, Mexico, described a general disposition of unease and depression that had ensued following her diagnosis of diabetes six years prior. In contrast with how her condition had been framed by the field of biomedicine, she emphasized the importance of being able to reframe this health condition in her own terms: "I was depressed and someone told me—my aunt, who has unfortunately passed on—she told me in my dreams to stop thinking this way [being depressed] or otherwise it would kill me. [She told me] that I would feel better if I acted like I was not suffering from anything, and this is how I've since gone about it. Under the idea that I don't have anything, I'm able to go about more relaxed." Here Camila claims that she decided to deal with her depression by choosing to focus less on her diagnosis. She avoided prescribed medications from her doctor in the United States, claiming, "I feel much worse [from the medication] ... it makes me more sick." Instead, like Paloma she preferred to eat "healthy" in the form of *cuidarse en la comida* and to take natural remedies that were mailed

Figure 14. Paloma preparing fish filets and rice for lunch. Photo by the author.

to her by her daughter-in-law in Mexico. Of course, some might consider Camila as being in denial about her health condition. Nonetheless, her refusal to succumb to the disease serves a practical purpose for her, as she associates the dyad of diabetes and depression with a complete loss of control over her life; her aunt forewarned Camila in her dreams that the depression would kill her. By applying her own language to her condition, and designing her own mode of treatment, Camila feels that she is actually able to reclaim some of this control.

Thus, aside from worrying about specific physical health ailments, the experience of being relegated to the precarious states of illegal, deportable, and abjective as everyday ways of being poses many risks to mental health (De Genova 2002; Gonzales and Chavez 2012; Hacker et al. 2011; Willen, Mulligan, and Castañeda 2011). Mental health specialists emphasize that although mental health problems afflict immigrant communities disproportionately, the stigma attached to these forms of suffering precludes possibilities for discussion, diagnosis, and appropriate treatment. In terms of access to mental health services, quality of care received, and outcomes, Maria-Rosa Watson and colleagues emphasize that in particular, Latinos in the United States with a mental disorder are "less likely than non-Latino Whites to utilize mental health services and are more likely to delay treatment" (2013, 671). In addition, there is also the question of having financial resources or other means through which to obtain a diagnosis.

NARRATIVE AS A MEDIUM OF HEALING

My informants' narratives of suffering imparted many entangled themes: physical estrangement from children (in the case of transnational mothers); abusive marital relationships; nostalgia for commensality, and for foods with *sabor* (flavor) that actually sated one's appetite; social isolation; concerns about health status; and diagnosis of a disease. Similar to Ruth Behar's (1993) use of life history as an emotional narrative that simultaneously elicits rage, suffering, and redemption, women's tales of *sufrimiento* were arguably as much about suffering as they were about healing and as much about the individual as they were about a collective. In imparting these narratives, my informants would often express gratitude for having found a willing listener. They often described some relief at being able to think through and talk about their life experiences in this context, as they noted the rarity with which they shared these details of their personal lives. When I asked in response why they did not feel more comfortable to reflect with others in their everyday lives, they insinuated that doing so would be deemed as selfish or shameful.

Although these women related what they perceived as therapeutic aspects of narrating *sufrimiento*, they also alluded to the gendered expectations governing social conduct that limited their own opportunities for self-expression. Perceptions among women in my research that such opportunities were scarce suggested that women's marginalization is partially enabled through moral codes that connote the expression of affect with shame and that require a particular political economy of the emotions (Scheper-Hughes 1992). In other words, women are generally expected to suppress their experiences of marginalization. Thus it is possible that the women viewed our one-on-one interviews as offering an exception to what were otherwise unspoken rules about individual comportment. Yet they also uncovered similar discursive opportunities in the context of focus groups. During the closing sessions of these groups some reflected on how participation in this research had affected them personally. For many, the sessions facilitated a path to healing. Malena, for instance, likened her experience to therapy, as she was able to open up to others and hear about how other women's experiences overlapped with her own:

> I don't have a stable place, right? Sometimes people have to move, they have to leave their place, or we have to move ourselves. But right now I feel very content and grateful to you all. I don't know how I will repay the favor, the attention that you have all given me. I see now that there are people interested in knowing others, of knowing of their lives, however [bad] they can be. It is like a therapy to speak, to share what one holds onto or the ideas that one thinks of. Even if it is just a little bit of sharing, it is a great help.

THE LOGIC THAT INDUCES SUFFERING

Although each of my informants' life histories had been shaped by particular circumstances and spoke to suffering in its variable forms, the culmination of these narratives illuminates a collective experience of displacement and marginalization characterizing the lives of many (im)migrant women. Food in this context is then more symbolic than literal, indexing a host of daily experiences and activities that contain affective meaning.

These narratives also brought attention to the imbricated layers of suffering that shape Mexican and Central American women's subjectivities in the United States. Without recognition by institutions of the "illness, loss, pain, and grief" (Todeschini 2001, 104) associated with displacement and marginalization, Nancy Scheper-Hughes argues that people search for meaning in suffering, that they seek to rationalize "suffering as penance for sin, as a means to an end, as the price of reason, or as the path of martyrs and saints" (1992, 529). In highlighting the political strategy that underpins the construction of such narratives, Maya Todeschini (2001) asserts, "The choke and sting of experience only becomes real—is heard—when it is narrativized" (20; see also Fassin and Rechtman 2009). I account for women's narratives of suffering here while desiring to exercise sensitivity with respect to the ways that women imagined and hoped these narratives would circulate beyond our research interactions.

The critique of neoliberalism—that it has rendered disproportionate suffering for the socioeconomically marginalized instead of enhancing the quality of life of all citizens—is by no means unfamiliar (see, e.g., Biehl 2005; Ong 2006; Rosas 2012). Yet the familiarity of this critique, emanating predominantly from ethnographic accounts in the social sciences, has not lessened support for the rhetoric of "empowerment" that continues to dominate mainstream media and policy (Cruikshank 1999). Thus, despite its familiarity (especially within academic circles), there is potentially more need now than ever before to document how the proliferation of neoliberal ideology is nourishing few and impoverishing many. This chapter has demonstrated the (gendered) embodied effects and forms of social suffering associated with this ideology. In chapter 4, I will illustrate how neoliberal logics have also infiltrated mainstream approaches of public and private food assistance programs to food insecurity in the United States. Rather than directing efforts toward redressing structural inequalities, these programs constitute a *biopolitical project of food security* that emphasizes "personal responsibility" and attempts to construct food insecurity as an individual problem.

CHAPTER FOUR

Disciplining Caring Subjects

Food Security as a Biopolitical Project

Field notes from October 21, 2010: I arrive at the community center's mobile food pantry minutes before the distribution commences. The site supervisor greets me and explains that volunteers of the food pantry—who are also clients—have first pick of the provisions. The cold, rainy weather is not at all pleasant for the dozens of women and children lined up outside waiting to collect the free food.

Today I learn that this particular mobile food pantry site has been in operation since 1997. The community center recently switched from a number system to allowing clients to collect provisions on a first come, first served basis. The supervisor explains that they get people "from all walks of life" including the disabled, elderly, students, families with children, and working adults, although he believes that the majority of clients are undocumented women. "Everyone gets the same amount," the supervisor assures me. He records data from each woman as she moves forward in the line, including details on household size, number of children, age, ethnicity, and whether or not she is a first-time participant. He tells me that this information is used for internal purposes only, and that his organization neither collects any information nor discriminates on the basis of employment or immigration status.

The volunteers are wearing latex gloves as they stack boxes of produce onto the tables and place items into clients' bags. Three clients at a time are allowed to approach the tables to collect provisions. Mothers walk through, many of them pushing baby strollers, as they pick up items from today's inventory: lettuce, cabbage, oranges, apples, potatoes, melons, sweet potatoes, onions, strawberries, blueberries, and tomatoes. I observe mothers stuffing bags of produce into the lower reaches of their strollers as older kids help with carrying the load. Some of the mothers struggle to squeeze everything into the bags they brought with them. Meanwhile, volunteers have to repeatedly recalibrate rations for each participant depending on the number of people still in line. Some clients wait patiently to go through the line again, as the event proceeds until clients have exhausted the inventory.

Prior to breaking down tables and dismissing volunteers, the supervisor shows me his clipboard reflecting the total number of attendees who registered today: sixty-seven. He suspects that the foul weather deterred additional people from coming.

DIETARY SURVEILLANCE

Public health practitioners and food system activists in the United States have both become concerned with the health consequences of a food system that they interpret as unregulated, particularly in terms of allowing for an abundance of calorie-dense, nutrient-poor, cheap foods (California Center for Public Health Advocacy et al. 2008). They highlight the relationship of malnutrition, in the form of consuming calorie-dense, nutrient-poor foods, to diet-related disease, including obesity, type 2 diabetes, hypertension, cardiovascular disease, metabolic syndrome, and cancer (Guthman 2011). Obesity prevention campaigns, as well as nutrition education and food literacy programs are now common, popularized for instance through first lady Michelle Obama's Let's Move!

Campaign and Jamie Oliver's hit television series *Food Revolution.* Many of these efforts cite the rises in obesity and noncommunicable diseases as threats to the future of the nation whereby health represents a matter of national security.

Kezia Barker (2012) critiques "health security" within broader, contemporary moves toward "securitization," a process described by Filippa Lentzos and Nikolas Rose as consisting of "border controls, regimes of surveillance and monitoring, novel forms of individuation and identification, notably those based on biometrics, preventative detention or exclusion of those thought to pose significant risks, massive investment in the security apparatus and much more" (2009, 231). The "US War on Fat" as interrogated by Susan Greenhalgh (2012) exemplifies this sort of national project of health security. Elsewhere I have suggested that these discourses commingle with extant beliefs about such things as a "Latino threat" (Chavez 2008) to the unfortunate disadvantage and stigmatization of Mexican American communities as well as Mexican and Central American (im)migrants living in the United States (Greenhalgh and Carney 2014).

The addition of food security to the list of national security threats, alongside other nonmilitary issues such as health security, constitutes another attempt to elevate public health to the level of national security with the effect of public health initiatives often justified as defensive measures against threats to the population (Barker 2012; Fidler 2003; Ingram 2005). Responses to food insecurity, similar to other projects of national security, are "imagined, justified, and conducted" (Barker 2012, 696) with securitization as an organizing logic, thereby positioning front-line public health workers as "proxies for the state" in enacting surveillance measures and disciplining the population (Horton and Barker 2009). Hence I suggest that we consider how dietary health interventions facilitate an "ongoing surveillance and management" of worrisome bodies—or in the case of my fieldwork, (im)migrant women's bodies—that aims to ensure what Jonathan Xavier Inda has described as "the welfare of the social body" (2007, 151). While diet may play a role in shaping an individual's health risks, there is a lack of consensus about whether if any of the so-called diet-related diseases are actually diet-related in origin. Nonetheless, public health concerns about these diseases have progressively overshadowed programmatic focus on the very real and important issues of hunger and food insecurity (Allen 2007; Guthman 2011; Poppendieck 2010). Unfortunately, public health attempts to prevent and address these diseases— namely, through modifications to individual behaviors—often fall into the trap of "blaming the victim" (Guthman 2008a, 2008b, 2008c, 2011).

This chapter delves into how food insecurity in the United States and some of the health problems observed in immigrant communities—but also in low-income communities of color— have been addressed by service providers. I approach this topic from my key informants' perspectives on a variety of food assistance programs and from my own experience of being a participant observer in these settings. I describe how service providers have begun to align with preventative health approaches in the name of preventing diet-related diseases. Programs approach this effort through tailoring services to meet several criteria: transmitting knowledge and skills to clients, challenging clients to reform individual behavior, and empowering clients to "take control" of their dietary needs and propensity for health problems. As interventions, these efforts promote the disciplined "health-conscious" consumer as a way of monitoring health risks and set in motion the biopolitical project of food security.

Although nutrition education has been a core component for decades of both public and private programs that provide nutrition assistance in the United States, I suggest that in the contemporary political economy of food assistance this practice implies deeper shifts in political ideology. I argue that the invocation of clients of private food assistance programs—that is, programs administered by nonprofit organizations—to assume a larger share of responsibility for diet and health precipitates the transfer of responsibility for care from the realm of the collective to the individual, implying further burdens for women who are the primary clients of these programs. Acting as proxies for the state, these programs are partially complicit with an ideology that enables the state to govern from a distance (Brockling, Krasmann, and Lemke 2011; Lemke 2012).

A SHORT HISTORY OF EMERGENCY FOOD ASSISTANCE

The neoliberal turn of the 1980s prompted major shifts in the structure of food aid in the United States. In response to widespread cuts in welfare, local communities founded food banks, food pantries, and soup kitchens (Poppendieck 1998). Emergency food assistance programs emerged as a temporary solution to fill the void left behind by reductions in public spending. Since many of these cuts have never been restored, however, the emergency food network in the United States has expanded and ossified to become a mainstay of the social safety net.

Many food banks and food pantries have historically depended on entitlement programs for supplying their inventory as they now also actively enroll clients in the Supplemental Nutrition Assistance Program (SNAP). Yet economic recession has prompted a curtailing of federal support and corporate donations for these private charities, which are now burdened with overseeing a larger share of the social safety net (Carney 2012). Meanwhile, the demand for private food assistance in all areas of the United States has not waned. For instance, in its 2010 *Hunger in America* report, the national association of food banks Feeding America found that more than thirty-seven million Americans and fourteen million children were relying on network members for food assistance. These figures represented an increase of 46 percent and 50 percent, respectively, from the previous report conducted in 2006.

With an annual clientele totaling more than one-quarter of Santa Barbara County's population, the Foodbank of Santa Barbara County (FSBC) had also witnessed a 35 percent annual increase in demand for services following the onset of the US economic recession in 2008 (Carney 2012). Yet economic recession had also hindered some of the FSBC's efforts in securing inventory. Specifically, recent cuts to federal programs such as the Emergency Food Assistance Program and declining donations from corporations that sought to redirect surplus food to cheap box stores and overseas markets (Young 2008) required that the FSBC identify alternative sources for procuring its inventory. As a result of these trends, the FSBC was required to purchase a larger share of the food it distributed, handle a larger volume of inventory, and coordinate distribution to a larger population. With support from the US Department of Agriculture (USDA) gradually deteriorating, food banks such as the FSBC have increasingly relied on grants through private foundations—agribusiness such as the ConAgra Foods Foundation issue some of the largest grants—and corporate food retailers such as Walmart. In my experience, funding from these foundations usually stipulates that nutrition education be a component of service delivery.

The strengthening of private food assistance in the United States has been linked to an eroding of state entitlement programs (Mares 2013; Poppendieck 1998). Janet Poppendieck (1998) suggests that private food assistance organizations remain apolitical with regard to the broader context of poverty, of which food insecurity is a symptom. In other words, instead of adopting a "comprehensive justice" (Sargent 2012) approach that views food insecurity as a problem of structural inequality, skeptics suggest that the sector of private food assistance is currently equipped to render at best short-term solutions. While there is certainly plenty of evidence to support these claims, the realm of private food assistance in the United States should not be interpreted as monolithic by any means. Moreover, it would be not only unfair but also inaccurate to suggest that all private food assistance organizations are staunchly apolitical in the work that they do. I say unfair because funders often prohibit political campaigning or lobbying activities of any kind; "apolitical" is thus an imposed label rather than a chosen one. And I say inaccurate because many food banks, including the FSBC, are very politically active; some are actually leading efforts to enroll people in SNAP as they also lobby at the state and federal levels for more robust funding in entitlement programs.

EATING AS A MEANS OF PREVENTION

During my fieldwork, I participated in a number of food distributions administered by private programs that featured nutrition classes and other resources for preventing or managing certain dietary health problems. The idea that carefully managed eating habits could serve as a means of disease prevention also characterized much of the health outreach, nutrition education, and

Figure 15. A poster issued by MyPyramid (USDA) promoting consumption of fruits and vegetables adorning the wall of a community center. Photo by the author.

social marketing offered at community sites regularly frequented by low-income and mixed-status households. Schools and community centers, in addition to private food distributions, hosted cooking and nutrition classes. Similarly, local YMCAs initiated the Healthy Family Home Program, through which they focused on promoting physical activity, healthy eating, and "healthy family time." The FSBC, collaborating with county public health officials, generously offered itself as the central conduit for coordinating curriculum across dozens of intervention sites and transmitting these forms of "knowledge assistance" to the low-income Latino population.

Figure 16. An FSBC booth at a local food festival in Santa Barbara. Photo by the author.

The FSBC provided many important resources and venues for connecting with mixed-status households who were relying on some form of food assistance. Celebrating its thirtieth year of operation in 2012, the mission of the FSBC as quoted on its website was "to provide nourishment to those in need by acquiring and distributing safe nutritious foods via local agencies and Direct-to-Client programs as well as providing food literacy training to solve hunger and nutrition problems." More than 102,000 county residents sought food assistance in fiscal year 2011 through the FSBC network of over 290 member agencies and programs and through its own direct-to-client programs. Of the 102,000 county residents that received support, 62,000 participated in more than one food program, resulting in 164,000 incidents of service; 44 percent of FSBC clients were children, 46 percent were working poor, and

10 percent were seniors. Agencies distributing food through the FSBC network did not collect information regarding the immigration status of clients; hence the absence of official data on this aspect of program demographics.

The FSBC operated from three remote locations countywide: warehouse facilities in the cities of Santa Maria and Santa Barbara, as well as an education and administration center in downtown Santa Barbara. As part of its response to increasing demand in recent years, the FSBC had expanded and renovated its facilities, including the opening of the Santa Maria warehouse in 2006 and the installation of a cooler and freezer at its Santa Barbara warehouse in 2008 to accommodate a larger inventory of fresh produce. With these structural improvements the FSBC was able to distribute more than eleven million pounds of food annually, over half of which was fresh produce.[1] The FSBC had actually made concerted efforts to increase the share of produce in its total annual distribution, proving its commitment to its Produce Initiative as well as to its more recent Children's Health Initiative.

The FSBC is a member of Feeding America, the national network of food banks. As of 2013, Feeding America included more than two hundred member food banks that collectively served thirty-seven million people annually. On its website, Feeding America claims that it "[promotes] better nutrition by increasing access to healthful foods like fruits and vegetables, raising awareness of the coexistence of hunger with other diet-related diseases, and by promoting nutrition education." Feeding America is an official partner of the USDA project MyPlate. Commenting on this partnership, Feeding America boasts of its national reach "to promote healthful food choices for our clients.... We can collaborate to increase awareness of both hunger and healthy eating, while building solutions that are appropriate and sustainable in the low income communities we serve" (Feeding America 2014b). As a condition of this partnership, members of the Feeding America network are expected to "work on a local level to reach consumers and help them make meaningful, sustainable, healthy dietary changes, based on the Dietary Guidelines" (Feeding America 2014a). The assumption underlying Feeding America's imposition of dietary guidelines on network members is that these guidelines hold legitimacy for catering to optimal health across all populations. Proponents of alternative food movements, however, underscore the "revolving door" political culture of the USDA and the inauthenticity of claims about concerns for consumer health being the priority in establishing official dietary guidelines. Marion Nestle (2007), reflecting on her own involvement with USDA procedures for establishing guidelines, alludes to the prevailing lack of consensus in discussions and reveals the industry politics that take precedence in the creation of consumer resources such as MyPlate.

The FSBC distinguishes itself both locally and nationally for its commitment to developing innovative solutions to food insecurity with a focus on dietary health—a cause that has garnered the FSBC a number of accolades in recent years. It won the Nonprofit of the Year Award from the Goleta, California, Chamber of Commerce in 2010, the Feeding America 2010 Child Hunger Program of the Year Award, and a Feeding America nomination for Food Bank of the Year in 2010 and 2011. These distinctions are perhaps all the more impressive in light of the extremely competitive nonprofit sector that dominates the region. Santa Barbara County has the highest density of nonprofits per capita (14.05 per 10,000), more than any other county in Southern California (with an average rate of 6.48 per 10,000), and 33 percent of the county's nonprofit sector provides health and human services; emergency food programs fall under this category (Costello and Manzo 2005). The abundance of nonprofits serving Santa Barbara County's population is arguably as much a reflection of the region's wealth and tradition of philanthropy as it is of the desperation and poverty that causes the demand for these services.

Rethinking the Role of Private Food Assistance

In early December 2009—after several months of rumors about the formation of a food policy council—local farmers, students, researchers, nutritionists, public health officials, school food advocates, university professors, institutional dining representatives, farmer's market managers, local food distributors, and food assistance program representatives convened at Casa de la Raza, a prominent Latino community center in downtown Santa Barbara, to share about the most pressing issues facing the local food system. About halfway into the meeting, as participants were going around in a circle to share their views, a prominent Anglo-American health expert stated, "Latinos just don't know how to cook." He then proceeded to emphatically convey his sympathy for the local Latino community whom he declared "does not know healthy from unhealthy food," arguing that cooking instruction should be a core component of outreach programs from service providers. His sentiments were echoed shortly thereafter by other Anglo attendees, who then dominated the latter half of the meeting to focus on this singular issue with the unfortunate result of diverting the rest of us away from the original agenda.

The health expert mentioned in the above vignette was not alone in his convictions. During my multiple years of involvement with the community food security, sustainability, and food justice movements in the United States, I have observed a tendency among health workers and activists to regularly generalize health risks to an apparently homogenous "Latino community" that ostensibly lacks the appropriate knowledge to deal with dietary health problems. Given the contemporary sociopolitical backdrop of media and legislative emphasis on "the Brown threat" (Rivera 2014), it is hard not to think that pressure to integrate educational components into programs imposed by funders and public health partners stems in part from concerns about the draining of public services by minority groups. Moreover, we might contemplate the extent to which such paternalistic thinking undermines the capacity of Latino communities to advocate on their own behalf or interferes with programs seeking to help, not harm, these communities.

Less than two years after the first meeting of the burgeoning food policy council, the FSBC had repositioned itself as a preventative health care organization with ambitions exceeding far beyond the simpler realm of "emergency food." Its reason for doing so was partly motivated by a desire to extricate itself from the stigmatized realm of emergency food assistance that had hindered its ability to establish credibility with many regional and national grant-based funding institutions, including health foundations that were becoming increasingly important amid declining federal support and growing service demand. They operationalized this new emphasis by delivering "food literacy training," defined by the organization as "how to shop, cook, and eat for optimal health." Hence, the FSBC coordinated a number of food literacy trainings in combination with food distributions. In pursuing a preventative health agenda, the FSBC aspired to generate long-term nutritional health outcomes for clients and to attract the financial capital to do so. Age and group appropriateness of trainings factored into the design of distinct programs offered through the FSBC; low-income families, high school students, schoolchildren, and even preschoolers each enjoyed their own unique curriculum. Across all ages and groups, programs promoted an ideology of self-care with regard to health. Direct-to-client programs coordinated by the FSBC included the Brown Bag program for seniors; the Mobile Farmer's Market, Mobile Food Pantry, and Healthy School Pantry for families; the Kid's Farmer's Market; the Picnic in the Park summer meal program for school-age children; and the Food Literacy in Preschool program. As part of a holistic approach to health, several of the direct-to-client programs also incorporated physical activities to promote exercise among clients.

The Healthy School Pantry program was hosted with parents and children of low-income families during after-school hours; at the end of its first year, more than a thousand families were reported to have participated. While distributing healthy food provisions was a core objective of the program, local health professionals—including *promotores* (bilingual community health workers)—demonstrated healthy recipes, conducted health screenings, and provided participants with basic lessons in nutrition and diet-related disease prevention. Sites offered this program on a monthly basis, but there was strong community support for offering the program with more regularity and expanding to additional sites.

Mobile food pantries and farmers markets, also organized by the FSBC for the distribution of fresh fruits and vegetables, doubled as sites of nutrition education. During my visits to several sites I repeatedly encountered Rethink Your Drink, a campaign developed by the US Centers for Disease Control and Prevention and the Network for a Healthy California. The central objective of this campaign was to reduce consumption of sugar-sweetened beverages. Rather than directing efforts toward an unregulated soft drink industry, however, Rethink Your Drink focused on reforming consumer behavior as a primary mode of disease prevention. To a certain degree, the bottled beverage industry even emerged as a partial "winner" in this campaign, as bottled water was featured as the ideal alternative in campaign materials.[2] While sitting in on the presentation at one site, I helped to distribute samples of fresh-squeezed orange juice to a room of some forty women and children as an employee of the FSBC delivered the Rethink Your Drink presentation in Spanish. These women and children also received plastic sandwich bags full of sugar cubes to experiment with by filling empty soda bottles to see how many grams of sugar were in different beverages, and they were encouraged by the FSBC employee to make their own beverages, such as *agua fresca* and orange juice, using fresh fruit at home.

As with many of the dietary health interventions I observed during the span of my fieldwork, proponents of Rethink Your Drink emphasized changes to consumers of all ages, but especially to youth. Many of these proponents were affiliated with Partners for Fit Youth, a coalition of over twenty-three agencies in the Central Coast region with a mission "to improve the health of youth and their families through education, intervention, outreach, and environmental changes, to prevent chronic disease, and to promote healthy weight" (Sansum Diabetes Research Institute 2014). The coalition had chosen to focus on Rethink Your Drink in response to recent findings that one in four children in Santa Barbara County was obese (Santa Barbara County 2011). In April 2011, at the coalition's monthly meeting, attendees addressed the matter of identifying summer sites at which to deliver the Rethink

¡PIENSA EN LO QUE TOMAS!

La persona típica consume casi 100 libras de azúcar al año - ¡o alrededor de un cuarto de libra de azúcar al día! La mayoría de esa azúcar proviene de refrescos azucarados. El exceso de calorías de toda esa azúcar pueden producir el aumento de peso, y exponen a la gente a enfermedades crónicas como la diabetes tipo 2 y enfermedades cardíacas.

¡HAGA UNA SELECCIÓN SALUDABLE!

- **AGUA** – ¡No tiene calorías! Póngale un toque de sabor con una rebanada de naranja, limón, lima o pepino!

- **LECHE SIN GRASA O LECHE BAJA EN GRASA 1%**

- **JUGO 100% DE FRUTA O**
- **VEGETALES** (limítese a media taza de jugo)

- **TÉ HELADO SIN AZÚCAR**

- **REFRESCO DE DIETA** (de vez en cuando)

¡Bebe AGUA!

¿SABÍA USTED?

El refresco es LA FUENTE NÚMERO UNO DE AZÚCAR en la dieta estadounidense.

Las bebidas azucaradas nos dan **30%** del azúcar no natural que consume diariamente.

¡Para quemar las calorías de un refresco de 20 onzas tiene que caminar a una velocidad moderada durante una hora, mas o menos!*

4 GRAMOS DE AZÚCAR = 1 CUCHARADITAS DE AZÚCAR

Vea cuanta azúcar hay en estos refrescos populares y considere beber agua:

	Refrescos 20oz.	Bebidas de Naranja 16oz.	Bebidas de fruta endulzada 16oz.	Bebidas de sabor a fruta 11.25oz.	Bebidas Deportivas 20oz.	Agua
Calorías	250	260	220	152	140	0
Gramos de Azúcar	68	60	52	38	36	0
Cucharaditas de azúcar	17	15	13	9.5	9	0

¡LO MEJOR ES BEBER AGUA!

GOLD COAST COLLABORATIVE FOR NUTRITION AND FITNESS
San Luis Obispo ◊ Santa Barbara ◊ Ventura
www.goldcoastnetwork.org

*Para una persona que pesa mas de 154 lbs (70kg) a quemar mas calorías que una persona que pesa menos. Adaptado de Dietary Guidelines for Americans 2005, pagina 16, mesa 4.

Adaptado de materias de Servicios de Salud de Contra Costa.
Para información sobre los Cupones para Alimentos, llame al 877-847-3663. Financiado por el Supplemental Nutrition Assistance Program del Departamento de Agricultura de los Estados Unidos, un proveedor y empleador que ofrece oportunidades equitativas.

CAMPEONES del CAMBIO

Figure 17. Educational flier from Rethink Your Drink.

Your Drink presentation. Previous Rethink Your Drink sites had included health and fitness fairs, schools in low-income neighborhoods, and CalFresh outreach events.

The Rethink Your Drink program had reached an impressively wide audience in Santa Barbara, and my informants often made subtle references to the messages they had gleaned from the campaign. They would often express support for "responsible" consumer practices by emphasizing the lengths they went to avoid soft drinks and by showcasing their own homemade concoctions, particularly *aguas frescas*. As Luisa explained, "I don't buy juices because both my son and daughter are chubby. We are all a bit overweight. So it's best that I make *agua* like *horchata* but I don't put in much sugar. I make them orange juice, hibiscus juice. I try to make these. If one buys these from the store they are too sweet. I don't buy them because we can't consume them, as we are already overweight. I try to buy that which is less sweetened."

Juliana was more overt in referencing how the campaign had influenced her to limit her family's consumption of sweetened drinks and to be more vigilant about her family's dietary health, commenting, "We don't buy many sugary foods and I avoid giving this to my children, I don't give them soda . . . yes, occasionally I'll let them have [something sweet], but not everyday. This would do them harm. They don't drink anything but water, and sometimes juice. [I do this] because of the nutrition classes they've provided me. [I never allow my children] more than an *agua fresca*."

In emphasizing how they were able to regulate the amount of sugar consumed by family members through preparing *aguas frescas* at home, these women demonstrated themselves as competent in executing the knowledge that had been shared with them through Rethink Your Drink as well as responsible consumers in the practice of self-care.

"Feeding Our Future": Youth-Centered Programs

Feed the Future was another initiative that the FSBC had implemented as part of its shifting away from emergency food distribution. Accordingly, the FSBC offered a suite of youth-centered programs, such as Picnic in the Park: A Summer Feeding Program, the Kid's Farmer's Market, the Food Literacy in Preschool program, and Pink and Dude Chefs, all of which sought to cultivate self-reliance among participants in the realm of diet. The development of these programs was also in response to concerns voiced within the public health community about childhood obesity in the region. The Santa Barbara County Department of Public Health and an array of nonprofits devoted much attention to obesity among children because, as one staff member explained, "adult obesity is not possible to prevent, but childhood obesity is preventable." The coalition Partners for Fit Youth formed in the early 2000s when "an avalanche of data on childhood obesity" came under public scrutiny and attracted the interest of public health officials.[3] Health assessments with county schoolchildren had also informed the regional health authority's decision to host an annual Child Obesity Summit, which launched in March 2009.

In early fall 2010, officials from the Department of Public Health convened parents into focus groups at schools in low-income areas to share results of a countywide health screening in which 37 percent of schoolchildren scored as obese or overweight for their age. In these focus groups, staff from the Department of Public Health, most of them registered dieticians and nutritionists, sought to incentivize more involvement from the low-income population in addressing this problem; they also announced plans to parents for the county's Obesity Prevention Plan and collected input to this effect. Notably, not all of the parents in attendance at these focus groups had children ranking in the "at risk" categories. Nonetheless, the county elected to present the survey findings to all of the parents in attendance.

Childhood obesity received much attention in the design and implementation of dietary health interventions, including those coordinated by the FSBC, and commanded a large share of monetary contributions from community members. The FSBC repeated a feature on the childhood obesity "epidemic" in several of its mailings to potential donors. Captivating its audience with a startling series of profile images of a child who gradually goes from being (excessively) thin to fat, the inscription that followed outlined how childhood obesity resulted from a lack of healthy food and that a diet more abundant in fresh fruit and vegetables would curtail the cycle of "hunger-poor diet-obesity."

Undeniably, the youth-centered programs offered by the FSBC encouraged youth to become more health-conscious consumers, but young people were not the only targets of these programs. Several volunteers and staff members informed me of how they hoped that youth participants would serve as agents of behavioral change within households by relaying campaign messages back to parents. YMCAs and Boys and Girls Clubs offered the Kid's Farmer's Market on a monthly basis during the school year. Each month elementary and middle school-age youth would receive a brief nutrition lesson and then learn how to prepare a healthy snack with a featured produce item of the month. The program would conclude with a mock farmer's market during which youth participants collected provisions to bring home to their families. The Picnic in the Park program substituted for the Kid's Farmer's Market during the months of June, July, and August; instead of arranging for provisions to take home, sites offered lunches to fill the meal gap created by the discontinuation of school meal programs during summer months. Youth attended sites of the program with family members, consumed a brown bag lunch on site, and participated in physical activities that were intended to

Figure 18. Ingredients for a healthy snack and the MyPyramid poster await youth participants at a Kid's Farmer's Market program site. Photo by the author.

encourage children to exercise. Finally, a more recent program, Pink and Dude Chefs, offered culinary training to high school students. The goal of this program was to bestow teenage participants with an appreciation for healthy food and the skills to prepare healthy meals.

Teach a Man to Fish: Foregrounding Empowerment in Programs

In September 2010, the executive director of the FSBC invited me to the Western Regional Conference of Food Banks, an annual gathering that brought together food banks in the Feeding America network to share best practices and to learn the latest in food bank technologies and research. As the FSBC was hosting the conference, the executive director delivered a keynote presentation in which he emphasized the transformative potential of "practical dietary health knowledge" for food bank clients. The audience—composed of other executive directors and CEOs of food banks both big and small—responded with mixed feedback. Some believed that playing the role of "nutrition police" (in the words of one woman) would not fit within the mission of their organization. Despite some pushback from the audience, this executive director's allegiance to promoting nutrition education as a means to empowerment soon framed almost all of the FSBC's outreach efforts and generated much enthusiasm within the larger community of Santa Barbara around the FSBC as an organization. Although it was perhaps an unanticipated benefit at the time, the FSBC's focus on empowerment proved to be an impressively effective strategy in garnering financial support.

Appeals to the agency of food-aid clients through the discourse of empowerment are both a reflection of the current funding climate for nongovernmental organizations, which prioritizes projects that focus on self-care and skill building (Guthman 2008c), and of an intensifying moralization of health as a matter of personal responsibility (Guthman 2011; Skrabanek 1994). The philosophy of the proverb "give a man a fish and he will eat for a day, teach a man to fish and he will feed himself for the year"—as paraphrased by the FSBC executive director during his keynote speech to other food bank CEOs and executive directors—now guides the funding criteria of several prominent US-based food and health foundations; the mantra has become even more relevant in light of the depreciated capacity of private food assistance programs to procure inventory. These food and health foundations include the Robert Wood Johnson Foundation, the Kellogg Foundation, the ConAgra Food Foundation, the Coca Cola Foundation, the Walmart Foundation, the Ronald McDonald House of Charities, and Share Our Strength, among other organizations.

One of the ways that I directly observed programs fostering a spirit of empowerment was in inciting clients to take partial ownership of programs by enlisting as volunteers. Natalia described how she became a volunteer shortly after participating as a client, noting, "I like it because I have been a volunteer there for four years. I like it because I get my vegetables. And because I get to chat with the other women. We all already know each other there. I had gone four times to stand in line, and during my fourth time the manager asked if I would also be interested in helping out. I told him yes, and so it's been since." While client-volunteers in private food assistance programs for the most part spoke fondly of volunteering, they also cited experiences of exploitation. For instance, some of my key informants reported unreasonable expectations that had been imposed on them by supervisors. These could include heavy lifting, an extension of one's shift without obtaining prior consent, and discouragement from bringing children to sites. As volunteering already constituted a time- and labor-intensive activity, such constraints on client-volunteer labor veritably dampened many women's hopes for empowerment within the programs. The negative aspects of volunteering as shared by client-volunteers did not necessarily reflect a shortcoming of the FSBC as an organization but rather of partner agencies that distributed provisions from the FSBC.

Aside from enlisting as volunteers, women actively participated in reproducing the language of empowerment they learned through programs by expressing their own desires for more nutritional knowledge. Paloma, for instance, appreciated learning at program sites about how to empower herself and her husband through "tratamos de comer saludable" (trying to eat healthy) following a diagnosis of diabetes. Notably, when enrolling as key informants in my study several of the women explained that they were motivated by the topic of nutrition. Although during recruitment I never advertised training or lessons in nutrition for the obvious reason that I have no formal background in this field, many women deduced nonetheless that this would ensue as part of the research. As Celina commented, "For me, I was interested [in participating in the research] to know what's healthy and I wanted to learn more about how to get good nutrition. Sometimes one attempts to cook nutritiously, but in reality they don't know if what they're eating is [nutritious], so I was interested for this reason."

Many of these women voiced an explicit demand for nutrition education. As one woman who did not have much direct experience with nutrition education stated to me, "I think that having nutrition classes would motivate people to care for their own bodies." Another woman explained how nutrition education served as a source of motivation. "I go because I like to be informed," she said. "I like to know more, for instance, about diabetes. This is something that has motivated me to eat healthy, and my children too. Because I want to see my children grow up. Sometimes I get them to watch the commercials, for them to get the message; even though some commercials advertise pure garbage, some say, 'It's for your health.' Sometimes I prohibit something, sweets for example, by saying, 'It's for your health.'" This woman believed that co-opting the language of nutrition education and public service announcements on television enabled her to hone her skills of persuasion around matters of health with her children. The women valorized to an extent these external influences that they viewed as enabling individuals to get on a path of self-care and to assume a larger share of personal responsibility in preventing health problems.

Apparently health workers had also observed this trend. In one public health official's description of a study on food access that was conducted by a group of Spanish-speaking, low-income women in three neighborhoods in the county,[4] she explained that these women traded their labor for nutrition classes and that they wanted more nutrition education as a result of collecting data. Follow-up nutrition classes had since continued with facilitation by local *promotoras*. Part of the appeal of such programs was presumably that they helped to assuage women's fears about the potential costs of managing chronic disease by empowering them with knowledge. Yet I could not understand why the women I met during my research were so preoccupied with obtaining this type of nutritional knowledge, especially when material constraints compromised the ability to put such knowledge into practice. Findings from research on *curanderas* (traditional healers) and modes of healing in migrant communities provide some possible insight. As these forms of healing become particularly important among those with limited access to biomedical care (Rogers 2010; Waldstein 2010), a nutritional approach to health may offer a glint of hope to women for becoming self-sufficient in the long term. This approach to health also readily resonated with women's practice of *cuidarse en la comida* (caring through food) or using food as an instrument of treating and preventing disease. In other words, *cuidarse en la comida* indexed a mode of disease prevention accessible to many, whereas barriers surrounded other modes of care (e.g., doctor visits and prescription medications). As most of the women in my fieldwork were charged with sole responsibility over household nutritional resources, they appreciated any attempt to further empower themselves in this realm as this effectively advanced their position within the household.

Observing how the imperatives for self-transformation fall most heavily on women, Rosalind Gill (2008) argues that women actually make the ideal neoliberal subjects. While finessing the repertoire of nutritional knowledge that had been shared with them by health workers, many of the women in my research boasted of their hopes for self-sufficiency and independence from public programs such as the Women, Infants, and Children (WIC) program and SNAP. Against the hopes of these women, however, several *promotores* expressed concerns to me about how much could really be communicated in a thirty- or forty-minute lesson (as with the Rethink Your Drink campaign) and that without adequate follow-up, short presentations offered small promise for long-term changes to food-related attitudes and behaviors.

Aside from purported health benefits, nutrition education was potentially valuable for another reason: women could access a semblance of social belonging through exhibiting nutritional knowledge. Although I think there is much supporting evidence for this claim, the following scene from my fieldwork is particularly illustrative. During a planned visit to Angela's home, I watched as she prepared a pasta *con pollo y verduras* (with chicken and vegetables). I had been surprised by her assertion that she prepared this meal multiple times per week given that other women in my research rarely cooked with pasta, preferring instead potatoes or rice. Two months later, in the context of one of our focus groups, Angela reflected on my aforementioned visit to her home and how she had actually solicited advice for a recipe beforehand from a health worker instead of preparing one of her typical meals.

"Truthfully," she said, "I was very uncomfortable because I didn't know if I was doing something wrong [to the food]. To me it seemed healthy, but I didn't know if from [Megan's] point of view it was healthy. I said, 'I'm going to make something that [Megan] likes, something that doesn't have too much spice.' But what do I make? Something healthy. A nurse from [the clinic] told me to make this pasta sauce but I had never made it before. It was with lots of vegetables." Angela was not the only woman to have admitted that she consulted with health workers to obtain "healthy" recipes for the purposes of this research. Other women admitted to reproducing recipes and regurgitating content from nutrition lessons in my presence for the reason that they thought I was there to evaluate them. Considering the broad forms of social exclusion encountered by immigrants in the United States, I interpreted these slight adjustments to culinary practices made by women as an extension of this desire for being recognized as responsible subjects and for social inclusion (Chavez 2008; Schmidt-Camacho 2008; Zavella 2011).

While those promoting nutrition education boast of its potential as a medium for social empowerment (Kent 1988), skepticism looms about how much the road to empowerment is paved by people in positions of power (Guthman 2011). The notion that immigrants drain the state of welfare resources is a common misconception and relates to the emergence of a new nativism that deems some but not all as entitled to public services (Zavella 2011). While the women in my research lamented lacking the means to acquire healthy food on a steady basis, the structural aspects of food insecurity and disease pathology rarely entered discussion within interventions and private food assistance programs. In generalizing about the health risks of the low-income population, preventative health programming within the realm of private food assistance resembled the structural violence of other public health interventions in the United States, which often exclude from care those who do *not* fit a specific category and subject those who *do* fit to unnecessary surveillance (Craddock 2000; Guthman 2011). As Julie Guthman notes, "The neoliberal state...redefines good citizenship as being a minimal consumer of state health and welfare services" (2011, 55). More than building skills, "empowering," or improving the health status of participants, such interventions arguably accomplish more in familiarizing immigrants with neoliberal notions of personal responsibility and self-reliance.

PROBLEMS WITH INTERNALIZING THE PROJECT OF FOOD SECURITY

While waiting to interview a health and nutrition educator from the Santa Barbara County Public Health Department in May 2011, I visited the WIC office, which—aside from providing food vouchers to low-income mothers with children ages five and under—offered nutrition assistance and counseling. Situated among the children's artwork that adorned the walls were instructions for parents on how to prepare quesadillas (purported as "a healthy alternative to Flaming Hot Cheetos") via use of a microwave. The instructions were offered in both English and Spanish and were accompanied by several illustrations. Any adult could likely imagine feeling patronized reading over this information written as if for children instead of the adult audience for which it was intended. In my own review of the instructions, I was reminded of criticisms made by my key informants about the cooking classes offered in Santa Barbara's public schools. Specifically, women with schoolchildren complained that these classes had insulted their knowledge by "teaching" them dishes they already knew how to prepare (and probably better than program staff), and that staff had overlooked the ways that demanding work schedules and limited household incomes constrained food purchasing decisions and the amount of time mothers had at their disposal for meal preparation.

My experience at the WIC office exemplifies one instance among many in which empowerment as the purported goal of dietary health interventions actually translates negatively toward the intended audience. Clients may experience the effects of structural violence when programs disregard how structural inequalities impede them from adopting so-called responsible consumer practices. In addition, clients may also experience epistemic violence when programs such as the after-school cooking classes fail to include opportunities for clients' knowledge to surface in the curriculum for the reason that these programs mistakenly misdiagnose the problem as one of inadequate knowledge among clients (Minkoff-Zern 2012).

In defense of these programs, there has been scant formal research on the lived experience of food insecurity in the United States. Most of the data available through large population surveys do not reveal how structures collide with human agency in producing this experience. By no means is this problem unique to misunderstandings of food insecurity in the United States. Critical medical anthropologists note that historically many public health interventions have attributed health problems among the working poor to individual moral failings while also operating on the assumption that with improved knowledge individuals will become empowered to change the fate of their health (Farmer 2005). Similar logics guide the realm of dietary health intervention in the United States. Contrary to assumptions about deficiencies in knowledge among clients, my research participants actually harnessed extensive culinary knowledge. As I discussed in chapter 3, women regretted lacking the time and resources to prepare meals from fresh, whole ingredients. Women had acquired this knowledge, or what Meredith Abarca discusses as "*sazón*, the knowledge of the senses" (2006), from other women in their families and communities beginning at a very early age. Yet recent pressure by public health advocates to devote more attention within both public and private food aid programs in the United States to dietary health assumes that the dietary practices of immigrant women demand intervention. These programs convey certain ideas—many of which stem from moral beliefs—about how to eat healthily and how to prevent or treat specific health problems. Greenhalgh (2012) suggests that such biopedagogy—instruction about the body—has the deleterious effect of colonizing one's subjectivity and actually foreclosing potential for empowerment.

The propensity of my key informants to blame other poor people for their own health problems demonstrated how more latent forms of epistemic violence in the delivery of dietary health information seeped into women's everyday discourses. When I spoke with women about how they perceived others' food-related behaviors in the Latino community, for instance, they often attributed health problems and consumption of *comida chatarra* (junk food) to a lack of or disregard for health-related knowledge:

MEGAN CARNEY: Are people in your community aware of possible effects on health from diet?

LINDA: Well, yes.

BRENDA: I think so.

LINDA: They are aware, but sometimes we don't want to understand.

Others confirmed these perceptions. As Tina commented, "People eat poorly because so often they don't know what the food contains." Pilar noted, "The food bank provides many classes where one goes to get produce. They explain how to eat healthfully. I think this is good because it helps one very much, especially low-income individuals. And [the food bank] teaches them how to eat well. I think it's good because it helps people with procuring food. They not only give out food, but they also teach people how to eat." Linda's statement that "a veces no queremos entender" (sometimes we don't want to understand) insinuated that health problems in the community related to individual choice.

It is interesting to highlight that the women in my research did not attribute blame for health problems within Latino communities to the food industry or government or implore these entities to implement changes. Rather, many viewed a need for interventions at the level of the individual. Yolanda remarked, "The meetings that they provide at school should be done in different neighborhoods to explain to people what nutrition is and how each meal should contain vitamins, calcium, iron, and one will know, because there are people that don't know these things." Another recommendation shared with me was to include cooking lessons into nutrition or eating (*alimentación*) classes for those women who cooked in an unhealthy manner. During a focus group, one woman shared her belief, clearly shaped by the "conventional wisdom" of nutrition in the United States, that people from Mexico were accustomed to cooking with a lot of oil and fat and that this translated to poor health. "I'd like to see a program that teaches us how to cook healthier," she said. "In Mexico we cook everything with a lot of oil and foods that get you fat. We use too much. For us, it tastes good but then we go to the doctor and they tell us 'you have high cholesterol, diabetes, et cetera,' because we don't know how to cook in a healthy manner." Pilar invoked a similar rationale in articulating demand for educational programs: "Perhaps [there should be] campaigns, bringing people to know that what they eat is not adequate and to offer them an eating group that could teach them how to eat well, because much of the time, what people eat, at large, does them harm, makes them fat."

In arguing for more nutrition education, it was curious how much these women's language and logic overlapped with the field of public health, demonstrating the efficacy of interventions within food assistance programs in reproducing "bootstraps" myths among clients. Similar to some of the attendees at the meeting of the food policy council discussed earlier in this chapter, these women speculated that others in their community did not know how to cook and did not recognize "healthy" from "unhealthy" food or how to incorporate unfamiliar foods that they found in the United States. Oddly enough, my research participants rarely called for any structural changes—such as access to health care, health facilities, or medical insurance—in constructing their answers to what could be done to improve the health of community members; instead they discussed this with me in terms of individual responsibility.

The concept of *habitus*, defined by Pierre Bourdieu as "the internalized form of class condition and of the conditionings it entails" ([1979] 1984, 101), captures how dominant ideologies and social locations become embodied, represented, and reproduced by marginalized groups (see also Ortner 2006). Dietary practices represent an important site of constructing this *habitus* with respect to the state, the family, and the community (Counihan 1999; Greenhalgh 2012; Himmelgreen and Crooks 2005; Narotzky 1997). Dietary advice from experts in biomedicine and health science may yield to particular subjectivities and technologies of self-governance (Rose 1996). Uncertainty about one's knowledge is but one consequence of dietary health projects that are themselves embedded in everyday negotiations of power, as "knowledge . . . presuppose[s] and constitute[s] at the same time power relations" (Foucault 1975, 27).

The impression bestowed on target audiences, however accidental, by many food assistance programs incorporating nutrition education was that eligibility for food assistance required assimilating to a particular *habitus*, a way of eating and knowing food. Programs implied that individual "deservingness" of food aid depended on one's conforming to or adoption of a certain dietary health ideology, wherein participants became "unknowing" subjects who were assumed to lack the knowledge for how to cook in a healthier manner. "Knowledge assistance" in the form of nutrition education encouraged women to assume practices of nutritional self-sufficiency and self-surveillance with regard to one's health. Instead of considering the ways that systematic changes could be made to redistribute resources and reduce health disparities, dietary health interventions focused on reforming the behaviors of individual eaters. Such interventions were successful in this endeavor to the extent that women I interviewed frequently relied on the rhetoric of individual responsibility in the disciplining of the self and others perceived as belonging to the broadly defined Latino community.

THE INSECURITY OF FOOD SECURITY AS A BIOPOLITICAL PROJECT

Many scholars and activists now regard food banks as big business, noting the partnerships that exist between large corporations and private food aid. As I've noted in this chapter, food banks increasingly rely on grants from private funders, many of which originate through agribusiness and corporate food retailers that require nutrition education be a component of service delivery. Food banks also partner with the USDA to deliver programs; for instance, the FSBC solicited input for curriculum development from the Network for Healthy California (funded by SNAP-Ed, a program of the USDA). Thus, I argue that private food assistance organizations face a double-edged sword in responding to food insecurity in the United States: given current funding schemes, they are limited in being able to contest the role of corporations or government in perpetuating the conditions of food insecurity. In other words, the capacity of private food assistance to respond to food insecurity, even if only in the short term, hinges on being complicit with the biopolitical project of food security. They also inevitably constitute part of this project in partnering with the field of public health to transmit dietary health messages to consumers.

In no way whatsoever do I mean to dismiss the benevolent intentions of service providers; quite honestly, our current social safety net would completely crumble without the hard work and dedication of these organizations. Given that possibility, however, we also need to think critically about the overall precarity of this system as the primary vehicle for dealing with food insecurity in the United States. My impression of many public health workers and private food-aid staff members has been that they strongly oppose the persistence of health disparities and seek to generate positive social change vis-à-vis increasing the life chances of target populations. It is also my impression, however, that neoliberal ideology has colonized even the realm of public health, isolating the individual in interventions as both cause and cure for health ailments. In other words, rather than eroding structures of inequality that make it difficult for poor people (often of color) to eat healthy food, the interventions described above tend to comply with schemes of structural violence that promote food security as a biopolitical project. Immigrants and migrants become the targets of such violence as they are also identified as the pathological "other" through interventions. Moreover, it is important to remember that food insecurity already constitutes a form of violence for those who experience it directly, so something like a focus on improving consumer knowledge without paying heed to one's limited purchasing power is only salt in the wound.

In chapter 5, I will discuss how immigrant women have responded to the biopolitical project of food security, which has also implied a further privatization of care, by focusing on expressions of agency—particularly in the ways that women push back against this project in the realms of public assistance, work, home, and family. In doing so, however, I will also question the notion of self-reliance as something that can be equally accessed by all.

CHAPTER FIVE

Managing Care

Strategies of Resistance and Healing

SUBVERTING A REGIME OF CARE

As I stated in this book's Introduction, the *biopolitics of food insecurity* and the *biopolitical project of food security* are concurrent processes shaping the lived experiences of women who have migrated from Mexico and Central America. To recapitulate this argument, the biopolitics of food insecurity are visible in the uneven distribution of life chances that impel many women to migrate in the first place; the biopolitical project of food security is an instrument of contemporary governmentality that structures how women are supposed to comport themselves and care for their families. These biopolitical modes do not operate independently of one another but are entangled in a dialectical relationship. The biopolitics of food insecurity produces a problem which calls for intervention through the biopolitical project of food security, which then reproduces the power relations inherent to a biopolitics of food insecurity, and so on.

Yet women are not passive recipients of these processes. The trope of all migrant women as victims, found for example in the literature on global trafficking, tends to overlook variation in women's experiences, denies women agency, and neglects to account for the nuanced motivations of those who migrate (Parreñas 2011). Contrary to this depiction, there are numerous examples taken from the ethnographic literature of women utilizing migration as a path toward autonomy, ascribing their own meanings to the work they do, and subverting different attempts to exploit them, even if in limited ways (Lee 2010). This chapter rejects the trope of migrant women as victims by underscoring the forms of resistance and quests for autonomy enacted by Mexican and Central American women through the materiality of everyday life in the United States (Das 2007; Das et al. 2001; Ong 1995, 2006; Otis 2011; Parreñas 2011). As Kim England and Isabel Dyck (2012) suggest, although migrants work in the lowest rungs of care hierarchies, it is imperative to understand their agency in both relational and instrumental caring activities. Thus, I suggest that immigrant women's strategies for "making do," which include a careful balancing of resources (the act of *economizar*), cooperating with others amid material scarcity, and navigating different forms of food assistance, contain social and political significance: they attest to a partial subversion of the biopolitical project of food security and associated attempts by the state to discipline "caring" subjects.

"SALIENDO ADELANTE"

Despite encounters with violence, scarcity, and repeated attempts by others or state institutions to constrain their agency, the women in my research rejected a narrative of "victimhood" in favor of one that would emphasize personal empowerment. The ways that women tailored the goals of private food assistance to align with their own interests, as was highlighted in chapter 4, serve as an example. However, this preference was also evident in women's descriptions of "getting ahead" (*saliendo adelante*) without the assistance of others—especially men. Malena for instance, whose conflicts with her husband after arriving to the United States (recall her story from chapters 1, 2, and 3) had erupted from his doubting that she could find work, commented on how even today she was determined to prove her husband wrong: "I said in my mind, 'I have the faith and hope that I will arrive at this place. I know that I can [migrate to the United States].' So I went full of this hope, repeating to myself, 'Yes I can . . . yes I can earn money . . . yes I can prove my husband wrong' who had said to me, 'You cannot work; what do you think you're going to do?' Indeed, it went differently from how he'd predicted."

Some women even advocated for avoiding intimate relationships with men altogether as a way of getting ahead. Camila lived with her daughter and grandchildren in a small apartment near downtown Santa Barbara. Her daughter was a single parent and neither she nor Camila had formal residency status. Camila had fled Acapulco almost twenty years earlier to escape an abusive husband with whom she had raised four children. Describing the decision to leave her husband following her mother's fatal battle with cancer, she said, "My life was very sad in Mexico. There were many problems with the father of my children. I ended [the marriage] because [my husband] drank so much and beat us. [I ended it when] my mom was sick; she died of cancer. And when she was very sick she said to me, "Daughter, no more, he is a very bad man"; she said this because he used to beat me in front of her and my father. He had no respect. He would hit and there'd be blood. [It was very] ugly." Camila explained that since coming to the United States she had avoided intimate relationships with men. "No más" (no more), she would repeat emphatically. She claimed to have advised her daughter to do the same after the separate fathers of her daughter's three children had failed to provide any financial support. In retelling their experiences of migration, both Malena and Camila exhibited pride for achieving their vision of coming to the United States, an accomplishment that marked the first step on a path toward autonomy.

Even as women recalled the most horrific encounters with violence, they reframed these experiences in terms of their own agency and resiliency. Pilar, for example, related her inner strength to the many life challenges she had faced. Her family had lived in an impoverished urban neighborhood in Guatemala. Her father was an alcoholic who regularly abused her mother, and her brother suffered from a disability that required twenty-four-hour supervision. In her early adolescence, Pilar became pregnant with the first of her three children. As a way of earning money and supporting her children, she sold food from a street cart in front of her family's home, with factory workers comprising the bulk of her customers. While working one afternoon Pilar witnessed the fatal shooting of a police officer. At the time of the incident she was pregnant with her third child. Soon after the shooting, local authorities pressed her for eyewitness testimony, and she also received threats from gang members associated with the incident who did not want her sharing information. Her mother offered to take in Pilar's two children, ages eight and two, and urged her to seek asylum in the United States. Pilar acquired a Mexican passport to cross the Guatemalan border into Mexico and then spent five days traveling to the US-Mexico border. Upon her arrival she was escorted away by US Border Patrol agents and held for four months in a detention center where she slept on a metal bed frame that was "como una mesa" (like a table), endured daily probing from psychiatrists and legal counselors about her fear of returning to Guatemala, and was denied adequate food and prenatal care. Against many odds, Pilar was able to convince officials of her story and in return received authorized entry into the United States.

I met Pilar some weeks after her release from the detention center. While she spoke openly about the gravity of her experience, she appeared determined to overcome the trauma of it all. Indeed, her positive disposition surprised and inspired many of those around her. In sharing with others her experience in the context of our focus group she reflected, "Much that I've seen has made me very sad, ultimately. Thankfully, however, I have the will to continue. I think that despite the experiences that have done me wrong and have tired me somewhat, I always think to tomorrow. I think that I am one of those people who will never give up easily. So here I am."

While my research participants often cited conditions of material insecurity or violence that precipitated the decision to migrate, they also stressed how they exercised autonomy in making the decision. Certainly, family members and significant others sometimes had a role in persuading the women toward making one decision or another, and the women relied on others in their social networks to help coordinate the logistics of this migration. Nonetheless, the women's decisions to migrate both indexed a specific moment of enacting autonomy and symbolized for many the beginning of a more autonomous path. The women characterized this autonomy as feeling more in control of their own circumstances, more self-sufficient, and less at the disposal of others.

"MAKING DO": PRACTICES
OF *ECONOMIZAR*

Brenda described needing to plan ahead to determine how foods in her household would be rationed so that she could stretch whatever limited resources they had over multiple days: "Sometimes we buy two gallons of juice, right? Like this past weekend, I had a visitor and I worried, 'What if this [juice] runs out before they go?' It gives me much shame to be without food. One is always thinking of how she can get what she needs for tomorrow. For example, if I buy a chicken, I always divide it in half—half for one day, half for the next day. So yes, one is worried that food will run out." Women's attempts to balance consumption of *comidas limitadas* (limited foods) serve as a poignant example of the strategies required for "making do" not just in the realm of food but in all efforts to become more self-sufficient. Women explained that household access to *comidas limitadas*—specifically, foods that were costly and required careful rationing among household members—constrained everyday consumption of *comida saludable* (healthy food). Thus, Brenda's concerns were motivated not only by a desire to provide for everyone in her household but also by the potential shame that could result from falling short in this endeavor.

In procuring and rationing *comidas limitadas* for family members, and children especially, women resorted to strategies of *limitar* (limiting) or *economizar* (economizing or saving) that required gatekeeping of household resources and depriving oneself of certain items or leisure. Take, for example, Juliana, who explained, "We try to limit ourselves. [We limit] our enjoyment, for example. Not buying a dress, not buying shoes, and placing more priority on food because of the children. Because the children don't know if there's money or not, they say, 'Give me, give me, give me,' but without really knowing what's possible or not." The "we" invoked by Juliana refers to women; her explanation illustrates the ways that women with limited financial resources are expected to make personal sacrifices while also shielding children from the realities of scarcity.

When I asked women about having enough to eat, their answers were often much like Carolina's: "We eat enough, but of *básicos* [basic foods]." Thus, lacking consistent access to *limitadas*, many of my research participants increasingly relied on a few *básicos*. Knowing which foods to prioritize and keeping a steady inventory of these foods were precautionary measures against financial disturbances. Juliana, for instance, claimed to live by her father's saying: "[Always] keep one's house stocked with rice and beans." Women's descriptions of *comida limitada* illustrated how "limited" in this context did not so much refer to quantity as it did to quality of food. Linda commented, "There is a lot of food, even though it may not be nutritious. Like, there are many potatoes and this we use in many ways, in tacos, in tortillas, you can do a lot with these, so there is never a shortage of food." Juliana explained that financial constraints sometimes required that she compromise quality for quantity: "I'm not always able to give [my children] balanced meals. I have to look for specials. I want what's cheap; I want to use what's cheap. I don't go to a single store, but I go to different stores looking for specials. I'm trying to save [*economizar*] on things."

As the monetary resources at one's disposal ultimately informed purchasing decisions, women were particularly sensitive to changes in food prices: "Price comes first, you always go for the items on special," noted Maya. Women conveyed concerns about

Figure 19. Santa Cruz Market, one of the popular *tiendas*, with locations in Santa Barbara and Goleta, displays price specials to passersby. Photo by the author.

sudden fluctuations in the prices of staples such as rice. Olivia commented, "People are worried when prices go up. Because when food prices increase, like rice when it is scarce, and they see the prices increase by four or five dollars, this represents a real problem." It is interesting how Olivia perceives the price change in certain foods like rice as a result of scarcity, perhaps illustrative of the efficacy of trade officials and retailers in assimilating consumers to the story of markets, thereby misplacing accountability rather than addressing the unfairness of a global food system dictated by speculation on commodities.

For women who had the time, surveying prices of foods at multiple stores and outdoor markets enabled "aprovechando las especiales" (taking advantage of specials). Among the retail options available there were discount stores (Smart and Final, Food 4 Less), farmers' markets, swap meets, bulk stores (Costco), and

Figure 20. Sunday shoppers pick through fresh produce at the Goleta Swap Meet. Photo by the author.

smaller Mexican *tiendas*. Linda summarized her purchasing decisions as follows: "We buy the cheapest foods in the store. It's to say that if something costs five dollars and another item costs three dollars, it's better to buy the item that costs less even though it's not the best." Betanía (whose failed shopping excursion opened chapter 1) identified the practice of shopping for items on sale as common among other Latinos, saying, "We watch prices to see when things go on sale. I don't buy anything not on sale because I don't have the money for it. There is very little money. And we Latinos, sometimes we go [for certain foods], sometimes not, because the prices go up. And food is already so expensive." Even amid the constraints posed by price, however, many women sought ways to gain some control over this process. For example, Juliana found many opportunities to introduce unfamiliar foods to her family, claiming that this practice had encouraged her children to develop a broad palate. Rather than representing herself as limited by the foods that she had to procure on sale, Juliana highlighted her own resourcefulness in overseeing her family's diet.

"THEY GIVE TO ME AND I GIVE TO THEM": THE SOCIAL DYNAMICS OF COOPERATION

Susana Narotzky notes that "food and information generally circulate in the same networks and often together" (1997, 114). The practices of pooling resources with others within households, or across extended family and social networks through ties of mutual aid, have been identified as important survival strategies of immigrants in the United States. Yet as I have alluded to in previous chapters, not all of the women in my research benefited from access to broad social networks. Despite this limitation, the women still referenced some forms of cooperation and reciprocity that they engaged in both within and across households. As expressed by Dora, distributing responsibilities among members of the household fostered conviviality and prevented resources from going to waste: "Yes, we share because sometimes [our housemates] don't have anything. And say that you have something, I say, 'Yes, soon I'll bring it for you' because I like conviviality, yes. To be able to help others, we're accustomed to this [practice]. My mother says don't throw out food because perhaps someone wants what you have."

Cooperating with others around food purchases, child care, and preparation of meals enhanced the capacity of my informants' households to cope with financial disturbances and temporal constraints. The women were sometimes able to stretch food budgets by procuring foods in bulk from warehouse stores such as Costco with contributions from other members of the household. Sometimes individuals or families living under the same roof alternated responsibilities for meal preparation or shared the contents of meals with others—the latter often in the case of leftovers. "Everyone cooperates for the meal," remarked Betanía. "They cooperate. When they have a meal, they share with me. They give a plate to my husband and me [if they have extra]. And if I have some [extra], I give to them." Narotzky claims that this type of "recurring commensality" translates to both nutritional and social benefits: "[T]he modest sense of sharing food where it is available between poor households is not only a way of incorporating much needed nourishment, but also a means of maintaining networks under stress situations" (1997, 114).

Sharing responsibility for preparing meals or child care with other women in the household comprised a form of support to mothers who were engaged in a double-duty workday, as in the case of Yolanda: "Sometimes when I'm getting home late, [my sister-in-law] makes the food. If I get home earlier, I make the food." Camila also helped her daughter, a single mother, by providing child care to her three grandchildren: "I don't work more than two days per week, and only a few hours. I don't have a job. I need to help my daughter, but I can't help her with the rent, with nothing [in terms of expenses]. All I can do is help with her children when they get home from school. Now they are at school and she is the only one who works. So I make the meals, look after the children because she works."

Indeed, many of my research participants had hoped to see more opportunities for cooperation and resource-sharing surface in the community. Despite the positive portrayals of sharing within households presented above, women also conveyed remorse that reciprocity was not a more common practice within the community at large. For example, rather than observing strengthened relations of mutual aid in the context of economic recession, the women perceived tensions in the community as eroding such ties. They believed that current economic conditions had heightened competition for resources among low-income households and that a hostile political climate had created distrust in social networks. However, the women were not in complete consensus around this issue. For instance, although Olivia lamented, "We do not have a sense of unity, the sense of being a *paisano* [compatriot]; we don't help each other like Latinos," her statement contradicted others' claims of generosity and convictions that one could ask for help in times of need. Linda, for example, proclaimed that people in her community were still willing to support each other: "There are times when one is desperate and can't give to one's family. One despairs for not having money. There are times that hunger arrives and times that one goes out and looks for people to give something. And one recovers some through what is given."

Finally, some women described avoiding these types of social interactions, even if they could result in exchanges of mutual aid, because they lacked the interest or time. Here it is interesting to consider the degree to which coordinating and nourishing relations of reciprocity represents a gendered labor that adds to the amount of unpaid labor already overseen by women (Glenn 2012). Perhaps then arguments in favor of strengthening women's social networks as a means to lessening the structural constraints of families or households fail to account for how this process implies its own forms of exploitation.

FROM "WELFARE QUEEN" TO "PUBLIC
CHARGE": UNDERSTANDING RESISTANCE
TO ENTITLEMENT PROGRAMS

Data on food-insecure households from specific geographic
regions of the United States reveal severe underutilization of federal food assistance programs (Shimada 2009). In California, for
instance, over 50 percent of households that are eligible for food
assistance in the form of Supplemental Nutrition Assistance
Program (SNAP) benefits do not apply (DeParle and Gebeloff
2009). Janet Poppendieck (1997) underscores some reasons for this
underutilization, noting that "people [are] unaware of their eligibility, [do] not believe that they [need] the stamps, or [feel] that
the costs of participation in terms of stigma, travel to the program office or the rigors of the certification process outweigh the
benefits" (1997, 155).

Undocumented individuals may apply to several government-
administered food and cash assistance programs on behalf of their
children assuming that they are US citizens. These include SNAP
(or CalFresh, as it has been rebranded in California), school breakfast and lunch programs, and the Women, Infants, and Children
(WIC) Nutrition Assistance Program. Although most of the
women in my research would have qualified to receive SNAP
through their children who were US-born, few elected to participate in the program. In particular, women cited social stigma
and fear of state surveillance as prohibitive variables.

Many of the stigma-generating myths applied to users of
food stamps—think "lazy," "irresponsible," "welfare queens,"
and "freeloaders"—have been fabricated by antiwelfare advocates
and neoconservative politicians (Chang 2000; Poppendieck 1998).
Whereas many people are actually employed while receiving food

stamps, the fact is that most food stamp recipients are too young or too old to work; as of 2011, 47 percent were under the age of eighteen, 8 percent were sixty or over, and 30 percent were employed (Food Research and Action Center 2011). One of the prevailing myths is that the primary users of food stamps are people of color, when in reality non-Hispanic whites represent the largest group enrolled in the program (Food Research and Action Center 2011). Such myths —about people enjoying the benefits of welfare over choosing employment, or that welfare is "that thing" that only people of color depend on—have had impressionable effects for groups in the lowest income brackets who would be most eligible for the program (Shimada 2009).

In recent years food banks across the United States have joined in the effort to promote SNAP enrollment. According to the logic of an antihunger approach, promoting the use of federal food assistance along with healthy eating habits may best address the "structural issues" around food insecurity because acting together these reduce the need for food banks as "welfare agencies" (Husbands 1999, 108). In theory, an antihunger approach also focuses on mitigating food insecurity through policy by conveying the needs of food-insecure households to legislators and recognizes that underserved food-insecure individuals desire self-sufficiency, have preferences in regard to what they eat, and want a more active role in improving their own food security (California Food Policy Advocates 2010; Husbands 1999).

The year that I began my fieldwork, the Foodbank of Santa Barbara County (FSBC) hired a young Mexican American woman, Amy Lopez, to do just those things articulated by an antihunger approach. Amy was charged with overseeing CalFresh outreach to clients who were mostly Spanish-speaking women and to serve as a local representative in communicating with policy makers in Sacramento and Washington, DC. With her bicultural and bilingual abilities and her past experience in social work, and as the daughter of a Mexican immigrant family and a native resident of the region, Amy was an ideal candidate for the position. Within only a few months of being hired she was quickly named "la reina de las estampillas" (the queen of food stamps) by her clients.

Compared with enrollment in CalFresh throughout the state, Santa Barbara County ranked forty-fourth out of fifty-eight counties for its low participation (California Food Policy Advocates 2003). As of 2008, only 16 percent of eligible households in the county—or 20,089 individuals—enrolled in the CalFresh program (California Food Policy Advocates 2010). In outreach efforts to promote CalFresh enrollment, the FSBC cited the rising demand for food provisions linked to economic recession and estimated losses from not injecting the local economy with federal dollars (Kaiser 2008).

A major aspect of Amy's job as CalFresh Outreach coordinator was to debunk myths about federal food aid (specifically SNAP)—particularly in regard to how it could interact with one's undocumented status. When I witnessed Amy on the job, she would distribute fliers that outlined in explicit terms the range of services that mixed-status households could receive without jeopardizing their petitions for formal immigration status or revealing themselves to the Department of Homeland Security. Conveying this information was of utmost importance, as about 80 percent of Amy's clients were undocumented women. Amy prioritized opportunities to connect with undocumented individuals, claiming that they were the most afraid to ask questions and thus less likely to seek assistance. She acted as a liaison with the Department of Social Services, filling out clients' applications and fielding their questions. She proudly reported to have helped 351 families enroll in the CalFresh program during her first year on the job. Her willingness to go above and beyond the demands of CalFresh outreach—such as assisting women in situations of domestic violence by connecting them with counseling services, or by helping them to find necessary household appliances such as refrigerators on Craigslist—contributed to her likability and to her eventual "coronation" as the queen (or sometimes "goddess") of food stamps. This title stands in stark contrast to the negative image of the "welfare queen" that was popularized by Republican political candidates in the late 1970s. Rather than symbolizing excessive hoarding, Amy's informal title connoted her benevolence.

Despite her glowing reputation, Amy struggled in her efforts to dismantle the perceptions of stigma held by clients. Many of my key informants explained that they were uninterested in Cal-Fresh because they associated enrollment with people who had failed in asserting self-reliance (and had thus jeopardized their potential for being recognized as ideal "caring" subjects). While twenty of the twenty-five women I formally interviewed had been or were currently enrolled in WIC, almost all of them vehemently opposed the prospect of accepting food stamps, unless they were experiencing serious financial problems.

Yolanda, who was receiving both WIC and CalFresh benefits, reported how these programs helped to placate worries about a potential depletion of household resources: "In this economy, food stamps are helping me a lot. WIC also, because it gives you cereal, milk; all day we have milk and cereal." Maya articulated how food stamps had relieved her of skipping meals and helped her to overcome her depression: "My experiences with [food] stamps have helped me very much because sometimes I was left without food.

And stamps have helped me to get through the month. Sometimes I have to pay rent and I can't buy food. Food stamps help me to buy lunch and to be more relaxed. Before I was very depressed because I didn't have [money] to eat or to feed my child."

Nonetheless, the women debated deservingness around program support. Even if people had low enough incomes to be eligible for the program, many of my informants stated that employment should negate one's eligibility. For instance, Malena did not plan to apply for CalFresh once she was no longer eligible for WIC through her US-born daughter because she had a paying job. "I haven't applied for the stamps because I can work," she said. "Perhaps it would be better if I did ask for help. I don't know. It could be good to ask for [food stamps], but as I say, I have work now, right, and I can do it, but perhaps when I don't have work it would be good to apply. Or perhaps if I had [all of] my kids here with me [in the United States] I would apply. I would have to ask for help then because I would have to pay more in rent [for a larger place to live]." Malena, like many of the other interviewees, had children living under someone else's care in her home country. Despite the role of structural violence, such as conditions of the global economy and of restrictive immigration policies, in creating her current economic predicament—and in physically dividing her family—Malena refused to utilize a program for which her US-born daughter qualified.

Commenting further on program stigmas, women explained that if given the option, they would opt for a paying job over receiving welfare benefits: "The truth is that I don't like to get [benefits]," Luisa explained. "I prefer to work, but now work is hard to find. I don't like asking for stamps. Only when there is really need, but the truth is that I really don't like it." Obviously aware of the stigmas around recipients of welfare, Luisa desired to feel less dependent on the government and more in control of her own circumstances, despite the extent to which the government (catering to private interests) was responsible for locking women into such circumstances.

Some women were more forthright in reproducing discourses about "freeloaders" or people who were perceived to abuse welfare programs. On several occasions I listened to women as they disapproved of people they knew to have permanent residency or citizenship (a perceived advantage in terms of finding employment) but continued to rely on welfare programs. These women articulated a moral boundary between people who "needed help" and people who "abused services." Both James Quesada (2011) and Grace Chang (2000) argue that denigration of welfare users by those who would also qualify acts as a form of symbolic violence in pitting people from the same group against one another instead of inciting them to demand entitlements from the state. On the one hand, we could think about women's abstention from enrollment in welfare programs as reflecting a desire for autonomy and recognition that they are not failed members of society. On the other hand, we also need to examine how the justifications women put forth in resisting welfare both constitute and are constitutive of the same moralizing rhetoric that enables the erosion of entitlement programs—and thereby the notion of entitlement altogether.

Finally, overriding all other concerns about enrollment in SNAP were women's fears about the consequences of participation for immigration status. My informants suspected state surveillance in these programs, citing the rigor of enrollment procedures. For instance, Dora did not want to apply for food stamps because her husband believed that by asking for help they would interfere with their planned petitions for asylum. With two of her children still living in Honduras, Dora was very hopeful that her family could be united through the documentation process. The amount of information required by programs also supported these women's suspicions of surveillance, and thus proved a significant deterrent to participation. While receiving food stamps for her children, Luisa described her own aversion to this aspect of the program: "I'm going to tell you that they ask you for a lot of information. How much money you have, how much you work, how much your husband earns, many things, and the truth is that I don't like it. Right now I need it. I'm going to look for work so I don't have to give away so much information." Mixed feelings of fear and frustration informed these women's skepticism of Cal-Fresh. Luisa feared being reported to authorities as a result of her enrollment in CalFresh, yet she was equally perturbed by what she perceived as government surveillance of her household. While she realized that a certain degree of disclosure was necessary in order to verify her eligibility for the program, she loathed how program officers required her to regularly prove her family's eligibility through submitting pay stubs, bank statements, and payment receipts for housing and utility bills. As I discovered through attempting to undergo the process of enrollment myself, individuals were required to submit quarterly reports on household income and major expenses such as medicine and child care. For Luisa, asking for help was enough of a personal and moral compromise without the invasive inquiries of program officers. Malena had also plainly described herself as someone "uninterested in something like [CalFresh]. I said that I didn't want to fill out these papers and make multiple trips [to program offices]."

In the context of Santa Barbara's low-income community, the legitimacy of staking claims on rights and entitlements comprised a realm of contestation. It was unclear whether or not food stamps could be considered worthwhile, especially when some but not all family members from households of mixed residency status qualified for public programs or when individuals outside of one's household "abused" such programs. The ambiguity surrounding one's rights fostered the women's distrust toward state institutions and subsequently prevented enrollment in public programs.

Less willing to pursue public assistance, women from low-income households increasingly sought support through private food assistance programs such as those discussed in chapter 4. It is important to note, however, the ways in which an unwillingness to enroll in federal programs has been cultivated by repeated attempts by the state to systematically block undocumented individuals' access to entitlement programs. As an example, the passing of the Personal Responsibility and Work Opportunity Reconciliation Act of 1996, which denied access by undocumented persons to public aid (including food stamps, federal welfare, and Social Security), precipitated an increased use of emergency food programs by this population (Poppendieck 1998).

In my asking women to compare public to private programs, they claimed to favor private programs for ostensibly permitting them invisibility from the state; in other words, women perceived such programs as occupying a place of neutrality. As I remarked in chapter 4, however, the contingencies of programs to meet the requirements of funders and the tendency to collaborate with non-state *and* state actors in implementing programs suggested that these sites were not so neutral after all. Aside from seeking provisions, the women utilized these programs because they required minimal information from clients and often sourced volunteers from within the community, catering to an environment of mutual aid and reciprocity, whereas reliance in the realm of entitlement programs such as food stamps connoted a lack of autonomy and an undesirable subjectivity. In addition, in making provisions free to all regardless of circumstances, private programs did not threaten participants with the stigma familiar to recipients of federal assistance. Instead, for many women these programs endowed them with increased social capital and offered a "third space" for constructing alternative forms of belonging (Caldwell 2004; Myeroff 1978; Zavella 2011).

This is not to say that these women did not perceive themselves as risking some shame in utilizing private programs. The distribution sites overseen by Catholic Charities, for instance, elicited much backlash from women because eligibility for assistance through this organization was conditional on one's having employment. Celeste explained how "a veces va uno con pena" (sometimes one goes with shame) and that being turned away from this program added insult to injury. Paloma remembered a time when her husband suffered an injury on the job and could not work, and she was thus refused assistance by a "tyrant-like" manager: "There was a girl, I asked if they could give me food; she asked, 'Do you work?' and I told her no. She said, 'Well, then you don't qualify,' but in such a tone! So I told my sister-in-law, pardon my language, 'They are such tyrants [*muy déspota*] here.'" From the perspective of these women, program managers did not recognize the personal and relational sacrifices endured by those coming to programs. Conversely, Dolores expressed some sympathy for program staff, suggesting that perhaps the insolence of clients provoked such hostility: "I've seen the complete opposite, the day I went to Unity Shop [another local agency]; what I saw there, I was thinking they treat us poorly because we are impolite toward them. Because yesterday I went, I saw a girl, she was Latina, being very demanding. "No, I want this!" [she kept exclaiming]. I think it's for this reason that they give us things unwillingly.

Figure 21. Dora in line with her daughter at a food distribution site in Santa Barbara. Photo courtesy of Dora.

While certain social aspects of programs contributed to feelings of solidarity and belonging among clients, the programs could just as easily become sites of conflict and contestation. A common complaint among women in my research who were clients of such programs had to do with volunteers. Specifically, program volunteers seemed to occupy an ambiguous space between being patrons of the program and informal program staff. They were often perceived as having an unfair advantage in having first pick of program provisions. There was also some concern around too much leniency in the screening process for becoming a volunteer. Angela, who had actually been volunteering for quite some time at one of the program sites, spoke against volunteer misconduct, an issue she attributed to a lack of program supervision. "I volunteer at the program and as volunteers we always try to pick the best," she said. "Before, it was the clients who went first and then the volunteers. It's not the same now. Like there is no one that supervises. There are people who fill their own box and keep it with them, and they are taking advantage. It should be that the clients go first and then the volunteers." Brenda even noted how program staff displayed favoritism toward certain clients or volunteers, which she contrasted with her respect for supervisors who practiced fairness: "This [one supervisor], she respected the rules. She wouldn't let you in first because you helped her. Everyone makes his or her sacrifice, they leave their things to come [here], and it's not fair that you want to go first, before someone who arrived here earlier than you. This [supervisor] didn't allow that, and that's what I liked about her. She didn't give priority to friends or people that helped her. [Her attitude was,] 'If you want to help me, help me, but you also need to go back outside and wait in line like everyone else.'"

Women who utilized such programs viewed others getting ahead in line as especially unjust when most program sites required arriving very early in the day or multiple hours before the food distribution commenced. Notably, many of these women expressed a desire for better management and *surveillance* of programs, noting the failures of sites to coordinate crowd control. One woman even appreciated that the site where she collected provisions had installed cameras to keep track of people's places in line.

Although women argued that staff should express more sensitivity in recognizing the hurdles associated with asking for help and work to ensure more fairness in programs, organizations were often unprepared to address the range of individual needs or to field individual complaints among clients. Language barriers and issues with translation, as well as a lack of bicultural training among some staff members, contributed to these misunderstandings while also generating even more demanding workloads for bilingual and bicultural staff members. Local *promotores* sometimes helped to address communication barriers in working with target communities, yet they entered agreements with participating agencies primarily on a volunteer basis. I do not cite these imbalances in service delivery to disparage the very important role served by these organizations, but there is obviously something very wrong with expecting only a few bilingual and bicultural staff members to field all requests from a very vast clientele. This pattern among organizations also suggests that real discrepancies exist between the perceptions of those with decision-making power in institutions and the actual needs of populations.

"VALUING OURSELVES": IDENTIFYING OPPORTUNITIES FOR SOCIAL CHANGE

The women in my research offered several suggestions in the context of focus groups for how programs could better align with the needs of populations and contribute to broader social change. Of particular prominence was the desire for opportunities to convene and converse with other women. There was a consensus in our focus groups that Latinas were seldom provided the opportunity to voice their opinions or to share their emotions, as both forms of communication were associated with shame: "We Mexican women, or Latinas, we don't give ourselves the opportunity to express ourselves. Many people do not give us the opportunity to explain ourselves because they are lecturing us."

In contrast to the women's feelings of being ignored in institutional settings, or even their home settings, the focus groups provided something quite different. As one focus group member put it, "I participated in a group once that was about children. But one does not speak because it gives one shame. One has to be brave enough to say something, but for shame she does not. I liked [the focus group] because everyone had the opportunity [to speak]." The focus group moderator and I observed how an interaction based on dialogue among women brought them to encourage one another on a path toward valuing their own self-worth: "We have worth," one participant commented. "I'd like more groups like this. As women, it teaches us that we should respect and value ourselves. That we should value ourselves as we are." Another woman noted that although she had also participated in other groups before, "it has never been like this, [right]?" This suggested that the women felt they had had more say in the overall direction of our conversations. In evaluating their own experiences with this process, the women asserted that they had the confidence to speak and to express themselves. As one commented, "Here we spoke the truth about what had passed [in our lives]. I don't know, we don't have to shame ourselves because we are not doing anyone harm. We just spoke truthfully about what has been our lives." Research is certainly not the only viable path to opening up this sort of dialogue; nonetheless, I wish to highlight that these women expressed a desire to replicate certain features of this space of exchange in other aspects of their social lives.

The focus group participants also described wanting to support other women outside the groups in overcoming marginalization and in connecting with resources. Juliana articulated the importance of this endeavor for her: "I'm interested in the rights of women. I know many women who are marginalized, who do not have a voice or a vote. I take an opposite stance. Because before I was in the same position." Other women called for programs that would link recently arrived migrants to essential resources, such as social services and jobs, and foster community building. Celeste, having migrated only two years before from Guerrero, was especially supportive of such a program:

> I'd like to see a program that coordinated groups open to the entire community because there are people who need help and we can help each other. When I arrived [in the United States], I didn't know about WIC or other programs. Sometimes my husband would work one week and not another. When I arrived, I went one year without work, looking and looking. In Mexico, I assumed that there was work in the United States and people went there to earn money, but I arrived and where [was the work]? So life here is not like how they paint it in Mexico. I wondered to myself, 'Why did I put myself through a week of suffering in the desert?' My husband learned of the bazaar, a service on the radio, the bazaar is really good [for finding work]. Because there are people who are looking for someone to clean their homes, or to do something else; that's how I found my boss. I found her through the radio and called her. I didn't know how to do anything. I cleaned houses in my country but not how one cleans here. Luckily my boss offered to help me. 'It doesn't matter [if you don't know what to do], I'll teach you,' [she said], and she helped me.

These insights from women in our focus groups highlighted the profound effects of social, political, and economic marginalization on the psychosocial well-being of immigrant women. As the targets of institutional racism and discrimination, these women had come to embody much of the discourse that had denied them a legitimate place in society. Yet they also countered this discourse in calling for social change through collective organizing and in recognizing their own worth as women. Arguments in favor of collective organizing are particularly powerful because in addition to rejecting the notion of poverty as a "natural" feature of contemporary life they resist the dominant narrative of "illegality" that seeks to delegitimize undocumented migrants.

ENACTING AN ALTERNATIVE SOCIAL ECONOMY

Women's calls for social change toward the end of my fieldwork, and specifically in the context of our focus groups, supported the notion that resistance was possible, and although structures constrained possibilities for social actions they could also enable them.

In identifying shared aspects of their lived experiences and forming friendships with one another (as I discussed in this book's introduction), these women resisted an imposed existence of social isolation and gestured to ways that they could enact the changes they wished to see. In closing this chapter, I will highlight a few examples of where such leadership among Mexican and Central American women has emerged, with the hope that similar models might be replicated or are already in the process of being developed elsewhere.

Since completing the fieldwork phase of this project, I have been conducting similar research in the state of Washington, another site in the United States with a deep history of migration from Latin America and a prominent battleground of contemporary organizing for immigration reform. Since beginning this research, I learned of the Women's Justice Circles that are organized by the Intercommunity Peace and Justice Center (IPJC), an interfaith nonprofit organization founded fourteen years ago. The Women's Justice Circles were developed with the intent of including the voices of low-income, immigrant, and migrant women who were living in crisis or on the margins in organizing for change that would best serve their needs. Today the circles, provided with technical support by the IPJC, assemble around the shared objective of disrupting the conditions that keep women poor and oppressed. The circles engage in a process of consensus building to identify key areas of intervention including housing, education, transportation, nutrition, domestic violence, and access to health services, among others.

The IPJC's Justice for Women project, as stated in its outreach materials, aims "to build relationships with others who want change, to claim our personal and collaborative power, to understand the issues that make life difficult for women who are low-income, to learn the skills of grassroots organizing and leadership, and to take action to create change." The circle model is based on the idea that women will begin to see themselves as effective agents of social change when they reflect on their sources of power and recognize the collective influence of other women in their lives. As of 2013, 75 percent of the circles comprised Spanish-speaking urban immigrants and rural migrant workers.

The Women's Justice Circles meet over eight sessions lasting two hours each and undergo a process of evaluation during the third and eighth sessions. The process of identifying and organizing around an issue emphasizes women's strengths. The women's justice coordinator from the IPJC trains women from the circles to act as facilitators, and these facilitators emphasize a safe environment in which women are comfortable sharing their life stories. Through this process of sharing during the first three sessions, the women begin to recognize commonalities with other women in the group as well as the differences that make them unique. During the fourth session, the women reflect on their strengths and choose a justice issue to address through concrete action.

The circles tend to range in size from eight to twelve women, and have been formed by women who are farmworkers, members of the LGBT community, mothers of children with disabilities, survivors of domestic violence or child abuse, and domestic workers. Circles have convened in community centers, public libraries, churches, and clinics. Although most of the circles are based in Washington, the IPJC has worked with circles in other states such as Michigan and Oregon, as well as internationally in the countries of Bolivia, El Salvador, Nicaragua, and Peru.

In 2012, one circle composed of Mexican and Central American women from south Seattle chose to focus on human rights violations at the Northwest Detention Center, some of them having been previously detained. The circle presented on the topic at the Northwest Detention Center Roundtable—an advocacy group for detainees—and prepared a brochure in Spanish (printed by the IPJC) explaining what to do when a relative is detained, later distributing the brochure through women's social networks and to other organizations. The circle was invited to be the guest of honor at the Day of the Dead celebration hosted by Latino City Employee, an organization providing resources to Latinos employed by the city of Seattle. Latino City Employee dedicated its Day of the Dead altar and proceeds to the women's circle. The circle decided to pass along these proceeds to the Northwest Detention Center Roundtable to establish a fund that would aid survivors of domestic violence who were released from the detention center.

In the past, some groups have focused explicitly on food access issues: planting a community garden, founding a food bank for farmworkers, and compiling a recipe book translated in five languages for clients of a food bank.

In addition, the IPJC hosts Latinas Connected for Change, an annual conference that in November 2011 convened three hundred Latinas in Seattle from forty cities and nine counties. Goals of the annual conference include celebrating the strengths of Latina women, building skills for leadership development and civic participation, developing an expanded Latina network, identifying and organizing ways to address the challenges that the Latino community confronts, and fostering citywide efforts and statewide collaborative opportunities that will better serve the Latino community.

Thus, although my research findings stem from only a few communities in Southern California, the experiences of Mexican and Central American women from these communities form part of a larger narrative of grassroots activism and social empowerment emerging from communities of historically marginalized women throughout the United States. Collectively, these instances of community-based activism inspire hope for confronting the social inequalities that translate to continued structural vulnerability of women migrating out of the Global South. Rather than accepting a fate of limited life chances, these women envision a radically different social economy in which they support one another in their aspirations to restore and reclaim a way of life that guarantees them more than the bare necessities.

Conclusion

I began this book by arguing that the lived experiences of women migrating from Mexico and Central America to the United States offer a unique vantage point from which to interrogate the overlapping biopolitical modes of food insecurity and the project of food security, but I do not suggest that this is the only place we can turn for analyzing these processes. Instead I have put forward this conceptual framework so that we might rethink how we approach studies of migration and food insecurity. Indeed, the pool of people vulnerable to and displaced by policy changes related to the deepening corporatization and liberalization of the global food system continues to expand and diversify.

The notion of care and what it means to provide caring labor comprises one thread of my analysis. There are several reasons for my decision to foreground this theme in talking about women's migration and food insecurity in the United States, but first and foremost were the cues provided to me by my empirical data. Whether in the context of women reflecting on the conditions that ultimately pushed them to come to the United States, their frustrations with the ways that daily barriers undermined their efforts to provide care, or their anxieties about being perceived as "failed" caregivers, care and caring labor connected these broad experiences. The other major reason stems from recent trends in theory on transnational migration. Whereas theorizing the migrant worker has been a central focus of this literature, scant attention has been to how migration articulates with social reproduction. Although the spheres of productive and reproductive labor are not so distinct as once imagined, one wonders what happens, or what is lost, when the always already devalued work of social reproduction is folded under the monolithic label of *production*. Part of my decision here to tease out reproductive, "caring" labors is thus not only analytical but also political. By capturing the nuances and injustices that structure reproductive labor, I hope to agitate for more comprehensive gender and reproductive rights.

Paying closer attention to the unevenness in the relations of social reproduction helps to elucidate the ways that health disparities are gendered. I argue that the pressures and perpetual barriers embedded in the relations of social reproduction tend to exacerbate women's feelings of marginalization and social exclusion while they also operate syndemically with poor health status and social suffering more generally to further compromise women's health, psychosocial well-being, and subsequent life chances. While I do not purport to suggest that (im)migrant women's suffering is a premeditated consequence of economic restructuring at, for instance, the levels of free trade agreements, neoliberal economic development, or the privatization of welfare, I do want to emphasize that in each of these schemes there are far more losers than winners. These policy shifts have palpable effects for individuals' subjectivities, most notably perhaps in the ways that inequality becomes embodied and interpreted as deserved by those in the most exploited and disadvantaged social classes.

There are thus several scales at which I hope that my preceding discussion intervenes in the literature on care, both in terms of its transnational dimensions and its undergoing privatization. First, I argue that an obligation to care, particularly as women operationalize a concept of care in the realm of foodwork, has been undertheorized as a motivation underpinning women's decisions to migrate—specifically from Mexico and Central America to the United States. I am increasingly convinced that this is the case with migrant populations the world over, thus meriting broader recognition by organizations monitoring global levels of food insecurity and its effects.

Second, I interpret that state responsibility for food security—as with other aspects of population well-being—is increasingly being transferred to individuals, a process that disproportionately implicates women and burdens them with overseeing this aspect of care. I suggest that the realm of private food assistance is playing an important role in this project. One appealing feature of private food assistance programs is that they offer undocumented women anonymity from the state in obtaining provisions (unlike the Supplemental Nutrition Assistance Program). These programs also provide opportunities for socializing in what otherwise feels like a hostile environment; the current political climate that has intensified policies around immigration enforcement and directed increasingly vituperative discourses at undocumented immigrants forces many of these women into social isolation. However, dietary health interventions within such programs also represent a site of biopolitics whose relations reveal a governing of life through conditioning clients toward neoliberal logics of personal responsibility. Thus, I claim that private food assistance programs have been called on to serve as proxies for the state in overseeing the transfer of care from the realm of the collective to that of the individual, especially in reifying an essentialist view of women as "caring subjects."

Third, I bring attention to how in the case of transnational mothers, the structural constraints around foodwork in the United States also place strain on women's capacity to care for others in their home countries. What emerges here is a portrait of how contemporary biopolitical modes continue to stratify reproduction (Colen 1995), even within a single family, so that we will observe, for instance, mothers feeling guilty about investing more in the lives of their US-born children than children in their home countries because even they can see that in the current scheme these lives will be essentially worth more. This is yet another source of immense grief and grave internal conflict for these women.

The emotional and psychological burdens associated with these women's caregiving practices have implications for their overall health status. As in the cases of many of the women I discussed in chapter 3, perceived caregiving "failures" or shortcomings become naturalized and embodied, thereby providing partial insight into how food insecurity as a technique of biopolitics shapes the subjectivities of socially and economically marginalized women. I invoked Lauren Berlant's (2007) concept of "slow death" in alluding to how society regards this suffering as "ordinary" and subsequently one reason for its remaining outside the purview of policy makers. This abject subjectivity of women, or "abjectivity" (Willen 2007), constrains them to reproducing life at the social margins whereby they are predisposed to health problems while also cut off from many of the possibilities for preventative care.

Biopolitical projects linked to food insecurity portend long-term devastation for the health and social fabric of the nation. As I discuss throughout this book, but particularly in chapter 3, neoliberalism has been critiqued extensively for its social failures (see, e.g., Biehl 2005; Ong 2006; Rosas 2012). Yet many critiques of neoliberalism valorize *autonomy* and *empowerment* as if these concepts were neutral and not also imbricated with underlying logics of neoliberal ideology (Cruikshank 1999; Gill 2008). Although my preceding discussion brings explicit attention to how this is operating in the realm of the *biopolitical project of food security*, which emphasizes "personal responsibility" and places responsibility for food security within the individual, there is mounting evidence that this ideology is seeping into and generating anxiety among all social classes. Thus, these projects portend repercussions for people from all walks of life, not simply the socioeconomically and politically marginalized, though those falling within these categories arguably endure the bulk share of social costs as the means to "self-reliance" represents a currency not equally accessible to all.

¡ADELANTE! THE WAY FORWARD

The food sovereignty movement has been an avid force in challenging the social—as well as ecological—consequences of an industrialized, global food system. First defined in 1996 by the international peasant organization Via Campesina, food sovereignty is the "people's right to healthy and culturally appropriate food produced through ecologically sound and sustainable methods, and their right to define their own food and agriculture systems" (Via Campesina 1996). From the perspective of Via Campesina (commonly regarded as the global leader in the food sovereignty movement), along with others mobilizing for alternative food movements, food security begins and ends with food sovereignty (Patel 2009). While *food sovereignty* represents a form of resistance to neoliberal economic development, industrial agriculture, and unbalanced trade relationships, and although some ambiguity surrounds the term, at its most basic understanding food sovereignty is the people's right to determine their own agricultural and food policies (McMichael 2008; Pimbert 2007). Proponents of food sovereignty seek to tackle the driving forces of food insecurity, claiming that as a movement "it proposes not just guaranteed access to food, but democratic control over the food system—from production and processing, to distribution, marketing, and consumption" (Holt-Giménez 2009, 146).

Given its heavy emphasis on rights, and particularly the rights of women, food sovereignty challenges state failures to guarantee the human right to food as it has been signed into international law. Food has appeared in the official language of human rights since the first signing of the Universal Declaration of Human Rights (UDHR) in 1948; article 25 of the UDHR states that everyone has "a right to a standard of living," including the right to food and the right to be free from hunger (Chilton and Rose 2009). The International Covenant on Economic, Social, and Cultural Rights of 1966 expanded on this notion to include "freedom from hunger" as a fundamental human right and the obligation of states to improve food production and distribution systems for equitable access to food. All countries except the United States and Australia agreed to recognize food as a basic human right at the Rome Declaration for World Food Security in 1996 (Chilton and Rose 2009). These terms were again ratified in 1999 to explicate the right to food and to oblige states in respecting, protecting, and fulfilling this right.

Right-to-food discourse and rights-based food system approaches remain controversial, particularly in the United States. While the US government officially embraces the UDHR, the Department of State insists that the constitution does not protect or recognize economic, social, and cultural rights, including the right to food (Messer and Cohen 2007), and repeatedly votes against the annual Right to Food Resolution in the UN General Assembly, "usually as the sole dissenter" (Messer and Cohen 2007, 16). Other reasons cited by the US government for voting against the Right to Food Resolution stem from concerns that the right to food is "associated with un-American socialist political systems" (Messer and Cohen 2007, 2), that fulfilling such legislation would be too expensive, and that the rights-based approach does not culturally resonate with the American model of self-reliance.

Since all human rights are mutually reinforcing, universal, and indivisible (Van Esterik 1999b), continued opposition on the part of the US government toward rights-based food system approaches has been argued to undermine all other commitment by the United States to the UDHR, upsetting the "basis for world civil and political order," reinforcing cultural relativist interpretations of human rights, and allowing for continued support of neoliberal economic policies as the path to global food security (Messer and Cohen 2007, 3). Furthermore, support by the US government of such entities as the World Trade Organization and others that are liberalizing trade and promoting neoliberal policies has been interpreted as a direct affront to the human right to food (Rosset and Martinez-Torres 2010). Instead of a rights-based approach, needs-based approaches frame welfare and charity, forcing citizens to become passive beneficiaries of nutritional handouts rather than as "claims-holders who mobilize around human right to food demands and hold governments accountable" (Messer and Cohen 2007, 18). Ellen Messer and Marc J. Cohen, in advocating for recognition of the human right to food in national and global policy and warning of the potential health implications of failing to do so, argue that "local small-farm agriculture should receive priority in national policies" and that "global trade agreements and aid policies must not undermine sustainable rural livelihoods in either the North or the South" (2007, 15).

One reason that food sovereignty advocates deem past and ongoing food security approaches to food insecurity and hunger as overall ineffective is because of the lack of participation on the part of marginalized food communities in every stage of the planning process, from defining and measuring to designing policies (Patel 2009; Pimbert 2007; Schiavoni 2009; Windfuhr and Jonsén 2005). For instance, multilateral donors that are shaping the emerging development field of global health have become some of the most outspoken proponents of food security but remain committed to "magic-bullet" solutions that are, overall, technocratic and based on a top-down approach. Many of these donors in fact are supporting the "Green Gene Revolution" for Africa, funded by the UK Department for International Development, the Rockefeller Foundation, and the Bill & Melinda Gates Foundation, with buy-in from multiple governments. As of 2011, the Gates Foundation had awarded over $160 million through its Agricultural Development program, which includes developing nutritionally enhanced crop varieties for this impending reiteration of the "green" revolution (Doughton 2011). Several critics have noted that such a narrow focus on single crops treads against the advice of expert panels on world hunger whose arguments around the difficulties in transferring technologies to resource-poor farmers resonate with critiques of the Green Revolution of the 1960s and '70s

(Doughton 2011). In the past decade, governments have increasingly prioritized these technocratic solutions to food insecurity, working closely with private donors to manufacture drought-tolerant, disease-tolerant, and biofortified crops as a primary way to alleviate famines. These public-private partnerships, however, generally fail to involve those most affected by food insecurity in any meaningful way in planning and implementing policies, and they also proceed outside the purview of ethics committees.

Alternative food movements are becoming increasingly popular in the United States (Allen 2004; Wekerle 2004), some emerging from marginalized communities that have adopted the rhetoric of food sovereignty as it has been used by Via Campesina (Rosset and Martinez-Torres 2010). The US Food Sovereignty Alliance, formed in 2010, is also championing broader adoption and implementation of food sovereignty principles throughout the country. These US–based alternative food efforts tread against the needs-based programs and policies dominated by the rhetoric of food security that have performed inadequately in responding to rising food insecurity (De Schutter 2009; Mittal 2009; Pimbert 2007).

There is looming skepticism about the potential of individuals to influence a system wherein power over food is concentrated in the hands of few, and recent events suggest that the capacity to do so may be slowly eroding (Nestle 2007). For example, in August 2012, one year and a few months after I completed my fieldwork, the Community Food Security Coalition—arguably one of the most vocal organizations for food justice in the United States—announced that it was disbanding, a decision met with considerable disapproval and anguish by coalition members. Meanwhile, corporate food industry behemoths such as Coca-Cola and McDonald's, which have captured new markets related to augmenting health anxieties and fears in recent years (Greenhalgh 2012), are also beginning to spearhead dietary health and antiobesity initiatives to get people to exercise more (Richardson 2013). Commenting on these sorts of trends, Peter Benson calls for mass scrutiny of the clear winners in this scheme:

> What if the energy and resources that go into dieting and worrying about weight were routed upward at the food and beverage industry as part of a social movement aiming to starve its profits and allay the stigma of obesity? What if the critical energies that all citizens direct at themselves and at others within the webs of governmentality were redirected at industries that are trashing the planet and filling it and human bodies with an endless flow of junk? This too would be a biopolitics of fat, of the bloated and grotesque and monstrous, in which the industrial powers, the biggest winners, would all of a sudden seem like big fat losers, although it would be a biopolitics that is quite differently concerned with the population and its welfare than the one reflected in the market-oriented discourse about choice, blame, and risk that these days dominates the conversation and incites reflection. (Benson 2012, 90)

Some readers may doubt the feasibility of what Benson is hoping to inspire through his provocative inquiry. Yet what he is gesturing toward is the need for a scaled-up social movement in order to incite structural change. One problem with a scaled-up, monolithic sort of movement, however, is that often the demands of specific groups get marooned by a more privileged class or become co-opted by the very powers such groups are fighting against (Guthman 2008a, 2011; Murphy 2012). These sorts of pitfalls inherent to large-scale social movements indeed contribute to my own doubts about their potential for stimulating meaningful social change. But that does not dismiss the value of activism on any scale toward challenging the expectations we have for ourselves as individuals and as a society.

Although the food sovereignty movement is one of the most powerful alternatives we currently have for countering the biopolitical project of food security, it also relies on a discourse of self-sufficiency and empowerment, virtues that remain out of reach for many. As only a movement, and without formal commitment from policy makers, it can only accomplish so much. In this regard the food sovereignty movement perhaps does not offer any immediate solutions to the women at the heart of this book.

ABJECT BIOPOLITICS

Nowhere are the biopolitics of immigration more abundantly clear, and especially as they intersect with the biopolitics of food insecurity, than in the current system of immigrant detention in the United States. In this context, food is a weapon through which the state shapes and produces an exploitable surplus population. The Department of Homeland Security screens and detains more than 30,000 people on any given day, and over 400,000 annually. Immigrant detention has also supported record-high deportations in recent years, with over two million people deported during the administration of president Barack Obama alone. Detention periods may last anywhere from one to two days to several weeks or months, sometimes even years. Bed quotas help to maintain a stable detainee population at centers, a practice that provides direct benefit to the private prison industry. Most of the men, women, and children who are detained on any given day have never committed a criminal offense but are merely there because they lack formal authorization to be in the United States. Despite the existence of detention standards issued by the US government, instances of torture and misconduct prevail in the testimonies of recently released detainees. Reports compiled by human and civil rights organizations, for instance, cite deprivation of food and water in addition to grossly inadequate health care, physical and sexual abuse, overcrowding, discrimination, and racism. The practice of detaining migrants, as part and parcel of a broader biopolitics, coaxes undocumented migrants to accept the conditions of their abjectivity, of their identification as "nobodies," (Green 2011) and of their corporeal suffering as natural and deserved.

Stripped as they are of political rights in this context (Agamben 1998), detainees have increasingly fought back with the limited means available to them: their bodies. Putting their bodies "on the line," detainees utilize the platform of voluntary hunger as a weapon against coerced orientation to poor food (Carney 2014b). On March 11, 2014, I attended a protest outside the Northwest Detention Center in Tacoma, Washington, that had been organized to support the twelve hundred or so detainees who had gone on a hunger strike some days before. On the handwritten list of demands submitted to private prison company GEO Corp by the detainees were better food, better treatment, better pay, lower commissary, and fairness. The number of *huelgistas de hambre* (hunger strikers) declined to 750 on the second day of the strike and 330 on the third day, until only a handful of detainees remained on strike on the day of the protest I attended. Immigration attorney Sandra Restrepo, speaking through a megaphone to an audience of protestors, shared her suspicion that detainees had likely withdrawn from the strike as a result of intimidation by guards. Although one of the largest to have ever taken place in the detention system, the hunger strike in Tacoma was not an isolated incident but was trailing not far behind another hunger strike that had been held the previous month at a detention facility in Arizona.

This book would certainly be incomplete, then, without some direct comment on the state of affairs related to immigration reform and border policies in the United States. Amid the nativist sentiments expressed by those who oppose open-door policies, there is fear of cultural change (Zavella 2011). Of course, much of the discussion of "culture" in this context is heavily racialized (Chavez 2008). I implore the opponents of more lenient border and immigration policies to consider how the experiences of unauthorized migrants in the United States index a vast array of inadequacies and failures in the structure of our society. Very few of us appear all that content with the status quo; indeed, many of us are already living our worst fears. It is a nightmarish scenario, even apocalyptic at times. Yet is our fear so valuable to us that we will hold onto it at any cost, even if it inevitably translates to widespread social suffering? In this respect, change would most definitely be a good thing, but getting there requires some imagination.

Imagine a society that is literate and knowledgeable about the repercussions of free trade and structural adjustment for the livelihoods of the poor in the Global South. Imagine that policy makers in Mexico and Central America reinvest in the livelihoods of subsistence communities, distribute resources evenly to populations in these countries, and make fewer concessions to the demands of global capital. Imagine that countries add food insecurity to the list of valid reasons for granting authorized entry to people fleeing from these problems, that the US government changes its stance on the human right to food, and that food insecurity stops being conceived of as an individual problem. Relatedly, imagine that we find more humanized and sociocentric alternatives to the project of food security. Imagine that all those eligible feel entitled to and deserving of welfare programs, that current efforts by the US Congress to decrease funding to the Supplemental Nutrition Assistance Program and the Women,

Infants, and Children program be stopped in their tracks, and that the realm of private food assistance increasingly finds ways to center the needs of clients in programs and connects with less restricted forms of funding so that it may detach itself from private interests. Imagine that public health workers advocate against the stereotyping of Latinos as unhealthy, uninformed, lazy, obese, and sick and instead redirect this energy toward regulating the junk food, processed food, and fast food industries. Imagine that cities and communities around the United States also reject policies like Secure Communities that only induce harm to communities by relegating individuals into further isolation, tearing families apart and orphaning children. Imagine that policy makers in the United States do not approve of further militarization of its border with Mexico as a condition of potential immigration reform, and that procedures for family reunification become more streamlined. Imagine that the Department of Homeland Security finds more humanized alternatives to the dehumanizing system of immigrant detention. Imagine that cities and communities like Santa Barbara prioritize the issue of affordable housing. Imagine that the United States becomes a global leader in recognizing and ensuring access to health care as a basic right and removes barriers to care for all classes of people. Imagine that society recognizes poverty as a moral wrong and elects to address its underlying causes systematically. Imagine that as a society we become more cognizant of how patriarchal thinking continues to shape the division of labor and contributes to gendered suffering so that we may dismantle this thinking. Imagine that social scientists, and especially anthropologists, continue to envision more participatory models for conducting research and find ways to collaborate with informants and to be more critical of projects that do not aspire toward generating social outcomes.

Epilogue

I recently heard a story on National Public Radio about a food bank somewhere in the middle of the country that was petitioning Walmart to provide higher wages to its workers instead of donating surplus food to charities. One Walmart employee was quoted as saying that he finds it absurd that the food he sees being discarded at work he later collects for his own consumption through a local food pantry. If Walmart could afford to donate this surplus, couldn't it afford to compensate its own employees with a living wage?

My students are often perplexed by the seeming contradictions of an economic system that denies working people a living wage but funnels essential resources through charitable channels. I tell them about how in Santa Barbara many of the individuals who provided cash contributions to the food bank were also likely employers of food bank clients. Every year I find that a larger portion of my students come from families that are working but still have to rely on food assistance. Some of these students are even becoming clients themselves at one of the dozens of food banks now appearing across US college campuses. The structural constraints that shape how most of us access the resources we need to survive have much to do with our values as a society. Perhaps there are more incentives for the CEO of any major food retailer such as Walmart to be recognized as a philanthropist, while also pleasing company shareholders, than to pay living wages to all of its employees.

Surprisingly, I encountered resistance from some funders and academics to my desire to offer modest stipends to key informants, as well as to my prioritizing social outcomes as part and parcel of my research design. Given the issues I sought to address through this research, I think any other approach to participant compensation and research design would have been exploitative. I am incredibly thankful to the University of California Institute for Mexico and the United States for recognizing the potential value of this project and for providing financial support.

As this research really developed a life of its own, it would be presumptuous to suggest that I have adequately accounted for all of its applied or social outcomes in this book. Nonetheless, I remain humbled by the few outcomes I was privileged enough to witness firsthand. For instance, staff members from the Foodbank of Santa Barbara County were generous in inviting me to share insights from my research for the purposes of developing and improving programs. In addition, my key informants availed themselves to forming friendships through focus group interactions and generously connected each other with different resources such as employment and child care. And the moderator of the focus groups, also serving as the executive director for an organization that acted as the "hub" for the Latino and Chicano community of Santa Barbara, noted to me that she planned to further develop or tinker with her organization's programs based on the feedback she received from research participants. Of course, these outcomes are not going to end suffering at all levels, but they do represent concrete steps forward.

GENERAL REGION CHARACTERISTICS (2010–12)

	US	California	Santa Barbara County	South County	North County
Poverty	15%	13.7%	18%	–	–
Poverty level for four-person household	$22,050	–	$53,700	–	–
SNAP/CalFresh enrollment (% of those eligible)	–	48%	16%	–	–
WIC enrollment (% of those eligible)	79.1%	–	56%	–	–
Free and reduced lunch (% that qualify)	–	56%	54%	–	–
Unemployment	8.3%	11.1%	8.7%	–	–
Food insecure*	14.5%	15.9%	37%	–	–
Median home price	$188,400	$458,500	$278,500	$662,500	$211,000
Latino (% of total population)	16.3%	37.6%	43%	–	–

SOURCES: Bureau of Labor Statistics, 2012; California Health Interview Survey 2009; Housing Authority of Santa Barbara County 2011; Food and Nutrition Service, US Department of Agriculture 2011; US Census Bureau 2010; WIC of California 2011.

* Figures for food insecurity in California and the United States reflect percent of total population. Food insecurity rate of prevalence in Santa Barbara County reflects percent of households at or below 185 percent of the federal poverty level.

APPENDIX TWO

LIST OF PARTICIPANTS

	Age	Country of origin	Years in the US	Occupation or occupational status	Number of children	Marital status	Immigration status
Angela	42	Mexico (Guerrero)	10	Housecleaner	4	Divorced	Unauthorized
Brenda	51	Mexico (Michoacán)	21	Property manager	3	Married	Permanent resident
Belén	23	Mexico (Guana-juato)	10	Unemployed	2	Married	Unauthorized
Betanía	62	Mexico (Guerrero)	9	Unemployed	8	Married	Unauthorized
Camila	56	Mexico (Acapulco)	20	Housecleaner	4	Divorced	Unauthorized
Celeste	25	Mexico (Guerrero)	2	Unemployed	2	Married	Unauthorized
Celina	36	Mexico (Veracruz)	13	Hotel housekeeper	1	Single	Unauthorized
Carolina	46	Mexico (Guerrero)	20	Unemployed	3	Married	Unauthorized

Name	Age	Origin		Occupation		Marital status	Legal status
Dolores	36	Mexico (Guerrero)	15	Unemployed	5	Married	Unauthorized
Dora	35	Honduras	6	Housecleaner	4	Married	Unauthorized
Gloria	54	Mexico (Guanajuato)	13	Unemployed	3	Married	Unauthorized
Pilar	28	Guatemala	<1	Unemployed	3	Single	Asylum seeker
Juliana	38	Mexico (Guerrero)	12	Unemployed	3	Married	Unauthorized
Linda	33	Mexico (Michoacán)	13	Housecleaner	3	Married	Unauthorized
Luisa	38	Mexico (Michoacán)	15	Unemployed	2	Married	Unauthorized
Marisol	30	Mexico/US	27	Unemployed	3	Single	Citizen
Margarita	29	Mexico (Guadalajara)	9	Food service worker	2	Married	Unauthorized
Maya	24	Mexico (Guerrero)	10	Unemployed	1	Single	Unauthorized

(continued)

(continued)

	Age	Country of origin	Years in the US	Occupation or occupational status	Number of children	Marital status	Immigration status
Malena	46	Mexico (Guerrero)	4	Hotel housekeeper	4	Divorced	Unauthorized
Natalia	48	Mexico (Oaxaca)	18	Housecleaner	4	Divorced	Unauthorized
Olivia	24	Mexico (Guerrero)	9	Unemployed	3	Married	Unauthorized
Paloma	41	Mexico (Guerrero)	24	Unemployed	0	Married	Permanent resident
Serena	23	Mexico (Guerrero)	4	Unemployed	2	Married	Unauthorized
Tina	49	Mexico (Sinaloa)	36	On disability	4	Divorced	Permanent resident
Yolanda	35	Mexico (Acapulco)	7	housecleaner	4	Married	Unauthorized

NOTES

INTRODUCTION

1. Data on monthly participation in the SNAP program may be found on the Food Research and Action Center's website, http://frac.org /reports-and-resources/snapfood-stamp-monthly-participation-data/.

2. The human subjects division at the University of California–Santa Barbara approved the research protocol, and a dissertation research grant from the University of California Institute of Mexico and the United States was awarded to cover the expenses of fieldwork. The women received a modest stipend for their participation in the research.

CHAPTER TWO

1. Predicting a labor shortage during wartime, the United States and Mexico signed a bilateral agreement that led to the formal recruitment of Mexicans to work on US farms as guest workers. For further reading see Cohen 2011.

2. The term *comadre* is used to address the mother of one's goddaughter or godson.

CHAPTER FOUR

1. FSBC development staff, personal communication with author.

2. This is the flyer that the Gold Coast Collaborative produced for distribution as part of the Network for a Healthy California's Rethink Your Drink campaign. The California Department of Public Health has since updated its Rethink Your Drink materials; they can be accessed online at http://www.cdph.ca.gov/programs/cpns/Pages/RethinkYour Drink-Resources.aspx.

3. Chair of Partners for Fit Youth, personal communication with the author.

4. This was the Communities of Excellence Study. https://www .countyofsb.org/uploadedFiles/phd/Health_Education/Network_for _Healthy_California/SBCountyCX3CommunityBriefSH6-1-09.pdf.

BIBLIOGRAPHY

Abarca, Meredith. 2006. *Voices in the Kitchen: Views of Food and the World from Working-Class Mexican and Mexican American Women.* College Station: Texas A&M University Press.

Agamben, Giorgio. 1998. *Homo Sacer: Sovereign Power and Bare Life.* Translated by Daniel Heller-Roazen. Stanford, CA: Stanford University Press.

Agriculture Future Trust. 2007. *Santa Barbara County Agricultural Resources Environmental/Economic Assessment (AREA) Study.* Accessed May 27, 2014. https://www.countyofsb.org/uploadedFiles/agcomm/agAdvisory/SB_AREA%20Study_Final_12_12_07-2.pdf.

Allen, Patricia. 2004. *Together at the Table: Sustainability and Sustenance in the American Agrifood System.* University Park, PA: Penn State University Press.

———. 2007. "The Disappearance of Hunger in America." *Gastronomica* 7 (3): 19–23.

———. 2008. "Mining for Justice in the Food System: Perceptions, Practices, and Possibilities." *Agriculture and Human Values* 25: 157–61.

Allen, Patricia, and Carolyn Sachs. 2007. "Women and Food Chains: The Gendered Politics of Food." *International Journal of Sociolology of Agriculture and Food* 15 (1): 1–23.

Anderson, Molly D. 2008. "Rights-Based Food Systems and the Goals of Food Systems Reform." *Agriculture and Human Values* 25: 593–608.

Anderson, S. A. 1990. "The 1990 Life Sciences Research Office (LSRO) Report on Nutritional Assessment Defined Terms Associated with Food Access: Core Indicators of Nutritional State for Difficult to Sample Populations." *Journal of Nutrition* 102: 1559–1660.

Appadurai, Arjun 1996. *Modernity at Large: Cultural Dimensions of Globalization.* Minneapolis: University of Minnesota Press.

"As the Cuts Hit Home" (editorial). 2013. *New York Times*, March 1.

Bank Muñoz, Carolina. 2008. *Transnational Tortillas: Race, Gender, and Shop-Floor Politics in Mexico and the United States.* Ithaca, NY: ILR Press.

Barker, Drucilla K. 2005. "Beyond Women and Economics: Rereading 'Women's Work.'" *Signs: Journal of Women in Culture and Society* 30 (4): 2189–2209.

Barker, Kezia. 2012. "Infectious Insecurities: H1N1 and the Politics of Emerging Infectious Disease." *Health and Place* 18: 695–700.

Beagan, Brenda. 2008. "'It's just easier for me to do it': Rationalizing the family division of foodwork." *Sociology* 42(4): 653–71.

Behar, Ruth. 1993. *Translated Woman: Crossing the Border with Esperanza's Story.* Boston: Beacon.

Behar, Ruth, and Deborah A. Gordon, eds. 1995. *Women Writing Culture.* Berkeley: University of California Press.

Beneria, Lourdes, and Shelley Feldman, eds. 1992. *Unequal Burden: Economic Crises, Persistent Poverty, and Women's Work.* Boulder, CO: Westview.

Benson, Peter. 2012. "Commentary: Biopolitical Injustice and Contemporary Capitalism." *American Ethnologist* 39 (3): 488–90.

Berlant, Lauren. 2007. "Slow Death (Sovereignty, Obesity, Lateral Agency)." *Critical Inquiry* 33 (4): 754–80.

Bernard, Russell H. 2006 *Research Methods in Anthropology: Qualitative and Quantitative Approaches.* Oxford: Altamira Press.

Biehl, Joao. 2005. *Vita: Life in a Zone of Social Abandonment.* Berkeley: University of California Press.

———. 2013. "Ethnography in the Way of Theory." *Cultural Anthropology* 28 (4): 573–97.

Biggerstaff, Marilyn A., Patricia M. Morris, and Ann Nichols-Casebolt. 2002. "Living on the Edge: Examination of People Attending Food Pantries and Soup Kitchens." *Social Work* 47 (3): 267–77.

Boehm, Deborah A. 2012. *Intimate Migrations: Gender, Family, and Illegality among Transnational Mexicans.* New York: New York University Press.

Bourdieu, Pierre. [1979] 1984. *Distinction.* Translated by Richard Nice. Cambridge, MA: Harvard University Press.

Brockling, Ulrich, Susanne Krasmann, and Thomas Lemke. 2011. *Governmentality: Current Issues and Future Challenges.* New York: Routledge.

Brown, Larry, Donald Shepard, Timothy Martin, and John Orwat. 2007. *The Economic Cost of Domestic Hunger: Estimated Annual Burden to the United States.* Accessed May 27, 2014. http://www.sodexofoundation.org/newsletter/pdf /economic_cost_of_domestic_hunger.pdf.

Bureau of Population Statistics. 2010. *Profile of General Demographic Statistics.* Bureau of Population Statistics.

Butler, Judith. 1998. "Performative Acts and Gender Constitution: An Essay in Phenomenology and Feminist Theory." *Theatre Journal* 40 (4): 519–31.

Caldwell, Melissa. 2004. *Not by Bread Alone: Social Support in the New Russia.* Berkeley: University of California Press.

California Center for Public Health Advocacy, PolicyLink, and UCLA Center for Health Policy Research. 2008. *Designed for Disease: The Link between Local Food Environments and Obesity and Diabetes.* Accessed May 27, 2014. http://www.publichealthadvocacy.org/PDFs/RFEI%20Policy%20Brief _finalweb.pdf.

California Department of Education. 2010. *Free/Reduced Meals Program and Cal-WORKS Data Files.* Sacramento: California Department of Education.

California Food Policy Advocates. 2003. *Touched by Hunger: A County by County Report on Hunger and Food Insecurity in California.* Oakland: California Food Policy Advocates.

———. 2010. *2010 Santa Barbara County Nutrition and Food Insecurity Profile.* Oakland: California Food Policy Advocates.

California Health Interview Survey. 2009. *California Health Interview Survey.* Accessed May 15, 2012. http://www.chis.ucla.edu.

Camarillo, Albert. 1979. *Chicanos in a Changing Society: From Mexican Pueblos to American Barrios in Santa Barbara and Southern California, 1848–1930.* Dallas: Southern Methodist University Press.

Cammarota, Julio. 2008. *Sueños Americanos: Barrio Youth Negotiating Social and Cultural Identities.* Tucson: University of Arizona Press.

———. 2011a. "'Food Security' and 'Food Sovereignty': What Frameworks Are Best Suited for Social Equity in Food Systems?" *Journal of Agriculture, Food Systems and Community Development* 2 (2): 71–87.

———. 2011b. "The Food Sovereignty Prize: Implications for Discourse and Practice." *Food and Foodways* 19 (3): 169–80.

Carney, Megan A. 2012. "Compounding Crises of Economic Recession and Food Insecurity: A Comparative Study of Three Low-Income Communities in Santa Barbara County." *Agriculture and Human Values* 29 (2): 185–201.

———. 2013. "Border Meals: Detention Center Feeding Practices, Migrant Subjectivities, and Questions on Trauma." *Gastronomica* 13 (4): 32–46.

———. 2014a. "The Biopolitics of 'Food Insecurity': Towards a Critical Political Ecology of the Body in Studies of Women's Transnational Migration." *Journal of Political Ecology* 21: 1–18.

———. 2014b. "Bodies on the Line: Fighting Inhuman Treatment with Hunger in Immigrant Detention." *Access Denied: A Conversation on Unauthorized Im/migration and Health* (blog). Accessed May 27, 2014. http://access deniedblog.wordpress.com/2014/05/04/bodies-on-the-line-fighting -inhumane-treatment-with-hunger-in-immigrant-detention-megan -carney/.

Castañeda, Heide. 2012. "'Over-Foreignization' or 'Unused Potential'? A Critical Review of Migrant Health in Germany and Responses toward Unauthorized Migration." *Social Science and Medicine* 74 (6): 830–38.

Chang, Grace. 2000. *Disposable Domestics.* Cambridge, MA: South End Press.

Chavez, Leo R. 2008. *The Latino Threat: Constructing Immigrants, Citizens, and the Nation.* Stanford, CA: Stanford University Press.

———. 2012. "Undocumented Immigrants and Their Use of Medical Services in Orange County, California." *Social Science and Medicine* 74 (6): 887–93.

Cheng, Shu-Ju Ada. 2006. *Serving the Household and the Nation: Filipina Domestics and the Politics of Identity in Taiwan.* Lanham, MD: Lexington Books.

Chilton, Mariana, and Donald Rose. 2009. "A Rights-Based Approach to Food Insecurity in the United States." *American Journal of Public Health* 99 (7): 1203–11.

Cho, Sumi, Kimberle W. Crenshaw, and Leslie McCall. 2013. "Toward a Field of Intersectionality Studies: Theory, Applications, and Praxis." *Signs: Journal of Women in Culture and Society* 38 (4): 785–810.

Cleveland, David A., Corie N. Radka, Nora M. Muller, Tyler D. Watson, Nora J. Rekstein, Hannah Wright, and Sydney C. Hollingshead. 2011. "The Effect of Localizing Fruit and Vegetable Consumption on Greenhouse Gas

Emissions and Nutrition, Santa Barbara County." *Environmental Science and Technology* 45 (10): 4555–62.

Cohen, Deborah. 2011. *Braceros: Migrant Citizens and Transnational Subjects in the Postwar United States and Mexico.* Chapel Hill: University of North Carolina Press.

Coleman-Jensen, Alisha, Mark Nord, Margaret Andrews, and Steven Carlson. 2011. *Household Food Security in the United States, 2010.* Economic Research Report No. ERR-125. Washington, DC: United States Department of Agriculture.

Coleman-Jensen, Alisha, Christian Gregory, and Anita Singh. 2014. *Household Food Security in the United States in 2013.* Economic Research Report No. ERR-173. Washington, DC: United States Department of Agriculture.

Colen, Shellee. 1995. " 'Like a Mother to Them': Stratified Reproduction and West Indian Childcare Workers and Employers in New York." In *Conceiving the New World Order: The Global Politics of Reproduction,* edited by Faye Ginsburg and Rayna Rapp, 78–102. Berkeley: University of California Press.

Costello, Kathleen, and Peter B. Manzo. 2005. *Southern California's Nonprofit Sector.* Accessed October 26, 2011. http://www.fullerton.edu/gcnr/SoCalNonprofitSectorReport.pdf.

Counihan, Carole M. 1999. *The Anthropology of Food and Body: Gender, Meaning and Power.* New York: Routledge.

———. 2004. *Around the Tuscan Table: Food, Family, and Gender in Twentieth Century Florence.* New York: Routledge.

———. 2005. "The Border as Barrier and Bridge: Food, Gender, and Ethnicity in the San Luis Valley of Colorado." In *From Betty Crocker to Feminist Food Studies,* edited by Arlene Voski Avakian and Barbara Haber, 200–217. Amherst: University of Massachusetts Press.

———. 2009. *A Tortilla Is Like Life: Food and Culture in the San Luis Valley of Colorado.* College Station: University of Texas Press.

County of Santa Barbara. 2008. *County Statistical Profile.* Accessed May 15, 2012. http://www.countyofsb.org/ceo/budgetresearch/documents/budget0809/200%2008-09%20Section%20B%20County%20Statistical.pdf.

Coutin, Susan B. 2007. *Nations of Emigrants: Shifting Boundaries of Citizenship in El Salvador and the United States.* Ithaca, NY: Cornell University Press.

Craddock, Susan. 2000. *City of Plagues: Disease, Poverty, and Deviance in San Francisco.* Minneapolis: University of Minnesota Press.

Cruikshank, Barbara. 1999. *The Will to Empower: Democratic Citizens and Other Subjects.* Ithaca, NY: Cornell University Press.

Crush, Jonathan. 2013. "Linking Food Security, Migration and Development." *International Migration* 51 (5): 61–75.

Das, Veena. 2007. *Life and Words: Violence and the Descent into the Ordinary.* Berkeley: University of California Press.

———. 2008. "Violence, Gender, and Subjectivity." *Annual Review of Anthropology* 37: 283–99.

Das, Veena, Arthur Kleinman, Margaret Lock, Mamphela Ramphele, and Pamela Reynolds. 2001. *Remaking a World: Violence, Social Suffering, and Recovery.* Berkeley: University of California Press.

De Genova, Nicholas. 2002. "Migrant 'Illegality' and Deportability in Everyday Life." *Annual Review of Anthropology* 31: 419–47.

De Schutter, Olivier. 2009. "Governing World Food Security: A New Role for the Committee on World Food Security." *Right to Food Quarterly* 4 (1): 2–3.

DeParle, Jason, and Robert Gebeloff. 2009. "Food Stamp Use Soars Across US, and Stigma Fades." *New York Times*, November 29.

DeVault, Marjorie L. 1991. *Feeding the Family: The Social Organization of Caring as Gendered Work.* Chicago: University of Chicago Press.

DeWalt, Kathleen M., and Billie R. DeWalt. 2002. *Participant Observation: A Guide for Fieldworkers.* Lanham, MD: AltaMira.

Dodson, Lisa. 2007. "Wage-Poor Mothers and Moral Economy." *Social Politics: International Studies in Gender, State and Society* 14 (2): 258–80.

Doughton, Sandi. 2011. "Could More-Nutritious Crops Help Fight Hunger?" *Seattle Times*, August 7, 2011.

Durand, Jorge, and Douglas S. Massey. 2010. "New World Orders: Continuities and Changes in Latin American Migration." *Annals of the American Academy of Political and Social Science* 630 (20): 20–52.

FAO (Food and Agriculture Organization of the United Nations). 2002. *The State of Food Insecurity in the World 2001.* Accessed August 8, 2014. http://www.fao.org/docrep/003/y1500e/y1500e00.htm.

———. 2003. *Trade Reforms and Food Security: Conceptualizing the Linkages.* Accessed August 8, 2014. http://www.fao.org/docrep/005/y4671e/y4671e00.htm.

————. 2013. *The State of Food Insecurity in the World: The Multiple Dimensions of Food Security.* Rome: Food and Agriculture Organization of the United Nations.

Farmer, Paul. 1996. *Infections and Inequalities.* Berkeley: University of California Press.

————. 2005. *Pathologies of Power: Health, Human Rights, and the New War on the Poor.* Berkeley: University of California Press.

Fassin, Didier. 2011. "Policing Borders, Producing Boundaries: The Governmentality of Immigration in Dark Times." *Annual Review of Anthropology* 40: 213–26.

Fassin, Didier, and Richard Rechtman 2009. *The Empire of Trauma: An Inquiry into the Condition of Victimhood.* Princeton, NJ: Princeton University Press.

Feeding America. 2014a. "MyPlate." Accessed August 7, 2014. http://feedin gamerica.org/how-we-fight-hunger/programs-and-services/nutrition /nutrition-myplate.aspx.

————. 2014b. "Nutrition and Feeding America." Accessed August 7, 2014. http://feedingamerica.org/how-we-fight-hunger/programs-and-ser vices/nutrition.aspx.

Fernandez-Kelley, Patricia, and Douglas Massey. 2007. "Borders for Whom? The Role of NAFTA in Mexico-U.S. Migration." *ANNALS of the American Academy of Political and Social Science* 610: 98–118.

Ferreti-Majarrez, Gwendolyn. 2012. "Attrition via Enforcement: Snuffing Latino Immigrants out of the Deep South." *Anthropology News* 53 (2): 5–6.

Fidler, D. 2003. "Public Health and National Security in the Global Age: Infectious Disease, Bioterrorism, and Realpolitik." *George Washington International Law Review* 35: 787–856.

Fitzgerald, Nurgul. 2010. "Acculturation, Socioeconomic Status, and Health Among Hispanics." *NAPA Bulletin* 34: 28–46.

Fitzgerald, Nurgul, Amber Hromi-Fiedler, Sofia Segura-Peréz, and Rafael Pérez-Escamilla. 2011. "Food Insecurity Is Related to Increased Risk of Type 2 Diabetes among Latinas." *Ethnicity and Disease* 21 (2011): 328–34.

Flores-Ortiz, Yvvette G. 2000. "Levels of Acculturation, Marital Satisfaction, and Depression among Chicana Workers." In *Las Obreras: Chicana Politics of Work and Family,* edited by Vicki L. Ruiz, 211–36. Los Angeles: UCLA Chicano Studies Research Center.

Food and Nutrition Service. 2011. "Supplemental Nutrition Assistance Program (SNAP), United States Department of Agriculture." http://www.fns.usda.gov/pd/supplemental-nutrition-assistance-program-snap.

Food Research and Action Center. 2011. *SNAP/Food Stamp Monthly Participation Data, Vol. 2011.* Washington, DC: Food Research and Action Center.

Foucault, Michel. 1975. *Discipline and Punish: The Birth of the Prison.* Translated by Alan Sheridan. New York: Random House.

———. 1978. *History of Sexuality, Volume 1: An Introduction.* Translated by Robert Hurley. New York: Random House.

———. 1991. "Governmentality." In *The Foucault Effect,* edited by Graham Burchell, Colin Gordon, and Peter Miller, 87–104. Chicago: University of Chicago Press.

Gill, Rosalind. 2008. "Culture and Subjectivity in Neoliberal and Postfeminist Times." *Subjectivity* 25: 432–45.

Gleeson, Shannon. 2010. "Labor Rights for All? The Role of Undocumented Immigrant Status for Worker Claims-Making." *Law and Social Inquiry* 35 (3): 561–602.

Glenn, Evelyn Nakano. 1992. "From Servitude to Service Work: Historical Continuities in the Racial Division of Paid Reproductive Labor." *Signs: Journal of Women in Culture and Society* 18 (1): 1–43.

———. 2012. *Forced to Care: Coercion and Caregiving in America.* Cambridge, MA: Harvard University Press.

Goldman, Roberta, Mary Kay Hunt, Jennifer Dacey Allen, Sonia Hauser, Karen Emmons, Marcio Maeda, and Gloria Sorensen. 2003. "The Life History Interview Method: Applications to Intervention Development." *Health Education and Behavior* 30: 564–81.

Gonzales, Roberto G., and Leo R. Chavez. 2012. "'Awakening to a Nightmare': Abjectivity and Illegality in the Lives of Undocumented 1.5-Generation Latino Immigrants in the United States." *Current Anthropology* 53 (3): 255–81.

Gottlieb, Robert, and Anupama Joshi. 2010. *Food Justice: Food, Health and the Environment.* Cambridge, MA: MIT Press.

Graham, Hilary. 1987. "Being Poor: Perceptions and Coping Strategies of Lone Mothers." In *Give and Take in Families: Studies in Resource Distribution,* edited by Julia Brannen and Gail Wilson, 56–74. Hemel Hempstead: Harvester Wheatsheaf.

Green, Linda. 2011. "The Nobodies: Neoliberalism, Violence, and Migration." *Medical Anthropology* 30 (4): 366–85.

Greenhalgh, Susan. 2012. "Weighty Subjects: The Biopolitics of the US War on Fat." *American Ethnologist* 39 (3): 471–87.

Greenhalgh, Susan, and Megan A. Carney. 2014. "Bad Biocitizens? Latinos and the US 'Obesity Epidemic.'" *Human Organization* 73 (3): 267–76.

Greves, H. Mollie, Paula Lozano, Lenna Liu, Katie Busby, Jen Cole, and Brian Johnston. 2007. "Immigrant Families' Perceptions on Walking to School and School Breakfast: A Focus Group Study." *International Journal of Behavioral Nutrition and Physical Activity* 4: 9.

Griswold del Castillo, Richard. 1984. *La Familia: Chicano Families in the Urban Southwest 1848 to Present*. Notre Dame, IN: University of Notre Dame Press.

Guthman, Julie. 2008a. "Bringing Good Food to Others: Investigating the Subjects of Alternative Food Practice." *Cultural Geographies* 15 (4): 431–47.

———. 2008b. "'If They Only Knew': Colorblindness and Universalism in California Alternative Food Institutions." *Professional Geographer* 60 (3): 387–97.

———. 2008c. "Neoliberalism and the Making of Food Politics in California." *Geoforum* 39 (3): 1171–83.

———. 2011. *Weighing In: Obesity, Food Justice, and the Limits of Capitalism*. Berkeley: University of California Press.

Hacker, Karen, Robert Marlin, Jocelyn Chu, Carolyn Leung, Robert Marra, Alex Pirie, Mohamed Brahimi, Margaret English, Joshua Beckman, and Dolores Acevedo-Garcia. 2011. "The Impact of Immigration and Customs Enforcement on Immigrant Health: Perceptions of Immigrants in Everett, Massachusetts, USA." *Social Science and Medicine* 73 (4): 586–94.

Haering, Stephen A., and Shamsuzzoha B. Syed. 2009. *Community Food Security in United States Cities: A Survey of the Relevant Scientific Literature*. Baltimore, MD: John Hopkins Bloomberg School of Public Health.

Hawkes, Corinna. 2007. "Globalization and the Nutrition Transition: A Case Study." In *Food Policy for Developing Countries: Case Studies*, edited by Per Pinstrup Anderson and Fuzhi Cheng. Accessed September 3, 2014. http://cip

.cornell.edu/DPubS?service=UI&version=1.0&verb=Display&handle
=dns.gfs/1200428200.

Himmelgreen, David, Nancy Romero Daza, Elizabeth Cooper, and Dinorah
Martinez. 2007. "'I Don't Make the Soups Anymore': Pre- to Post-Migration
Dietary and Lifestyle Changes among Latinos Living in West-Central
Florida." *Ecology of Food and Nutrition* 46 (5–6): 427–44.

Himmelgreen, David A., and Deborah L. Crooks. 2005. "Nutritional Anthro-
pology and Its Applications to Nutritional Issues and Problems." In *Applied
Anthropology: Domains of Application*, edited by Satish Kedia and John van
Willigan, 149–88. Westport, CT: Praeger.

Himmelgreen, David A., and Nancy Romero-Daza. 2010. "Eliminating 'Hunger' in the US: Changes in Policy Regarding the Measurement of Food
Security." *Food and Foodways* 18 (1): 96–113.

Holmes, Seth M. 2012. "The Clinical Gaze in the Practice of Migrant Health:
Mexican Migrants in the United States." *Social Science and Medicine* 74 (6):
873–81.

———. 2013. *Fresh Fruit, Broken Bodies: Migrant Farmworkers in the United States.*
Berkeley: University of California Press.

Holt-Giménez, Eric. 2009. "From Food Crisis to Food Sovereignty: The Challenge of Social Movements." *Food First Monthly Review*, July–August 2009.
Oakland: Food First.

Holt-Giménez, Eric, and Raj Patel, eds. 2009. *Food Rebellions: Crisis and the Hunger for Justice.* Oakland: Food First Books.

Hondagneu-Sotelo, Pierrette, and Ernestine Avila. 2007. "'I'm Here, but I'm
There': The Meanings of Latina Transnational Motherhood." In *Women
and Migration in the US-Mexico Borderlands: A Reader*, edited by Denise A.
Segura and Patricia Zavella, 388–412. Durham, NC: Duke University Press.

Horton, Sarah, and Judith C. Barker. 2009. "'Stains' on Their Self-Discipline:
Public Health, Hygiene, and the Disciplining of Undocumented Immigrant Parents in the Nation's Internal Borderlands." *American Ethnologist* 36
(4): 784–98.

Housing Authority of the County of Santa Barbara (HACSB). 2010. Accessed
May 15, 2014. http://www.hasbarco.org/index.htm.

Hubert, Annie. 2004. "Qualitative Research in the Anthropology of Food: A
Comprehensive Qualitative/Quantitative Approach." In *Researching Food*

Habits: Methods and Problems, ed. Helen Macbeth and Jeremy MacClancy, 41–54. New York: Berghahn.

Husbands, Winston. 1999. "Food Banks as Antihunger Organizations." In *For Hunger-Proof Cities: Sustainable Urban Food Systems*, edited by Mustafa Koc, Rod MacRae, Luc J. Mougeot, and Jennifer Walsh, 103–9. Ottawa, Ontario, Canada: International Development Research Centre.

Imhoff, Daniel. 2007. *Food Fight: The Citizen's Guide to a Food and Farm Bill*. Berkeley: University of California Press.

Inda, Jonathan X. 2007. "The Value of Immigrant Life." In *Women and Migration in the US-Mexico Borderlands: A Reader*, edited by Denise A. Segura and Patricia Zavella, 134–57. Durham, NC: Duke University Press.

Ingram, Alan. 2005. The New Geopolitics of Disease: Between Global Health and Global Security. *Geopolitics* 10 (3): 522–45.

International Food Policy Research Institute. 2002. *Green Revolution: Curse or Blessing?* Accessed May 27, 2014. http://www.ifpri.org/sites/default/files/pubs/pubs/ib/ib11.pdf.

Irazabal, Clara, and Ramzi Farhat. 2008. "Latino Communities in the United States: Place-Making in the Pre–World War II, Post War, and Contemporary City." *Journal of Planning Literature* 22 (3): 207–28.

Johnston, Josée, and Lauren Baker. 2005. "Eating Outside the Box: FoodShare's Good Food Box and the Challenge of Scale." *Agriculture and Human Values* 22 (3): 313–25.

Jowett, Madeleine, and Gill O'Toole. 2006. "Focusing Researchers' Minds: Contrasting Experiences of Using Focus Groups in Feminist Qualitative Research." *Qualitative Research* 6 (4): 453–72.

Kaiser, Lucia. 2008. "Why Do Low-Income Women Not Use Food Stamps? Findings from the California Women's Health Survey." *Public Health Nutrition* 11 (12): 1288–95.

Kaufman, Frederick. 2010. "The Food Bubble: How Wall Street Starved Millions and Got Away with It." *Harper's*, July 2010, 27–34.

Kearney, Michael. 1995. "The Local and the Global: The Anthropology of Globalization and Transnationalism." *Annual Review of Anthropology* 24: 547–65.

Kent, George. 1988. "Nutrition Education as an Instrument of Empowerment." *Journal of Nutrition Education* 20 (4): 193–95.

Kenworthy, Nora J. 2012. "Asylum's Asylum: Undocumented Immigrants, Belonging, and the Space of Exception at a State Psychiatric Center." *Human Organization* 71 (2): 123–34.

Kieffer, Edith C., Sharla K. Willis, Angela M. Odoms-Young, J. Ricardo Guzman, Alex J. Allen, Jackie Two Feathers, and Jimena Loveluck. 2004. "Reducing Disparities in Diabetes among African-American and Latino Residents of Detroit: The Essential Role of Community Planning Focus Groups." *Ethnicity and Disease* 14 (3): 27–37.

Kimura, Aya H. 2013. *Hidden Hunger: Gender and the Politics of Smarter Foods.* Ithaca, NY: Cornell University Press.

Kleinman, Arthur. 1989. *The Illness Narratives: Suffering, Healing, and the Human Condition.* New York: Basic Books.

Langness, Lewis L., and Gelya Frank. 1981. *Lives: An Anthropological Approach to Biography.* Novato, CA: Chandler and Sharp.

Larchanche, Stephanie. 2012. "Intangible Obstacles: Health Implications of Stigmatization, Structural Violence, and Fear among Undocumented Immigrants in France." *Social Science and Medicine* 74 (6): 858–63.

Lauren Schlau Consulting. 2008. *Santa Barbara: The American Riviera. Santa Barbara County Visitors Survey and Economic Study.* Accessed August 12, 2014. http://www.santabarbaraca.com/includes/media/docs/Visitor-Survey-and-Economic-Impact---Executive-Summary.pdf.

Lee, Charles T. 2010. "Bare Life, Interstices, and the Third Space of Citizenship." *WSQ: Women's Studies Quarterly* 38 (1–2): 57–81.

Lemke, Thomas. 2012. *Foucault, Governmentality, and Critique.* Boulder, CO: Paradigm.

Lentzos, Filippa, and Nikolas Rose. 2009. "Governing Insecurity: Contingency Planning, Protection, Resilience." *Economy and Society* 38 (2): 230–54.

Li Ching, Lim. 2008. Overhaul of Agriculture Systems Needed. Third World Network. Accessed September 3, 2014. http://www.twnside.org.sg/title2/susagri/susagri032.htm.

Lopez, Mark Hugo. 2014. "In 2014, Latinos Will Surpass Whites as Largest Racial/Ethnic Group in California." Accessed August 12, 2014. http://www.pewresearch.org/fact-tank/2014/01/24/in-2014-latinos-will-surpass-whites-as-largest-racialethnic-group-in-california/.

Lopez, Mark Hugo, Ana Gonzalez-Barrera, and Seth Motel. 2011. *As Deportations Rise to Record Levels, Most Latinos Oppose Obama's Policy.* Accessed August 11, 2014. http://www.pewhispanic.org/2011/12/28/as-deportations-rise-to-record-levels-most-latinos-oppose-obamas-policy/.

Maher, JaneMaree. 2010. "Motherhood: Reproduction and Care." In *The Globalization of Motherhood: Deconstructions and Reconstructions of Biology and Care,* ed. JaneMaree Maher and Wendy Chavkin, 16–27. London: Routledge.

Mankekar, Purnima. 2002. "'India Shopping': Indian Grocery Stores and Transnational Configurations of Belonging." *Ethnos* 67 (1): 75–97.

Mannur, Anita. 2007. "Culinary Nostalgia: Authenticity, Nationalism, and Diaspora." *MELUS* 32 (4): 11–31.

Mares, Teresa. 2012. "Tracing Immigrant Identity through the Plate and Palate." *Latino Studies* 10: 334–54.

———. 2013. "'Here We Have the Food Bank': Latino/a Immigration and the Contradictions of Emergency Food." *Food and Foodways* 21 (1): 1–21.

———. 2014. "Another Time of Hunger." In *Women Redefining Food Insecurity: Life Off the Edge of the Table,* ed. Janet Page-Reeves, 45–64. Lanham, MD: Lexington.

McMichael, Philip. 2008. "Food Sovereignty, Social Reproduction, and the Agrarian Question." In *Peasants and Globalization: Political Economy, Rural Transformation and the Agrarian Question,* ed. A. Haroon Akram-Lodhi and Cristóbal Kay, 288–311. London: Routledge.

———. 2009. "A Food Regime Genealogy." *Journal of Peasant Studies* 6 (1): 139–69.

Medina, F. Xavier. 2004. "'Tell Me What You Eat and You Will Tell Me Who You Are': Methodological Notes on the Interaction between Researcher and Informants in the Anthropology of Food." In *Researching Food Habits: Methods and Problems,* ed. Helen Macbeth and Jeremy MacClancy, 55–62. New York: Berghahn.

Mendenhall, Emily. 2012. *Syndemic Suffering: Social Distress, Depression, and Diabetes among Mexican Immigrant Women.* Walnut Creek, CA: Left Coast.

Menjívar, Cecilia. 2011. *Enduring Violence: Ladina Women's Lives in Guatemala.* Berkeley: University of California Press.

———. 2013. "Central American Immigrant Workers and Legal Violence in Phoenix, Arizona." *Latino Studies* 11 (2): 228–52.

Messer, Ellen, and Marc J. Cohen. 2007. *The Human Right to Food as a US Nutrition Concern, 1976–2000*. IFPRI Discussion Paper No. 731. Washington, DC: International Food Policy Research Institute.

Minkler, Meredith, and Nina Wallerstein. 2003. *Community-Based Participatory Research for Health*. San Francisco: Jossey-Bass.

Minkoff-Zern, Laura-Anne. 2012. "Knowing 'Good Food': Immigrant Knowledge and the Racial Politics of Farmworker Food Insecurity." First published online June 22, 2012. *Antipode*. Accessed September 25, 2014. http://onlinelibrary.wiley.com/doi/10.1111/j.1467-8330.2012.01016.x/abstract.

Mittal, Anuradha. 2009. *The 2008 Food Price Crisis: Rethinking Food Security Policies*. New York: United Nations Conference on Trade and Development.

Morgan, David, and Richard Krueger. 1998. *Focus Group Kit*. Thousand Oaks, CA: Sage.

Murphy, Michelle. 2012. *Seizing the Means of Reproduction: Entanglements of Feminism, Health, and Technoscience*. Durham, NC: Duke University Press.

Myeroff, Barbara. 1978. *Number Our Days*. New York: Simon and Schuster.

Nally, David. 2011. "The Biopolitics of Food Provisioning." *Transactions of the Institute of British Geographers* 36: 37–53.

Narotzky, Susana. 1997. *New Directions in Economic Anthropology*. London: Pluto.

Nestle, Marion. 2007. *Food Politics*. Berkeley: University of California Press.

Neuberger, Zoe, and Robert Greenstein. 2013. *The Impact of the Sequester on WIC: Will WIC Be Able to Serve All Eligible Low-Income Women and Young Children Who Apply?* Accessed August 11, 2014. http://www.cbpp.org/cms/?fa=view&id=3909.

Nicholson, Melanie. 2006. "Without Their Children: Rethinking Motherhood among Transnational Migrant Women." *Social Text* 24 (3): 13–33.

Nixon, Ron. 2013. "Food Stamp Program Faces Deeper Cuts Under House Farm Bill." *New York Times*, May 8.

Nord, Mark, Margaret Andrews, and Steven Carlson. 2009. "Household Food Security in the United States, 2008." United States Department of Agriculture.

Ong, Aihwa. 1995. "Women Out of China: Traveling Tales and Traveling Theories in Postcolonial Feminism." In *Women Writing Culture*, edited by Ruth Behar and Deborah Gordon, 350–72.

———. 2006. *Neoliberalism and Exception: Mutations in Citizenship and Sovereignty*. Durham, NC: Duke University Press.

Ortner, Sherry. 2006. *Anthropology and Social Theory: Culture, Power, and the Acting Subject*. Durham, NC: Duke University Press.

Osypuk, Theresa L., Ana V. Diez Roux, Craig Hadley, and Namratha Kandula. 2009. "Are Immigrant Enclaves Healthy Places to Live? The Multi-Ethnic Study of Atherosclerosis." *Social Science and Medicine* 69 (1): 110–20.

Otis, Eileen M. 2011. *Markets and Bodies: Women, Service Work, and the Making of Inequality in China*. Stanford, CA: Stanford University Press.

Page-Reeves, Janet. 2014. "Conceptualizing Food Insecurity and Women's Agency: An Introduction." In *Women Redefining Food Insecurity: Life Off the Edge of the Table*, edited by Janet Page-Reeves, 3–41. Lanham, MD: Lexington.

Palerm, Juan Vicente. 2002. "Immigrant and Migrant Farmworkers in the Santa Maria Valley." In *Transnational Latina/o Communities: Politics, Processes, and Cultures*, edited by Carlos Vélez-Ibáñez, Anna Sampaio, and Manolo González-Estay. Lanham, MD: Rowman and Littlefield.

Park, Lisa Sun-Hee. 2011. *Entitled to Nothing: The Struggle for Immigrant Health Care in the Age of Welfare Reform*. New York: New York University Press.

Parreñas, Rhacel Salazar. 2001. *Servants of Globalization: Women, Migration and Domestic Work*. Stanford, CA: Stanford University Press.

———. 2011. *Illicit Flirtations: Labor, Migration, and Sex Trafficking in Tokyo*. Stanford, CA: Stanford University Press.

Passel, Jeffrey S., and D'Vera Cohn. 2011. *US Unauthorized Immigration Flows Are Down Sharply Since Mid-Decade*. Accessed August 11, 2014. http://www.pewhispanic.org/2010/09/01/us-unauthorized-immigration-flows-are-down-sharply-since-mid-decade/.

Passel, Jeffrey S., D'Vera Cohn, and Ana Gonzalez-Barrera. 2012. *Net Migration from Mexico Falls to Zero—and Perhaps Less. Pew Research Center*. Accessed September 5, 2014. http://www.pewhispanic.org/2012/04/23/net-migration-from-mexico-falls-to-zero-and-perhaps-less/.

Patel, Raj. 2009. "What Does Food Sovereignty Look Like?" *Journal of Peasant Studies* 36 (3): 663–706.

Patil, Vrushali. 2013. "From Patriarchy to Intersectionality: A Transnational Feminist Assessment of How Far We've Really Come." *Signs: Journal of Women in Culture and Society* 38 (4): 847–67.

Pechlaner, Gabriela, and Gerardo Otero. 2010. "The Neoliberal Food Regime: Neoregulation and the New Division of Labor in North America." *Rural Sociology* 75 (2): 179–208.

234 / Bibliography

Pérez, Rachel L., and Meredith E. Abarca. 2007. "Cocinas Públicas: Food and Border Consciousness in Greater Mexico." Food and Foodways 15 (3): 137–51.

Pfeiffer, James, and Rachel Chapman. 2010. "Anthropological Perspectives on Structural Adjustment and Public Health." Annual Review of Anthropology 39: 149–65.

Phillips, Lynne. 2006. "Food and globalization." *Annual Review of Anthropology* 35: 37–57.

Pimbert, Michel. 2007. *Transforming Knowledge and Ways of Knowing for Food Sovereignty.* London: International Institute for Environment and Development.

———. 2008. *Towards Food Sovereignty: Reclaiming Autonomous Food Systems.* London: International Institute for Environment and Development.

Plascencia, Luis. 2012. *Disenchanting Citizenship: Mexican Migrants and the Boundaries of Belonging.* New Brunswick, NJ: Rutgers University Press.

———. 2013. "Attrition through Enforcement and the Elimination of a 'Dangerous Class.'" In *Latino Politics and Arizona's Immigration Law SB 1070,* edited by Lisa Magaña and Erik Lee, 93–127. New York: Springer.

Poppendieck, Janet. 1997. "The USA: Hunger in the Land of Plenty." In *First World Hunger: Food Security and Welfare Politics,* edited by Graham Riches, 134–64. New York: St. Martin's.

———. 1998. *Sweet Charity? Emergency Food and the End of Entitlement.* New York: Viking.

———. 2010. *Free for All: Fixing School Food in America.* Berkeley: University of California Press.

Pothukuchi, Kami. 2004. "Community Food Assessment: A First Step in Planning for Community Food Security." *Journal of Planning Education and Research* 23: 356–77.

Pottier, Johan. 1999. *Anthropology of Food: The Social Dynamics of Food Security.* Cambridge: Polity.

Quesada, James. 2011. "No Soy Welferero: Undocumented Latino Laborers in the Crosshairs of Legitimation Maneuvers." *Medical Anthropology* 30 (4): 386–408.

Quesada, James, Laurie K. Hart, and Philippe Bourgois. 2011. "Structural Vulnerability and Health: Latino Migrant Laborers in the United States." *Medical Anthropology* 30 (4): 339–62.

Rae, Isabella. 2008. *Women and the Right to Food: International Law and State Practice.* Rome: Food and Agriculture Organization of the United Nations.

Razavi, Shahra. 2002. *Shifting Burdens: Gender and Agrarian Change under Neoliberalism.* Bloomfield, CT: Kumarian.

Richardson, Jill. 2013. "New Rule: Coca-Cola Doesn't Get to Tell Us to Exercise." Accessed May 27, 2014, http://www.lavidalocavore.org/diary/5369/new-rule-cocacola-doesnt-get-to-tell-us-to-exercise.

Ricoeur, Paul. 2004. *Memory, History, and Forgetting.* Chicago: University of Chicago Press.

Rivera, Christopher. 2014. "The Brown Threat: Post-9/11 Conflations of Latina/os and Middle Eastern Muslims in the US American Imagination." *Latino Studies* 12 (1): 44–64.

Robinson, William I. 2008. *Latin America and Global Capitalism: A Globalization Perspective.* Baltimore, MD: Johns Hopkins University Press.

Rogers, Anissa T. 2010. "Exploring Health Beliefs and Care-Seeking Behaviors of Older USA-Dwelling Mexicans and Mexican-Americans." *Ethnicity and Health* 15 (6): 581–99.

Rosas, Gilberto. 2012. *Barrio Libre: Criminalizing States and Delinquent Refusals of the New Frontier.* Durham, NC: Duke University Press.

Rose, Nikolas. 1996. *Inventing Ourselves: Psychology, Power, and Personhood.* Cambridge: Cambridge University Press.

Rosset, Peter M., and María Elena Martinez-Torres. 2010. "La Via Campesina: The Birth and Evolution of a Transnational Social Movement." *Journal of Peasant Studies* 37 (1): 149–75.

Sansum Diabetes Research Institute. 2014. "Youth Programs." Accessed August 7, 2014. http://www.sansum.org/community-outreach-and-education/youth-programs/.

Santa Barbara County. 2011. *Santa Barbara County 2010 Children's Scorecard: Data on Our Children's Physical, Emotional, Educational and Social Well-Being over Time.* Accessed August 7, 2014. http://www.countyofsb.org/WorkArea/DownloadAsset.aspx?id=33148.

Sargent, Carolyn. 2012. "Special Issue Part 1: 'Deservingness' and the Politics of Health Care." *Social Science and Medicine* 74: 855–57.

Sargent, Carolyn, and Stephanie Larchanche. 2011. "Transnational Migration and Global Health: The Production and Management of Risk, Illness, and Access to Care." *Annual Review of Anthropology* 40: 345–61.

Sarkisian, Catherine A., W. Neil Steers, Mayer B. Davidson, Arleen F. Brown, Keith C. Norris, Robert M. Anderson, and Carol M. Mangione. 2005.

"Using Focus Groups of Older African Americans and Latinos with Diabetes to Modify a Self-Care Empowerment Intervention." *Ethnicity and Disease* 15 (2): 283–91.

Sauter, Michael B., Ashley C. Allen, and Charles B. Stockdale. 2012. "The Nine American Cities Nearly Destroyed by the Recession." Accessed February 1, 2012. http://247wallst.com/2012/01/19/the-nin-cities-that-havent-recovered-from-the-recession/3/.

Scheper-Hughes, Nancy. 1992. *Death without Weeping: The Violence of Everyday Life in Brazil.* Berkeley: University of California Press.

Schiavoni, Christina. 2009. "The Global Struggle for Food Sovereignty: From Nyeleni to New York." *Journal of Peasant Studies* 36 (3): 682–89.

Schmidt-Camacho, Alicia. 2008. *Migrant Imaginaries: Latino Cultural Politics in the Mexico-US Borderlands.* New York: New York University Press.

Segura, Denise A. 1993. "Ambivalence or Continuity? Motherhood and Employment among Chicanas and Mexican Immigrant Women." In *Las Obreras: Chicana Politics of Work and Family*, edited by Vicki L. Ruiz, 181–209. Los Angeles: UCLA Chicano Studies Research Center.

Segura, Denise A., and Patricia Zavella. 2007. "Introduction." In *Women and Migration in the US-Mexico Borderlands: A Reader*, edited by Denise A. Segura and Patricia Zavella, 1–32. Durham, NC: Duke University Press.

Seremetakis, C. Nadia. 1996. *The Senses Still: Perception and Memory as Material Culture in Modernity.* Chicago: University of Chicago Press.

Shimada, Tia. 2009. *Lost Dollars, Empty Plates: The Impact of Food Stamp Participation on State and Local Economies.* Oakland: California Food Policy Advocates.

Simmonds, Norman, and Joseph Smartt. 1999. *Principles of Crop Improvement.* Oxford: Blackwell.

Singer, Merrill. 2009. *Introduction to Syndemics: A Systems Approach to Public and Community Health.* San Francisco: Jossey-Bass.

Singer, Merrill, and Scott Clair. 2003. "Syndemics and Public Health: Reconceptualizing Disease in Bio-Social Context." *Medical Anthropology Quarterly* 17 (4): 423–41.

Singer, Merrill C., Pamela I. Erickson, Louise Badiane, Rosemary Diaz, Dugeidy Ortiz, Traci Abraham, and Anna Marie Nicolaysen. 2006. "Syndemics, Sex and the City: Understanding Sexually Transmitted Diseases in Social and Cultural Context." *Social Science and Medicine* 63: 2010–21.

Skrabanek, Petr. 1994. *The Death of Humane Medicine and the Rise of Coercive Healthism.* London: Social Affairs Unit.

Sloane, David C., Allison L. Diamant, LaVonna B. Lewis, Antronette K. Yancey, Gwendolyn Flynn, Lori Miller Nascimento, William J. McCarthy, Joyce Jones Guinyard, and Michael R. Cousineau. 2003. "Improving the Nutritional Research Environment for Healthy Living through Community-Based Participatory Research." *Journal of General Internal Medicine* 18: 568–75.

Spieldoch, Alexandra. 2007. *A Row to Hoe: The Gender Impact of Trade Liberalization on Our Food System, Agricultural Markets and Women's Human Rights.* Geneva: Friedrich-Ebert-Stiftung.

Stanford, Lois. 2014. "Negotiating Food Security along the US-Mexico Border: Social Strategies, Practice and Networks among Mexican Immigrant Women." In *Women Redefining Food Insecurity: Life Off the Edge of the Table,* edited by Janet Page-Reeves, 105–24. Lanham, MD: Lexington.

Stephen, Lynn. 2007. *Transborder Lives: Indigenous Oaxacans in Mexico, California, and Oregon.* Durham, NC: Duke University Press.

Stewart, David W., Prem N. Shamdasani, and Dennis Rook. 2007. *Focus Groups: Theory and Practice.* Thousand Oaks, CA: Sage.

Stewart, Kathleen. 1992. "Nostalgia—A Polemic." In *Rereading Cultural Anthropology,* edited by G. Marcus, 252–66. Durham, NC: Duke University Press.

———. 2007. *Ordinary Affects.* Durham, NC: Duke University Press.

Sukovic, Masha, Barbara F. Sharf, Joseph R. Sharkey, and Julie St. John. 2011. "Seasoning for the Soul: Empowerment through Food Preparation among Mexican Women in the Texas Colonias." *Food and Foodways* 19 (3): 228–47.

Tauber, Maya, and Andy Fisher. 2002. *A Guide to Community Food Projects.* Venice, CA: Community Food Security Coalition.

Ticktin, Miriam. 2011. *Casualties of Care: Immigration and the Politics of Humanitarianism in France.* Berkeley: University of California Press.

Todeschini, Maya. 2001. "The Bomb's Womb? Women and the Atom Bomb." In *Remaking a World: Violence, Social Suffering, and Recovery,* edited by Veena Das, Arthur Kleinman, Margaret Lock, Mamphela Ramphele, and Pamela Reynolds, 102–56. Berkeley: University of California Press.

United Nations Department of Economic and Social Affairs Population Division. 2013. *International Migration Policies 2013.* Accessed August 11, 2014.

https://www.un.org/en/development/desa/population/publications/pdf /policy/InternationalMigrationPolicies2013/InternationalMigration Policies2013_WallChart.pdf.

US Census Bureau. 2010. "American Community Survey." Accessed August 11, 2014. http://www.census.gov/acs/www/.

—. 2014. "State and County QuickFacts: Santa Barbara County, California." Accessed August 11, 2014. http://quickfacts.census.gov/qfd/states /06/06083.html.

US Department of Agriculture. 2014. *FY 2014: Budget Summary and Annual Performance Plan.* Accessed March 11, 2014. http://www.obpa.usda.gov/budsum /FY14budsum.pdf.

Van Esterik, Penny. 1999a. "Gender and Sustainable Food Systems: A Feminist Critique." In *For Hunger-Proof Cities: Sustainable Urban Food Systems,* edited by Mustafa Koc, Rod MacRae, Luc J. Mougeot, and Jennifer Walsh, 157–61. Ottawa, Ontario, Canada: International Development Research Centre.

—. 1999b. "Right to Food; Right to Feed: Right to Be Fed. The Intersection of Women's Rights and the Right to Food." *Agriculture and Human Values* 16: 225–32.

Van Hook, Jennifer, Frank D. Bean, and Jeffrey S. Passel. 2005. *Unauthorized Migrants Living in the United States: A Mid-Decade Portrait: Migrant Information Source.* Washington, DC: Migration Policy Institute.

Vauthier, Barbara. 2011. "Food Insecurity Improves Slightly but Remains High." *Foodlinks America,* September 9.

Vélez-Ibáñez, Carlos G. 1996. *Border Visions: Mexican Cultures of the Southwest United States.* Tucson: University of Arizona Press.

Via Campesina. 1996. "The Right to Produce and Access to Land (Statement on Food Sovereignty)." Accessed September 3, 2014. http://www .voiceoftheturtle.org/library/1996%20Declaration%20of%20Food %20Sovereignty.pdf.

Waldstein, Anna. 2010. "Popular Medicine and Self-Care in a Mexican Migrant Community: Toward an Explanation of an Epidemiological Paradox." *Medical Anthropology* 29 (1): 71–107.

Wamala, Sarah, and Ichiro Kawachi. 2007. "Globalization and Women's Health." In *Globalization and Health,* edited by Sarah Wamala and Ichiro Kawachi, 171–86. Oxford: Oxford University Press.

Watson, Maria-Rosa, Stacey Kaltman, Tiffany G. Townsend, Taware Goode, and Marcela Campoli. 2013. "A Collaborative Mental Health Research Agenda in a Community of Poor and Underserved Latinos." *Journal of Health Care for the Poor and Underserved* 24 (2): 671–87.

Weigel, M. Margaret, Rodrigo X. Armijos, Yolanda Posada Hall, Yolanda Ramirez, and Rubi Orozco. 2007. "The Household Food Insecurity and Health Outcomes of US-Mexico Border Migrant and Seasonal Farmworkers." *Journal of Immigrant and Minority Health* 9 (3): 157–69.

Wekerle, Gerda R. 2004. "Food Justice Movements: Policy, Planning, and Networks." *Journal of Planning Education and Research* 23: 378–86.

WIC of California. 2011 California Department of Public Health. Accessed September 2, 2014. http://www.cdph.ca.gov/programs/wicworks/Pages /default.aspx.

Willen, Sarah S. 2007. "Toward a Critical Phenomenology of 'Illegality': State Power, Criminalization, and Abjectivity among Undocumented Migrant Workers in Tel Aviv, Israel." *International Migration* 45 (3): 8–38.

———. 2012. "Migration, 'Illegality,' and Health: Mapping Embodied Vulnerability and Debating Health-Related Deservingness. Special Issue Introduction." *Social Science and Medicine* 74 (6): 805–11.

Willen, Sarah S., Jessica Mulligan, and Heide Castañeda. 2011. "Take a Stand Commentary: How Can Medical Anthropologists Contribute to Contemporary Conversations on 'Illegal' Im/migration and Health?" *Medical Anthropology Quarterly* 25 (3): 331–56.

Williams, Eddie N., and Angela Glover Blackwell. 2004. *Community-Based Strategies for Improving Latino Health*. Oakland: Joint Center for Political and Economic Studies.

Windfuhr, Michael, and Jennie Jonsén. 2005. *Food Sovereignty: Towards Democracy in Localized Food Systems*. Rugby, Warwickshire, England: ITDG.

Wunderlich, Gooloo S., and Janet L. Norwood. 2006. *Food Insecurity and Hunger in the United States: An Assessment of the Measure*. Washington, DC: National Academies Press.

Young, Sophie. 2008. "Season of Hunger: A Crisis of Food Inflation and Shrinking Safety Nets in the US." Retrieved August 11, 2014, http://www .oaklandinstitute.org/node/2568.

Yow, Valerie Raleigh. 2005. *Recording Oral History: A Guide for the Humanities and Social Sciences*. 2nd ed. Lanham, MD: AltaMira.

Zambrana, Ruth E., Claudia Dorrington, and David Hayes-Bautista. 1995. "Family and Child Health: A Neglected Vision." In *Understanding Latino Families: Scholarship, Policy and Practice*, edited by Ruth E. Zambrana, 157–77. Thousand Oaks, CA: Sage.

Zavella, Patricia. 2011. *I'm Neither Here Nor There: Mexicans' Quotidian Struggles with Migration and Poverty*. Durham, NC: Duke University Press.

Zimmerman, Mary K., Jacquelyn S. Litt, and Christine E. Bose. 2006. *Global Dimensions of Gender and Carework*. Stanford, CA: Stanford University Press.

Zlolniski, Christian. 2006. *Janitors, Street Vendors, and Activists: The Lives of Mexican Immigrants in Silicon Valley*. Berkeley: University of California Press.

INDEX

"The Food Bubble: How Wall
  Street Starved Millions and
  Got Away with It" (Kaufman), 7
food insecurity, 4; biopolitical
  projects linked to, 36; defined, 5;
  global interventions for, 5–6;
  health status and, 102, 103–4;
  immigrant detention and,
  204–7; immigration status and,
  72, 76–78; individual blame for,
  9; migration and, 1–2, 9–12,
  52–61; needs-based approach to,
  9; politics of, 13–14; reproductive
  labors of women and, 11; return
  migration and, 61–64; statistics
  on, 212; structural inequality
  and, 16–17; as structural
  violence, 49–53; subjectivities
  and, 34–35, 102, 103–4; in the
  United States, 12–17; women and
  people of color and, 7. *See also*
  biopolitics of food insecurity
food justice, 37–38
Food Literacy in the Preschool
  program, 143, 147
food literacy training, 142–43
food pantries, 130–31, 134
food preparation: empowerment
  and, 64; resettlement and, 65–66
food prices, 170–73
Food Research and Action Center,
  14
Food Revolution (television series),
  132
food security: biopolitical project
  of, 11, 18, 164, 198; defined, 4–5,
  13–14; dietary health and, 17–19;
  food sovereignty movement
  and, 198–204; insecurity of,
  161–63; internalizing project of,
  156–61; needs-based approaches
  to, 200–201; transfer of state

responsibility to individual, 196.
  See also biopolitics of food
  security
food shopping, 170–73
food sovereignty movement, 8–9,
  198–204
food stamps, 14. *See also* Supplemental Nutrition Assistance
  Program (SNAP)
food system, structural violence
  and, 6–7
food utilization, 5
Foodworks, 33, 50–51
Ford Foundation, 5
Foucault, Michel, 17–18
foundations: funding food
  assistance, 135, 162; Green Gene
  Revolution and, 201; moralization of health and, 150–51
framing of lived experience, 11
French illness clause, 65
FSBC. *See* Foodbank of Santa
  Barbara County

gang violence, working mothers
  and, 88–89
gender, foodwork and, 33
gendered dimensions of social
  reproduction, 34
gendered effects: of neoliberalism,
  45–53; of structural violence, 33
gendered migration, food and,
  53–61
gendered social suffering, 12
General Agreement on Tariffs and
  Trade, 8
Genova, Nicholas de, 76
GEO Corp., 205
Georgia House Bill 87, 75
Gill, Rosalind, 154
global food crisis (2007–9), 7
global health, 201

global interventions to food
  insecurity, 5–6
globalization, food and, 3–4, 7
Gloria (informant), 85–86, 107–8,
  109, 215
Gonzales, Roberto, 76
government: fear of surveillance
  by, 181–82; Green Revolution
  and, 202
governmentality, 17–18; social
  death and, 96–97
government food assistance, 14–17,
  134–35; erosion of, 136; schools
  meals program, 14, 21–22;
  underutilization of, 176. *See also*
  Supplemental Nutrition
  Assistance Program (SNAP);
  Women, Infants, and Children
  Supplementary Nutrition
  (WIC) program
grants, for private food assistance,
  135, 162
Green Gene Revolution, 201–2
Greenhalgh, Susan, 132, 158
Green Revolution, 5–6, 201–2
Guatemala, migrants from, 23, 104
Guthman, Julie, 156

Habitus, 160–61
Haering, Stephen, 13
Harper's magazine, 7
Head Start programs, 22
healing: narratives as medium of,
  126–27; traditional, 153–54
health: economic marginalization
  and disparities in, 101–5; food
  insecurity and, 102, 103–4; food
  security and dietary, 17–19;
  global, 201; immigration status
  and, 97–98; junk food and,
  78–82; lack of social support
  and, 112; of migrant women, 197;

migration and, 97–98; moralization of, 150–51, 157–60; resettlement and, 100; social suffering
  and, 118–26; stress and, 119–26
Health School Pantry program
  (FSBC), 143
health security, 131–34, 132
Healthy Family Home Program,
  137
healthy food. *See comida saludable*
  (healthy food)
Honduras, migrants from, 23
housing, for migrants, 91–92
Hubert, Annie, 26
human right, food as, 7–9, 199–201
Hunger, 13
Hunger in America report, 135
hunger strikers, immigrant
  detainees and, 205

illegality, food insecurity and state
  of, 72, 76–78
illness clause, French, 65
IMF. *See* International Monetary
  Fund
immigrant detention, 204–7
immigration: migration *vs.,* 32–33;
  reform policies, 205–6; state-
  level legislation on, 75–76; US
  deterrence and deportation
  measures against, 75
Immigration and Customs
  Enforcement (ICE) informants,
  77
Immigration and Reform Control
  Act (1986), 75
immigration regime, 75
immigration status: concern about
  enrollment in SNAP and,
  181–82; food insecurity and, 72,
  76–78; health and, 97–98; of
  migrant women, 214–16. *See also*

Latina migrants' narratives
(continued)
  93, 215; Marisol, 215; Maya, 170,
  179–80, 215; Natalia, 78–79, 93,
  151, 216; Olivia, 82, 87, 96, 171, 175,
  216; Paloma, 123–24, 125, 151–52,
  184, 216; Paula, 39–44; Pilar, 123,
  159, 160, 167–68, 215; Serena, 90,
  216; Tina, 68–69, 71, 92, 159, 216;
  Yolanda, 62–64, 67–68, 114,
  159–60, 174, 179, 216
Latinas Connected for Change, 193
Latinas/Latinos: mental disorders
  and, 126; in Santa Barbara
  County, 20, 73–74
Latino City Employee, 192
Lentzos, Filippa, 132
Let's Move Campaign, 131–32
life history interviews, 24, 26
Linda (informant), 54–56, 86–87,
  119–20, 158, 159, 170, 172, 175, 215
Litt, Jacquelyn, 68
lived experience, framing of, 11
Lopez, Amy, 177–79
loss, migration and feelings of, 107–13
low-income households: defined,
  21; nutrition education aimed at,
  137, 139–40; private food
  assistance education programs
  aimed at, 141–49
Luisa (informant), 56–58, 77, 79–80,
  99, 146, 180–81, 182, 215

Maher, JaneMaree, 69
"making do," 36
Malena (informant), 1–2, 58–61, 90,
  91, 105–7, 127, 166, 167, 180, 216
malnutrition, diet-related disease,
  131–32
Mankekar, Purnima, 65
Mannur, Anita, 115
Mares, Teresa, 51, 65

Margarita (informant), 93, 215
marginalization: of migrants, 195;
  neoliberalism and, 128–29;
  women and experience of,
  126–27
Marisol (informant), 215
marital status, of migrant women,
  214–16
Massey, Douglas, 45, 46
Maya (informant), 170, 179–80, 215
McDonald's, 202–3
meals: migration and changes in,
  109–12; shared responsibility for
  preparing, 174
Medina, F. Xavier, 27
men: alcoholism and, 89; domestic
  violence and, 115–18, 166–67;
  interference with women's
  efforts to provide healthy food,
  83–84; migrant women's
  relationship with, 166–67
Mendenhall, Emily, 102
Menjívar, Cecilia, 104, 105
mental health problems, 101, 102,
  125–26
Messer, Ellen, 201
Mexico: Green Revolution and, 6;
  migration from, 9–12, 23, 46–47
migrants: criminalization of by
  state, 75–76; effect of recession
  on, 90–95; housing issues for, 91;
  improvement in diet since
  coming to US, 41, 44; social
  isolation of, 107–13; structural
  vulnerability of, 101, 102–5. See
  also Latina migrants
migration: chronic food insecurity
  and, 1–2; feminization of, 45–46;
  food insecurity and, 9–12,
  52–64; health and, 97–98;
  immigration vs., 32–33; from
  Latin America, 23, 45–46; from

structural inequality, food insecurity and, 16–17
structural violence, 6–7; food insecurity as, 49–53; gendered effects of, 33; nutrition and preventive health programming and, 155–56, 157, 163
structural vulnerability: constraints on nutritional needs as, 44; of migrants, 101, 102–5
students, food banks and, 208–9
study participants, 23–25, 114–16, 214–16. *See also* Latina migrants' narratives
subjective transnationalism, 66
subjectivities: food insecurity and, 102, 103–4; layers of suffering and, 128; migrant women's, 195–96, 197; resettlement and, 100
suffering: collective experience of, 99; embodied effects of social, 118–26; narratives of, 100, 105–18; subjectivities and, 128
Sukovic, Masha, 50, 64, 66
Supplemental Nutrition Assistance Program (SNAP), 14, 15, 21, 134–35, 136, 154, 196, 205; enrollment in, 176, 177, 212; immigration status and, 181–82
surveillance of individual diet, 133
Syed, Shamsuzzoha, 13
symbolic violence, denigration of welfare users and, 181
syndemics, 35, 103

Ticktin, Miriam, 65
Tina (informant), 68–69, 71, 92, 159, 216
Todeschini, Maya, 128
trade rules, food insecurity and, 8
transnational commodity, mothering as, 70–71

transnational migration, 195
transnational mothers, 58–59, 61, 62–63, 70–71, 93–95, 105–6, 197
transoceanic migration, 45

undocumented status, 23; entitlement programs and, 176; experience of nonbelonging and, 118–19; families split between countries and, 93–95; food insecurity and, 72, 76–78, 95; health effects of, 125–26; lack of protection from violence and, 117–18
unemployment, 212; recession and, 90–95
United Nations, 45
United States: criminalization of migrants in, 75–76; food insecurity in, 12–17; immigrant detention in, 204–7; needs-based approach to food insecurity, 9; right-to-food discourse and, 199–200; structural violence and food system in, 6–7
United States Centers for Disease Control and Prevention, 143–44
United States Department of Agriculture (USDA), 12, 95, 135, 162
United States Food Sovereignty Alliance, 202
"US War on Fat," 132
Universal Declaration of Human Rights, 199, 200
University of California Institute for Mexico and the United States, 209
USDA. *See* United States Department of Agriculture